THE EXTENDED MIND:
THE EMERGENCE OF LANGUAGE, THE HUMAN MIND,
AND CULTURE

ROBERT K. LOGAN

# The Extended Mind:

## The Emergence of Language, the Human Mind, and Culture

*To Lou*
*My partner in*
*collaboration and crime.*
*It was great to see you at*
*the launch. Hope we can*
*collaborate around*
*the Bowl*

*Bob Logan*
*Dec 4, 2007*

UNIVERSITY OF TORONTO PRESS
Toronto   Buffalo   London

ISBN 978-0 8020-9303-5

Printed on acid-free paper

Toronto Studies in Semiotics and Communications
Editors: Marcel Danesis, Umberto Eco, Paul Perron, Peter Schultz,
and Roland Posner

---

**Library and Archives Canada Cataloguing in Publication**

Logan, Robert K., 1939–
  The extended mind: the emergence of language, the human mind
  and culture / Robert K. Logan.

  (Toronto studies in semiotics and communication)
  Includes bibliographical references and index.
  ISBN 978-0-8020-9303-5

  1. Language and languages – Origin.   2. Language and culture.
  3. Human evolution.   I. Title.   II. Series.

  P107.63 2007      401      C2007-901647-2

---

University of Toronto Press acknowledges the financial assistance to its publishing
program of the Canada Council for the Arts and the Ontario Arts Council.

University of Toronto Press acknowledges the financial support for its
publishing activities of the Government of Canada through the Book Publishing
Industry Development Program (BPIDP).

This book has been published with the help of a grant from the Canadian
Federation for the Humanities and Social Sciences, through the Aid to Scholarly
Publications Programme, using funds provided by the Social Sciences
and Humanities Research Council of Canada.

# Contents

THE EXTENDED MIND:
THE EMERGENCE OF LANGUAGE, THE HUMAN MIND,
AND CULTURE

# Introduction

And as imagination bodies forth. The form of things unknown, the poet's pen turns them to shapes, and gives to airy nothing a local habitation and a name.

William Shakespeare, *A Midsummer Night's Dream*

The origin and evolution of human language is one of the great mysteries confronting contemporary scholarship and science. A problem-centred rather than a discipline-centred study, it is not a subject that can be addressed by one discipline but rather requires the input from a host of fields including linguistics, computational linguistics, psycholinguistics, evolutionary biology, evolutionary psychology, primatology, cultural anthropology, archaeology, physiology, phonology, neurophysiology, cognitive science, and media ecology. I must confess to the reader that I am not an expert in any of these fields with the exception of the last one, through my study of the evolution of notated language, namely, writing, mathematics, science, computing, and the Internet (Logan 1995, 2004a, 2004b). In some of my earlier works (1995 and 2004b), I showed that speech, writing, mathematics, science, computing, and the Internet form an evolutionary chain of six languages. My thesis was that a new form of language emerged as a bifurcation from an older form of language each time an information overload was created that the older form could not handle.

The study in which posited that the notated forms of language emerged from speech led naturally to the question of how speech, the first form of verbal language, emerged. So I must confess that I virtually stumbled into the origin of language field as a result of my earlier research with notated language. However, I believe, that I have something new to contribute to this field through my experience of working with the historical data associated with the notated languages within the context of media ecology, a field of study pioneered by Marshall McLuhan and Harold Innis. Given the paucity of data available to the origin of language field, I believe there are things that can be learned from the historical data set associated with notated language. I hope that the reader will find my approach of value. I certainly come to the field with new eyes.

My goals in this book are threefold. First, I wish to present the Extended Mind Model, which I developed to explain the emergence of language. I first presented this model to an academic audience in 1997 (Logan 1997) at a conference on the role of chaos theory in psychology and the life sciences and published on it for the first time in an academic journal three years later (Logan 2000). Second, I wish to supplement my simple model, which only partially explains the emergence of language, with other models that I feel are consistent with my approach. In achieving the second goal I will first review the extensive literature that has emerged in the past fifteen years, critiquing it from the perspective of my approach. I believe that the Extended Mind Model sheds some light on a number of controversies raging in the evolution of language field, but I will leave that judgment to the reader. Finally, my third goal is to use the insights in my work and that of others to draw parallels between language and culture and develop the notion of Universal Culture, which is to culture what Chomsky's Universal Grammar is to language.

I have divided my book into five parts. In part 1, I formulate the objectives of my study and provide the reader with a history of the study of the origin and evolution of language as well as the history of my entry into this field. I also provide the framework within which I will review the literature, namely, Tinbergen's Four Why's, which are four questions that need to be answered to understand a biological phenomenon such as the emergence and evolution of human language. In part 2, I review my earlier work in the evolution of notated language (chapter 2), in which language is shown to be both a communication medium and an informatics tool and develop the Extended Mind Model to explain the origin of verbal language (chapters 3 and 4).

The origins of speech and the human mind are shown to have emerged simultaneously as the bifurcation from percepts to concepts and a response to the chaos associated with the information overload that resulted from the increased complexity of hominid life. As our ancestors developed toolmaking, controlled fire, lived in larger social groups, and engaged in large-scale coordinated hunting, their brains could no longer cope with the richness of life solely on the basis of its perceptual sensorium and as a result a new level of order emerged in the form of conceptualization and speech. Speech arose simultaneously as a way to control information and as a medium for communication. Rather than regarding thought as silent speech, one may just as well regard speech as vocalized thought.

The mechanism that allowed the transition from percept to concept was the emergence of speech. The words of spoken language are the actual medium or mechanism by which concepts are expressed or represented. Words are both metaphors and strange attractors uniting many perceptual experiences in terms of a single concept. Spoken language and abstract conceptual thinking emerged simultaneously, as the bifurcation from non-verbal communication skills and the concrete percept-based thinking of prelingual hominids.

The transition from percept-based thinking to concept-based thinking represented a major discontinuity in human thought and entailed three major stages or breakthroughs in hominid cognition:

1 Manual praxic articulation (or toolmaking and tool use)
2 Social organization (or the language of social interaction)
3 Preverbal communication, which entails the use of hand signals, mime, gesture, and prosodic vocalization.

It is shown that these cognitive breakthroughs represent three distinct percept-based preverbal forms of proto-language. They were the cognitive laboratory in which the skills of generativity, representation, and communication developed and, hence, were the source of the cognitive framework for speech.

We use our dynamic systems model of the mind to understand the connections between technology, commerce, artistic expression, narratives, and science and to generate what we have playfully called the

Grand Unification Theory of Human Thought and Culture. The three percept-based preverbal forms of language represent more than just the transition to spoken language and abstract conceptual thought. Transformed by spoken language and the abstract thought that followed in its wake, they also served as the prototypes of three fundamental activities of modern humans, namely, technology which emerged from toolmaking, commerce which emerged from social organization, and the arts which emerged from mimetic communications. In this way we link these activities to those associated with the verbal languages of speech, writing, mathematics, science, and computing. Language is the link that united all the activities of human enterprise.

A model to address the mind-body problem is developed in which it is assumed that the mind came into being with the advent of verbal language and, hence, conceptual thought. Language is a tool that extended the brain and made it more effective, thus creating the human mind.

In part 3, I first critique Chomsky's notion of the hard-wiring of the Universal Grammar and the Language Acquisition Device (chapter 5). I then review the evolution of language literature within the framework of Tinbergen's Four Why's, identifying the contentious issues in the field and suggesting ways in which the Extended Mind Model might resolve some of them (chapters 6 to 9), thereby identifying those models that I believe are compatible with my own approach.

In part 4, a synthesis of the Extended Mind Model is made with a number of other compatible approaches (chapters 10 and 11). Although the Extended Mind Model is limited in its scope and does not account for all aspects of spoken language, it does complement a number of other models that more fully describe the emergence and evolution of language. I also show how the Extended Mind Model supports some of these models and critiques others and vice versa show how certain models (Christiansen 1994; Christiansen and Devlin 1997; Christiansen and Ellefson 2002; Christiansen and Kirby 2003; Clark 1997, 2003; Donald 1991, 1998; Deacon 1997, 2003; Jackendoff 2002; Schumann 2003a, 2003b; and Tomasello 1999) support and complement the Extended Mind Model. The synthesis that emerges from this analysis provides a feasible model or narrative for the way in which human language with all its complexities and many functions may have emerged.

In part 5, I explore the relationship of language and culture and the parallels that can be drawn between these two phenomena. In chapter 12, I focus on the co-evolution of language and culture. In chapter 13, the role of altruism in the emergence of language is examined. By extending Christiansen's notion that language may be treated or represented as an organism to culture, I show in chapter 14 that culture, like language, should have universal features and therefore propose the existence of Universal Culture as an analogue to the Universal Grammar. A survey of the literature on culture is made to support this hypothesis.

## A History of My Study of the Emergence and Evolution of Language

I am not a linguist or a cognitive scientist but rather a physicist who morphed into a media ecologist. I became interested in the impact of science on society as the result of a course I taught beginning in 1971 at the University of Toronto called the 'Poetry of Physics.' I was fascinated by the problem posed by Joseph Needham, in his book *The Grand Titration* (1979) of why abstract science began in the West even though so much of technology originated in China. I proposed that since monotheism and codified law were unique to the West and that together they give rise to a notion of universal law that this might explain the Needham paradox. I shared these thoughts with Marshall McLuhan, who immediately pointed out that the alphabet, which served as a model for analysis, classification, coding, and decoding, was also unique to the West. We combined our ideas and developed the hypothesis that the phonetic alphabet, codified law, monotheism, abstract science, and deductive logic were ideas unique to the West, and while they were not causally linked, they were self-supporting or autocatalytic (McLuhan and Logan 1977). I carried away from this work on the alphabet effect (Logan 2004a) the understanding that the way in which a language was notated could affect the way its users think and develop concepts.

The next project that I began was to study the impact of computer use on learning and work and, hence, cognition. Once again I came to the conclusion that the way in which language is notated affects the way in which we think and that language, like computing, is both a medium of communication and an informatics tool which I (Logan 1995, 2004b) formulated in terms of the equation:

$$\text{language} = \text{communications} + \text{informatics.}$$

A collaboration with Denise Schmandt-Besserat, who investigated the origin of writing and numerical notation (see Schmandt-Besserat 1992), led me to the conclusion that speech, writing, mathematics, science, and computing were each individual languages with their own unique semantics and syntax. A chance meeting with Ilya Prigogine, while visiting Schmandt-Besserat at the University of Texas, led to another conclusion – namely, that these five languages form an evolutionary chain and that each new language emerged as a new level of order in response to the chaos of an information overload that arose in conjunction with the use of the earlier languages (Logan 1995; also see chapter 2 herein for more details). I subsequently added the Internet to this evolutionary chain of languages as the sixth language (Logan 2004b).

This line of research led me to wonder how the first language, speech, might have come into existence. I made use of Prigogine's ideas once again and concluded that the complexity of hominid life, as detailed by Merlin Donald (1991), became so great that speech emerged as a transition from percept-based thought to concept-based thought. I further hypothesized that the first words were our first concepts and that they acted as strange attractors uniting the various perceptual experiences associated with that word. But more of this later when I present my Extended Mind Model in chapters 3 and 4, which I hope will stimulate discussion and dialogue with others in this field.

Because the origin of language took place tens of thousands of years ago there is, of courses, a dearth of empirical data to shed light on these events. My work with the evolution of notated language can provide a source of empirical data, which to date has been largely overlooked and perhaps provide some insights into our understanding of the emergence of language. I welcome all comments and criticisms of this work, which by its nature of trying to reconstruct events of our deepest past, is speculative. I invite readers to contact me with their thoughts and comments by email at logan@physics.utoronto.ca.

The second aim of this study is to review, juxtapose, compare, and synthesize the large body of work of the linguistic community on the origin of language, using the Extended Mind Model for the emergence of language (2000), which is based on my theory of the evolution of notated language (Logan 1995, 2004a, 2004b). These two bodies of work can inform each other. The thesis that will be developed in this essay is that historical data relating to the evolution of language after the advent of speech and beginning with the emergence of writing can shed light on the origin and evolution of human language and resolve some of the controversies and differences of opinion that exist in this field. At the same time, the origin of speech body of work can enrich our understanding of the evolution of notated language.

There are two basic assumptions from my previous work on notated languages that I would like to bring to this study of the origin of spoken language. One is the notion that language is at the same time both a medium of communication and an informatics tool used to represent abstract thoughts and that these two functions of language emerged simultaneously and co-evolved. As a result the question as to which came first, communication or representation, becomes moot. The language of thought – *mentalese*, as defined by Gerry Fodor (1975) – is nothing more than the natural language used for everyday communications.

As language allowed humans to communicate abstract concepts to each other they were also able to use these concepts for the internal dialogue of conceptual thinking. The two activities emerged simultaneously. The creation of verbal language represents a bifurcation from perceptual mental activity to one based on abstract concepts. For this reason, ideas from complexity or emergence theory will be used to suggest that the emergence of verbal language was a classical example of punctuated evolution in which the non-verbal, mimetic, percept-based preverbal forms of the language of hominids evolved into verbal concept-based speech and the inner voice that we call conscious thinking.

A second notion that I would like to bring to this study of the origin of language from my work on the evolution of notated language is the idea that new elements of language (and, hence, language itself) emerge from a response to an information overload due to an increased complexity in human life. Thus, the origin of speech represents a bifurcation from perceptual thinking to conceptual thinking brought on by the increased complexity of hominid life resulting from toolmaking, the control of fire, and the increased complexity of cooperative social structures that arose to take advantage of the hearth and large-scale coordinated hunting. I will go into the details of my Extended Mind Model later in this study (chapter 3).

In pursuing this project and offering my ideas to the reading public based on my work with the evolution of notated language, I am comforted by the following words of Derek Bickerton 'The sooner we start building bridges between the study of language, on the one hand, and studies of human evolution and human neurology on the other, the better. To be sure, our earliest proposals on the subject will probably be naive and misguided. This does not matter as long as we realize that those proposals are first approximations that will have to be revised countless times' (1995, 76).

I also regard as a mandate for the approach I have taken the following comment by Michael Tomasello, whose model for the emergence of language entails the process of sociogenesis, whereby something new is created through the social interaction of two or more individuals: 'Ideally we should know much more than we do about the processes of sociogenesis in different domains of activity in human history. Cultural psychologists, who should be concerned with this problem, have mostly not spent great effort in empirical investigations of the historical processes by means of which particular cultural institutions in particular cultures have taken shape ... Perhaps the most enlightening investigations of these processes are studies by intellectual historians concerned with such things as the history of technology, the history of science and mathematics, and language history' (1999, 209–10). My analysis of the evolution of notated language and its application to the origin of language problem is precisely the kind of knowledge that Tomasello is calling for here.

I have already confessed to the reader that, as far as the field of linguistics goes, I am autodidactic and not an expert. As a consequence, I have made liberal use of direct quotations and allowed the experts in the field to speak in their own words so as not to misrepresent their positions. Nevertheless, I want to apologize at the outset for any misrepresentations that many have occurred because of the context in which I have quoted them. I give all the authors full credit for their ideas that I have woven into my narrative and take responsibility for any errors or misrepresentations. This manuscript is part report on original research and part documentary.

One of the lessons of my work with the evolution of notated languages is that the emergence of new media change the nature of older media (Logan 2004b). Such is the case with the impact of the printing press, the airplane, and the Internet on the book. The printing press allowed identification of the author of a book to emerge and this led to correspondence between scientists who read each other's books. The airplane facilitated face-to-face meetings of scientists at conferences where ideas could be exchanged. The Internet allows the instantaneous exchange of ideas between the author and the reader. I hereby invite readers to communicate with me at logan@physics.utoronto.ca with their comments and criticisms.

Earlier versions of the Extended Mind Model, which is presented chapters 3 and 4, were first presented at the 7th Annual Conference of the Society for Chaos Theory in Psychology and the Life Sciences at Marquette University, Milwaukee, Wisconsin, on 1 August, 1997 (Logan 1997) and at the 57th Annual Convention of the New York State Communication Association, Monticello, New York, 8–10 October, 1999, but first appeared in print later (Logan 2000).

In closing, I wish to thank a number of experts in the field who have taken the time to comment on my ideas or have shared their ideas with me in various academic venues. These include Morten Christiansen, Rick Dale, Terry Deacon, Robert Este, Randy Goebel, David Hobill, Stuart Kauffman, Paul Levinson, Mark Lipton, John Locke, Maria Ielenszky Logan, Gary Lupyan, Alex Manu, Bruce Powe, Dwight Read, Dominique Scheffel Dunand, Denise Schmandt-Besserat, John Schumann, Ilya Shmulevich, Louis Stokes, Lance Strate, David Sloan Wilson, and Frank Zingrone.

# PART 1

## On the Origin and Evolution of Language

# 1 The History of the Study of the Origin of Language

The study of the origin of language has a fascinating history. In the nineteenth century, because of the dearth of data and a lack of a theoretical framework, all attempts to explain the origin of language were highly speculative and of little scientific value. The work that was presented became so arbitrary that the Linguistic Society of Paris, one of the most renowned linguistic societies of its day, banned, in 1866, the presentation of any papers that dealt with the origins of language. Linguists in the twentieth century, with the exception of a few neo-Darwinians, were quite content to describe the structures of languages, the way in which they operate, how they are learned, how they change, and so forth, carefully avoiding the question of their origin or why they exist. Noam Chomsky, no doubt the most influential linguist of the past fifty years, also avoided the question of the origins of language and was particularly sceptical about the possibility of a Darwinian explanation, asserting at one point that 'Darwinian theory is so loose it can incorporate everything' (in Horgan 1995, 154). Not all linguists (see Burling 1986; Calvin 1983; Hurford 1989; Krebs and Dawkins 1984; Lieberman 1973, 1975, 1984; Pinker and Bloom 1990), despite their respect for Chomsky's work, were ready to give up on 'natural selection' and accept that a universal grammar was hard-wired into the human brain by some mysterious mechanism.

Although most scholars now believe natural selection has played an important role in the emergence of language, opinions differ as to whether natural selection operated solely on the human genome has, as been suggested by Steven Pinker and Paul Bloom (1990), or whether it acted on both the human genome up to a certain point after which language and/or culture evolved so as to be easily acquired, as I find to be the case, and as has been suggested by Morten Christiansen (1994), Terrence Deacon (1997), Michael Tomasello (1999), Andy Clark (1997, 2003), as well as others.

In addition to this basic division, there are still a great many different approaches and hypotheses to explain the emergence of language. Each model seems to emphasize a different aspect of human language as the starting point for the origin of language. Some start with phonology, others with social interactions and/or social intelligence. There is debate as to whether the primary function of speech is as a medium of communication or as a medium of thought. Some maintain that language evolved extremely gradually over millions of years, while others posit a sudden or catastrophic appearance of speech. Some suggest that language evolved from hand signals or other forms of mimetic communication; others hold that language began with vocalization. Furthermore, there is debate as to which came first: a lexicon or syntactic structure?

Ib Ulbaek, commenting on his work and that of others who accept a Darwinian approach wrote, 'Each has put his own fingerprint on the general outlook' (1998, 32). All of these many approaches draw upon a variety of data sets, but none examine the evolution of notated language for which there exists excellent documentary and/or historical evidence which I make use of in my approach.

Although I have developed my own independent model for the emergence of language based on my earlier work, I must confess that as I read the cogent arguments presented by the proponents of other approaches to this problem I have come to the conclusion that there is a great deal of merit in their work. In many cases, I find the arguments made by those with different points of view very compelling, if perhaps a bit overstated or too single-minded. I have conclude that their conflicts are due in part to a difference of emphasis or perhaps a familiarity or bias with their own field of specialty. This is not to paper over some of the real differences, but rather to represent my view that a synthesis of the different models is in order. I was reminded of the three blind men who came to different conclusions as to the nature of an elephant on the basis of each separately examining the trunk, a leg, and the tail, and they concluded respectively that the elephant was a snake, a tree, and a rope. So it is that linguists have come to different conclusions as to the nature of language that range from the idea that it is (1) a social mechanism of communication, (2) a medium of thought, (3) a phonological phenomenon, (4) a semantic tool, and (5) a generative grammar. We shall see that, like the elephant, language is all of these things, indeed, language is a multidimensional phenomenon.

It was extremely appropriate that Tecumseh Fitch opened the Fourth Evolution of Language Conference at Harvard University in the spring of 2002 with the following statement from Susanne K. Langer: 'The chance that the key ideas of any professional scholar's work are pure nonsense is small; much greater the chance that a devastating refutation is based on a superficial reading or even a distorted one, subconsciously twisted by a desire to refute.' Like the blind men inspecting the elephant we approach the questions of the origin of language without a complete picture of the phenomenon. Our blindness stems from the fact that the emergence of language is buried in the very distant prehistoric past and the empirical evidence at our disposal is limited. If, however, we take a lesson from the three blind men and try to synthesize the views of scholars who have studied the origin and nature of language with the data and tools at their disposal, perhaps we can arrive at a picture that incorporates the best of the many models that have been proposed in this fascinating field.

Before proposing my own model I would like to clearly state my biases in undertaking this task. All biological processes, including the origin of speech, are governed by both Darwinian natural selection and plectic processes. *Plectics* is a word coined by Murray Gell Mann (1996), and it is the generic term for chaotics, complexity theory, emergence theory, complex adaptive systems theory, or any of the other flavours of nonlinear dynamics theory. Examples of plectic processes include Ilya Prigogine's (1997) idea of order out of chaos for processes far from equilibrium, Stuart Kauffman's (1995) notion of life emerging from autocatalytic sets of organic chemicals that self-organized, and Per Bak's (1996) idea of self-organizing criticality. Christiansen's (1994) notion of language as an organism, Deacon's (1997) model for the emergence of symbolic representation, Tomasello's notion of sociogenesis and joint attention, and Clark's model of embedded cognition also contain examples of emergence or plectic processes.

Perhaps making a distinction between Darwinian natural selection and plectics is unnecessary. I believe, as do many others, that the ultimate explanation of Darwinian natural selection will be in terms of plectics. In this stage of our understanding of biological processes, natural selection and complexity or emergence theory seem to some like two independent approaches, but with time they will eventually converge and be shown to be equivalent.

When speaking of Darwinian natural selection, we usually think of the genetic evolution of a biological system. But, as pointed out by Linnda Caporael (2001, 612): 'Natural selection is a powerful general principle in the world of living things. What makes a theory 'evolutionary' or 'Darwinian' is not that it is based in biology, but rather the integration of three interacting principles of change: variation, selection, and retention. What varies, what are the conditions for selection, and what are the mechanisms for retention may differ: neuronal selection, selection in the immune system, and learning are all examples of selection (Cziko 1995). Cultural artifacts, practices, and even scientific theories may be selected (Campbell 1997).'

Deacon pointed out human speech 'is an evolutionary anomaly, not merely an evolutionary extreme' (1997, 34) and therefore human speech represents a discontinuity, a quantum leap, in the behaviour of animal life. The communication behaviours of non-human animals are not languages but, because we are so used to thinking of communication in terms of language, some make the mistake of identifying animal communication as language despite its lack of generativity and its extremely small number of independent signals.

Generalization is one of the primary goals of science and a key component of the scientific method. This does not mean that all natural phenomena are necessarily the same or unified. The first attempts to explain the nuclear force were in terms of electromagnetic forces. After many failures it was realized that the nuclear force was not an extreme of the electromagnetic forces but a new phenomenon. Similarly human communication through verbal language is not an 'evolutionary extreme' of animal communication; it is a new phenomenon. The same is true of non-linear dynamics; it is not an extreme form of linear dynamics but the new phenomenon of chaotics or emergence. The discontinuity in communication in the transition from animal to human communication is in part a product of the discontinuity between linear and non-linear dynamics.

Non-linear systems and linear systems both belong to the class of dynamic systems, but as soon as one introduces a single non-linear element one moves through a discontinuity in behaviour into the domain of chaotic systems. The non-linear system is not an extreme (or a more complicated form) of a linear system, as was once claimed by physicists. Non-linear systems exhibits emergent behaviour. The butterfly effect is anomalous. The same is true of animal communication; as soon as one introduces a single conceptual or symbolic element one moves through a discontinuity in behaviour into the domain of language systems as opposed to communication systems. A non-linear system is still a dynamic system, but its behaviour is anomalous when compared with a linear system. By the same token, a human linguistic system is still a communication system, but it is an anomalous systems compared with an animal communication system.

This analysis leads naturally to the question: Was the emergence of language a Darwinian process or a process dominated by complexity or plectics? I am of the opinion that self-organization plays an important role in the emergence of language and is certainly a product of non-linear dynamic processes, but this does not preclude the possibility that neo-Darwinian mechanisms operated on both the human genome and on language itself. It is also certainly the case that the origin of language cannot be explained by a single causal factor. The nature of language is extremely complex, and language is the product of many different mechanisms all of which had to be in place for it to have emerged. These include phonemic articulation, phonemic generativity, lexical creation, conceptual representation, comprehension, a theory of the mind, syntax, and generativity of propositions. Speech serves two functions: social communication and as representation of and a medium for abstract thought.

As to the order in which these functions and mechanisms emerged, it is neither prudent nor practical to assume that they emerged in a linear sequential manner like a string of beads on a necklace. There is certainly good evidence from ecology and genetics to conclude that the Darwinian process of the evolution of species is one of co-evolution. There is no reason to believe that the biological processes that led to the emergence of human language should be any different and, therefore, I believe, that the functions and mechanics cited above co-evolved. In developing my model for the emergence of language, and in attempting to synthesize it with the others models of the origin of speech, I will take the tack that the communicative and cognitive functions of human language and the multiple mechanisms that made speech possible co-evolved together as an autocatalytic system of communication and thought.

**Tinbergen's Four Why's**

After the publication of the article by Pinker and Bloom (1990), which reconciled the conflict between Chomsky's approach and that of the neo-Darwinians, many other articles began to appear, each proposing a different model for the origin of speech. Although each model was based on natural selection each focused on a different aspect of human language. An interesting way to analyse the strength and weaknesses of these different schemes is to make use of Nikolaas Tinbergen's (1963) identification of four kinds of questions (known as the Four Why's) that need to be addressed to understand any biological phenomenon, in this case, human language. They are questions about: (1) function (or purpose), (2) mechanisms (or machinery), (3) ontogeny (or development), and (4) phylogeny (or evolutionary history).

Most models for the origin of speech address only one or two of these categories, but rarely do they consider all four at once which is necessary, I believe, to understand a phenomenon as complex as speech. Some phonologists, for example, assert that language began as the ability to enunciate phonemes which led to the functionality of language as a social and cognitive tool, whereas the social theorists put it the other way around – that functions related to social needs motivated the use of language which then created a selective pressure to be able to expand the phonology. Experts often see the phenomena that they study as the starting point of language and the other factors as consequences: 'Depending on which aspects of language are deemed to be most complex, different prior adaptations are invoked to explain how language became possible' (Deacon 1997, 25). No doubt I am guilty of a similar bias as a physicist, who makes use of complexity or emergence theory and the notion that speech and conceptualization emerged simultaneously as a result of the complexity of hominid life. This bias also motivates my assumption that language is both a medium of social communication and an informatics tool used for the representation of abstract concepts.

The Extended Mind Model, which will be developed in chapters 3 and 4, simultaneously considers all four of Tinbergen's Four Why's and incorporates the notion that the functions and mechanisms of language co-evolved. In other words, mechanisms emerge to serve functions and functions emerge from mechanisms that perhaps served as pre-adaptations for those functions. The ontogenetic and phylogenetic relationship of functions and mechanisms is that of elements of a non-linear dynamic biological system. Another advantage of this position is that it reconciles a number of conflicts between competing models, each of which have much merit, and allows them to be synthesized. Rather than taking an either/or position on competing models I prefer a both/and approach. Andrew Carstairs-McCarthy shares a similar sentiment vis-à-vis the debate as to whether grammar is adaptive. He finds that 'what both sides in this debate have generally had in common, so far, is an all-or-nothing attitude: either grammar is adaptive or it is not. But from the point of view of evolutionary biology, that attitude seems oversimple' (2000, 249).

For language to have emerged, there must have been an important function that it served and, hence, was selected for. There had to be mechanisms to allow language to be realized. To understand the relationship between the functions and the mechanisms of language, it is useful to consider Marshall McLuhan's aphorism: 'The medium is the message.' It incorporates the notion that independent of its content or messages, a medium has its own intrinsic effects on our way of thinking which are its unique message: 'The medium is the message because it is the medium that shapes and controls the scale and form of human association and action' (1964, 9).

The effects of a medium impose a new environment and set of sensibilities upon its users. It is helpful to consider the function of language as its message and the mechanisms of speech as its medium. McLuhan observed that not only is the medium the message, but the medium is also an extension of the psyche. One cannot consider the message, or the function of language as separate from its mechanisms or medium. The medium (or mechanisms) not only makes it possible for messages to exist, but it also influences the nature of the message or the function of language. Conversely, the need for the message or function creates the medium or the mechanisms. Necessity is the mother of invention, but each new invention or machinery, in turn, creates new needs and, hence, more inventions. The process and the relationship between the two is non-linear, continuous, and never ending.

In addition to considering the function and the mechanisms of language, as well as their relationship, we must also consider the ontogeny (or development) and the phylogeny (or evolutionary history) of speech because we are dealing with a biological system and not with a technology that can be designed and built by a sentient being. Not only must the mechanisms we identify be able to achieve the function of language, they must satisfy two other conditions: (1) they must be something that can be easily learned by a child and (2) they must have evolved from some of the features of a simpler biological system, namely, those of our hominid ancestors.

Most of the models we encounter in the literature start with either a function of speech or with a mechanism. The two initial functions of language that are exclusively cited are social communication and conceptual or representational thinking. Those who hold that the development of a mechanism led to speech often cite phonology (and phonemic generativity) or syntax (and syntactical generativity). Other models start with some form of non-human primate or prehuman hominid behaviour such as hand signalling, vocalizing, socializing, throwing, or toolmaking. The only model that takes ontogeny as its starting point is Chomsky's, where it is assumed that the human brain is hard-wired with the Universal Grammar (UG) and a Language Acquisition Device (LAD) and, hence, actually avoids dealing with the phylogeny of language and assumes that the ontogeny is automatic.

In the next chapter I will summarize my previous work with the evolution of notated language and its emergence from speech to set the stage for my model for the emergence of speech itself.

# PART 2

## The Extended Mind Model

# 2 The Evolution of Notated Language

Every particular notation stresses some particular point of view.

Ludwig Wittgenstein

## The Six Modes of Language

The computer and the Internet are the most recent techniques for organizing human thought in a long series of techniques and technologies, beginning with speech, for communicating, storing, retrieving, organizing, and processing information. The series includes spoken language, pictures, tallies, clay tokens, picture writing, logographic (pictographic or ideographic) writing, syllabaries, the alphabet, abstract numbers, numerals, mathematical signs (+, −, ×, =), the concept of zero, geometry, mathematics, logic, abstract science, maps, graphs, charts, libraries, the printing press, encyclopedia, dictionaries, bookkeeping techniques, the scientific method, photography, the telegraph, the telephone, cinema, radio, audio recording, television, video recording, optical disks, computers, control theory, cybernetics, and the Internet.

Computing and the Internet, however, are more than just new technologies. They represent new forms of language, if we accept that language is defined as a system for both communications and informatics. Computing and the Internet, which encompasses the World Wide Web, are part of an evolutionary chain of languages, which also includes speech, writing, mathematics, and science. To establish my hypothesis, I will show that these six modes of language are distinct, each with its own semantics and syntax. Through historical analysis, I will demonstrate that each new mode of language evolved from the previous forms as new information-processing needs arose and that each new language subsumed the structures and elements of the earlier languages (Logan 2004b).

## A New Concept of Language

Traditionally, the sole focus of linguists in defining language has been on communication. One example is Edward Sapir's (1921) definition of *language*: 'a purely human and non-instinctive method of communicating ideas, emotions, and desires by means of a system of voluntarily produced symbols.' While it is true that the main function of language has been communication, this is not its only function; language also plays a key role in the processing of information, including its storage, retrieval, and organization. Language is a tool for developing new concepts and ideas; it is an open-ended system. Since writing, mathematics, science, computing, and the Internet permit the development of ideas that could never have arisen through the use of speech alone, we must consider these other modes as distinct, albeit related, languages.

Generalizing and extending Sapir's definition, I define *language* as a purely human and non-instinctive method of communicating ideas, emotions, and desires, as well as processing, storing, retrieving, and organizing information by means of a system of voluntarily produced symbols. Given this definition of language, it is necessary to recognize that speech is not the only form of language. My suggestion that speech and writing, for instance, are two distinct but related forms or modes of language differs from the beliefs of traditional linguists who consider speech as the primary form of language and writing as merely a system for transcribing or recording it. This tradition dates back to Aristotle, who postulated that 'the sounds ... are symbols of ideas evoked in the soul and writing is a symbol of the sounds' (Bandle et al. 1958, 95).

Ferdinand de Saussure (1967), one of the founders of the field of linguistics, formulated the modern attitude of linguistics towards writing when he wrote in 1916: 'Language and writing are two different systems of signs; the latter only exists for the purpose of representing the former ... The subject matter of linguistics is not the connection between the written and spoken word, but only the latter, the spoken word is its subject.' De Saussure's position was reinforced later by another immensely influential linguist, Leonard Bloomfield, who stated that 'writing is not language, but merely a way of recording language by means of visible marks' (1993, 21).

The relationship between writing and language, as posited by de Saussure and Bloomfield, is far too confining for understanding the implications of microcomputers and the Internet for the future of communication, work, and education. Their definitions are restricted to a model in which the sole purpose of language is communication; they do not take into account the information-processing capabilities of language. The definitions of Bloomfield and de Saussure have been re-evaluated by a modern generation of linguists, who view language from the perspective of informatics and, hence, understand the multitasking nature of language.

Michael Stubbs critiques Bloomfield's definition, making the observation that 'writing is not merely a record ... I know from personal experience that formulating ideas in written language changes those ideas and produces new ones' (1980, 53). Joyce Hertzler concurs, noting that 'people often find that their thoughts are clarified and systematized, and that necessary qualifications and extensions appear, when they subject them to the more rigorous test of exactness and completeness demanded by the written form' (1965, 444). Frank Smith, too, agrees stating that 'ideas develop from interaction and dialogue ... especially with one's own writing' (1982, 204). Wallace Chafe suggests that 'language is used in a variety of ways, each of which affects the shape that language takes. Since the 1970s, ever-increasing attention has been paid to differences between spoken language and written language, and it has become clear that each of these two broad categories allows for diverse uses and forms' (1998, 96).

While it is true that written language is derived from spoken language, it is useful to regard writing and speaking as two separate language modes because they process information so differently. Arguments that support the notion that writing is a separate mode of language can also be made for mathematics, science, computing, and the Internet. These five additional modes of language each have unique strategies for communicating, storing, retrieving, organizing, and processing information. I have, therefore, extended the notion of those linguists who consider speech and writing as separate modes of language to claim that speech, writing, mathematics, science, computing, and the Internet are six separate modes of language, which are distinct but interdependent. They form an evolutionary sequence in which the later modes are derived from and incorporate elements of the earlier modes of language. They form a nested set of languages in which the later forms contain all of the elements of the earlier forms.

Speech, the first form of human language, is the basis of all other linguistic modes of communication and information processing. We can define *spoken language* as the sum of information uttered by human speakers. *Written language*, which is derived from speech, is defined as the sum of information that has been notated with visual signs. Writing differs from speech in that it involves a permanent record, whereas speech disappears immediately after it is uttered. We shall distinguish five different modes or forms of written language: writing (or literature), mathematics, abstract science, computing, and the Internet. Writing and mathematical notations were the first forms of written language; both grew out of the system of recording payments of agricultural tributes using clay accounting tokens in Sumer, just over five thousand years ago. The language of science and its methodology emerged from writing and mathematics in ancient Greece some twenty-five hundred years ago. The methods and findings of science are expressed in the languages of writing and mathematics, but science may be regarded as a separate form of language because it has a unique way of systematically processing, storing, retrieving, and organizing information, which is quite different from either literature or mathematics. A little more than sixty years ago, the next system for processing information emerged from science and mathematics in the form of computing, with its own unique cybernetically based and automated methods for processing and organizing information. Finally, the latest form of language emerged from computing and telecommunications in the form of the Internet and the World Wide Web.

Whether these six modes of information processing and communication should be regarded as separate languages or whether they are merely six different aspects of the human capacity for languaging are questions I will not attempt to answer. For the purposes of this analysis, I will consider speech, writing, mathematics, science, computing, and the Internet as six distinct modes of language, which form an evolutionary chain of development. What these modes of language share is a distinct method for the communication and processing of information, each of which changes our world-view. Just as Sapir argues that cultures dissect nature along the lines dictated by their native languages, so the six languages of information processing each provide a unique framework for viewing the world.

## A Model for the Evolution of Thought from Language

In *Thought and Language,* Lev Vygotsky (1962) shows that language plays both a communication and an information-processing role. In his attempt to demonstrate the relationship between thought and language, Vygotsky posits three phases in a child's development of verbal thought: social speech, egocentric speech, and inner speech.

Vygotsky's first form of speech – 'social speech' – is purely for the purpose of communication and is non-intellectual. After using language as a tool for communication and social intercourse, the child discovers that language is also useful for facilitating her thought processes. The child then begins to display a phenomenon known as 'egocentric speech,' in which he is basically talking to himself. The child vocalizes but is not addressing anyone in particular. This form of speech, which commences at about age three, continues to about age seven, when it suddenly disappears and is replaced by 'inner speech' – or thought. At first, egocentric speech does not differ greatly from social speech, but as the child matures, the speech takes on more and more of the aspects of inner speech. Vygotsky's observations of children ages three to seven reveal that human beings resort to egocentric speech whenever they are confronted with a puzzling situation they need to think through. Vygotsky concludes that egocentric speech is basically the child thinking out loud and that it naturally evolves into inner speech once the child realizes that the vocalization is not necessary for the main function of this form of speech, namely, problem-solving or thinking: 'We came to the conclusion that inner speech develops through a slow accumulation of functional and structural changes, that it branches off from the child's external speech simultaneously with the differentiation of the social and the egocentric functions of speech, and finally that the speech structures mastered by the child become the basic structures of his thinking' (Vygotsky 1962, 51).

Vygotsky's model is based on the notion that speech or language has two components: communication and informatics. Language in the form of social speech in children younger than age three is pure communication and social interaction. With egocentric and inner speech, language becomes a tool for processing information or assisting the child to think. The only difference between egocentric and inner speech is that the former, which appears first, is vocalized, and the latter is not. But both serve the same function. Once inner speech emerges and is used solely for the purposes of thought, egocentric speech disappears, and vocalized speech is used exclusively for communication purposes except in times of stress, when even adults sometimes think out loud by talking to themselves.

### The Evolution of the Six Modes of Language

The two principle uses of speech are for communication and abstracting experience through conceptualization. In preliterate societies speech was the medium for social interactions and a tool for the coordination of activities that require cooperation, such as hunting or food gathering. Spoken language evolved more complex functions and was used in the cultural apparatus of a society to tell stories and sing songs. Eventually, speech was used as a medium to record (or store) and retrieve cultural information in the form of poems, folk tales, and folk songs. As stories became more complex, speech was used to organize the information stored in these formats. Organizational forms such as rhyme, rhythm, meter, and plot, in turn, became information tools, which permitted larger amounts of data to be stored and successfully retrieved (Havelock 1963).

Eventually, however, speech and the human capacity for memorization encountered limits as to how much data could be recorded in this manner. Writing systems and numerical notations emerged, which allowed the amount and type of data being stored to expand enormously. The invention of writing and mathematical notations had a tremendous impact on the informatics capacity of human language and thought. Written records gave rise to new forms of classification, analysis, and other forms of information processing. The increase in the information-processing capacity that mathematical notations make possible is easily confirmed by comparing the complexity of mathematical calculations that can be done with pencil and paper with calculations done solely in one's head.

The increase in the amount and sophistication of data that writing and mathematics make possible eventually gave rise to a new form of language and information processing – the language of science. Scientific activity, whether it is concrete or abstract, is confined to literate societies. Science is not just the gathering of new knowledge about nature; it also consists of giving a shape to that knowledge by organizing it systematically. Science is a form of knowledge management. The effective storage and information processing that writing and mathematics make possible allowed scholars to gather and collect so much data that the only way to deal with the ensuing complexity and the information overload was to develop a new mode of organization known as the scientific method. Science and the scientific method, however, also became a tool for generating still more information-gathering activities. The information overload that modern science and the scientific method helped to generate became so great in the twentieth century that it led to the development of computers as a way to help scientists cope with the enormous amounts of data they accumulated and the complex calculations they needed to execute.

Vygotsky's work shows how children discover that language, a medium of communication, can also be used as a tool to process information and solve problems. One can easily extend this notion backwards in time and assume that, at some point, humans discovered that their system of vocalized verbal signals could be used internally, as a tool for thinking. It might even be the case that speech arose to make conceptual thinking possible and was then used for communication purposes. And a third possibility is that language emerged simultaneously as both a tool for thinking and a medium for communication.

The extension of speech and its concretization in the form of writing, mathematics, science, computing, and the Internet leveraged language as a tool for thinking and amplified its informatics capacity while preserving its communication function. The motivation for the emergence of new forms of language, however, seems to have been strictly the need for a greater informatics capacity, not a need for increased communication.

Writing was first used not for communication but for the keeping of accounting records. For the period just after the emergence of writing, 'few literary documents [have been] excavated, although the same period has yielded tens of thousands of economic and administrative tablets and hundreds of votive inscriptions' (Kramer 1959). The very first words to be assigned a written form in the Sumerian language were the words for agricultural commodities that were collected as tribute by the priesthood who administered the irrigation system. They used writing to record who paid their taxes to the state. Written numerals were invented at the same time as writing to keep track of the amounts of each commodity that were given in tribute.

The invention of writing and abstract numerals illustrates cyberneticist Ross Ashby's (1957) Law of Requisite Variety, as well as the notion that necessity is the mother of invention. According to Ashby, managers can only control a system if they can create a model of it that contains the requisite variety or complexity to accurately describe it. The priests running the irrigation system in Sumer needed to collect tribute from farmers in order to feed the irrigation workers. They, therefore, needed to store and keep track of a complex set of data. Given that human memory has difficulty coping with more than seven, plus or minus two, elements at a time, the only way the priests could remember who had paid their tribute and who had not was to create permanent records of the tributes. It was only after the invention of writing for the purposes of economic control that writing was also used for the purposes of communication, and eventually, for other informatics applications such as the composition of stories or written poems.

The development of science was also motivated by purely informatics considerations. Abstract science permitted greater control of nature through better organization of information and the ability to make predictions. The scientific method provided scientists with the requisite variety to control a body of knowledge that the languages of writing and mathematics had not been able to manage.

The invention of computing is still another example of informatics driving the development of language. Without computing, natural and social scientists would not have been able to manage the information overload created by their disciplines. It was only after its initial application as an informatics device that computing was also used for communications, and hence, its name in English is 'computer' (as in calculator) and not 'word processor,' even though by now far more users process words with computers than compute or calculate numbers with them.

The Internet is another example of a new form of language that emerged from an information overload. Computing increased the sheer number of messages that needed to be communicated as well as the number of people that needed to be communicated with. As the world shrunk to the dimensions of a global village, the number of people in the village with whom one wanted to communicate increased dramatically. This information overload or traffic jam of messaging gave rise to networking, client-server systems, and finally, the Internet. The Internet, as opposed to client-servers systems, was able to encompass the entire global community in a single electronic embrace. As is so often the case, a quantitative change created a qualitative change, and as a result a new language emerged: the Internet, or the sixth language.

Starting with the ability to record ideas through writing and mathematical notation, human thought has become increasingly more complex. The need to model more complex phenomena has driven the development of the six modes of language. Consequently, each new mode of language is informatically more powerful than its predecessors, but at the same time a little less poetic, with the exception of the Net, which because of its visual and audio elements is able to incorporate the arts and an artistic mode of expression. Our model of the evolution of language is one in which the information-processing capacity of language becomes more and more important as the complexity of human thought increases. It is essential to remember, however, that all forms of language possess a dual capacity for communication and information processing. Computers and the Internet are also communication devices and the spoken word has an informatics capacity. Both of these features of language must be addressed when we consider the origin of language.

**The Semantics and Syntax of the Six Modes of Language**

The claim made here that writing, mathematics, science, computing, and the Internet are distinctive modes of human language is based on the notion that a language is defined by both its information-processing powers and its capacity for communication. To strengthen the claim that these five modes of language may be regarded as languages in their own right, and not just derivatives of speech, I will demonstrate that they qualify for this distinction solely on the basis of the criteria established by traditional linguists. According to Allan Paivio and Ian Begg, 'semantics and syntax – meaning and grammatical patterning – are the indispensable core attributes of any human language' (1981, 25). Semantics is the relationship between linguistic signals and their meaning or, in other words, a lexicon: 'Naming is undoubtedly the most straightforward and dramatic example of such semantic behavior' (ibid.). Syntax is the structure or relationship among linguistic signals.

New modes of language evolved to model increasingly more complex phenomena and, hence, according to Ashby's Law of Requisite Variety, they required more complex structures to function. We, therefore, expect the semantics and the syntax of the new forms of language to retain the older structures and add their own new unique elements to those structures.

If writing, mathematics, science, computing, and the Internet are distinct modes of human language, which deserve to be differentiated from speech, then they must have distinct semantic and syntactical features above and beyond those of speech. In the case of writing, the semantics of the written word are quite similar to those of the spoken word, although there are examples where a construction that is acceptable in oral language is not valid in prose and vice versa. Oral contractions such as 'don't' or 'can't' are not widely used in formal prose writing. As a rule, one's written vocabulary is considerably greater than one's oral vocabulary. We often use words in our written communications that we would never use in our oral discourse. Written signs, however, have an additional semantic feature above and beyond the spoken words they represent in that they denote at the same time spoken sounds (phonemes), spoken syllables, and spoken words, and hence, carry a double level of abstraction: a written sign denotes a spoken word which, in turn, denotes a concept from the real world. In logographic systems such as hieroglyphics, visual signs denote whole words. In syllabic systems, the visual signs represent syllables, and in phonetic alphabets, the letters represent phonemes (Logan 2004a). Words in the latter two systems are represented respectively by some combination of either syllables or letters, depending on the system.

It is at the syntactical level that written language begins to more radically distinguish itself from speech. Punctuation serves a function beyond semantically reproducing the natural pauses and reflections of speech; mainly, it provides a syntactical structure to language that is quite different from that of speech. Writing encourages a formal structuring of language consisting of sentences, paragraphs, sections, and chapters largely absent in spoken language. Analysis of the transcription of most oral discourse reveals that spoken language is not generally organized into grammatically correct sentences. In fact, the very term *grammar* betrays its association with writing through its etymology. The Greek term for *letter*, as in letters of the alphabet, is *gramma*. There are similar associations in other languages – grāmatas in the Latvian language means books. In short, grammar was not formalized before writing, just as there was no such thing as spelling before writing, and no uniform spelling before the printing press.

Grammars are not exact sets of rules: 'Were a language ever completely "grammatical" it would be a perfect engine of conceptual expression. Unfortunately, or rather luckily, no language is tyrannically consistent. All grammars leak' (Stubbs 1980, 39). Before writing, rigorous grammatical conventions were not necessary because any ambiguities could be resolved either by tone, facial expression, or dialogue. Listeners could always ask for an explanation if they did not understand what was said. This is not the case with writing, where readers are, basically, on their own.

In addition to the formal distinctions between written and spoken language, there is also the empirical change of semantics and syntax that the storage features of writing encourage. Within the semantic domain, one observes a marked increase in abstract words and terminology as a language acquires a written form. A comparison of the lexicon of Homer (as found in the transcriptions of his orally composed poems) and that of the ancient Greek philosophers and playwrights of the fifth and fourth centuries BCE reveals the development of a new written vocabulary. The new lexicon of written words is rich in abstract terminology appearing in the language for the first time, and old words take on additional new abstract meanings (Havelock 1963).

M.A.K. Halliday regards written and spoken languages as quite distinct: 'Written language never was, and never has been, conversation written down' (1989, 41). He distinguishes content words from function or grammatical words such as *the, and, then, to* (ibid., 61). He next points out that the ratio of content words to function words is much higher for written language as compared with spoken language, and as a result the information density of written language is much greater than that of speech. Another interesting distinction that Halliday has identified is that 'written language represents phenomena as products. Spoken language represents phenomena as processes ... A piece of writing is an object; so what is represented by written language is also given the form of an object ... But when you talk, you are doing; so when you represent by talking you say that something happened or something was done' (ibid., 81). To contrast the two forms of language Halliday considers the written and oral expression of the same basic proposition. One might write, '*Opinion in the colony greeted the promised change with enthusiasm,*' instead of saying, '*The people in the colony rejoiced when it was promised that things would change in this way.*' The written sentence contains one verb and has a content word-to-grammatical word ratio of six to four, whereas the spoken sentence contains three verbs and has a content word-to-grammatical word ratio of seven to ten.

Tomasello, too, believes there are significant differences between written and oral expression: 'One finds that SSS [spontaneous spoken speech] and written language are very different grammatically (Miller and Weinert 1998). Many constructions occur only or mainly in speech, for example, imperatives and interrogatives, or only in writing, for example, some types of complex nominals, but not in both' (2003a, 4).

Within the syntactical domain, the major structural change with writing is the appearance of the prose system, which incorporates many more analytical features than the oral tradition. With writing, not only do visual syntactical elements appear, such as the spaces between words and the separations of sentences, paragraphs, and chapters, but the creation of permanent records through writing also gave rise to new syntactical elements such as charts, tabulations, tables of contents, and indexes:

Givo´n (1979) ... and many others have suggested that the use of subordinate clauses increases dramatically with literacy. The major study along these lines is Kalma'r (1985), which maintains that Samoyed, Bushman, Seneca and various Australian languages rarely employ subordination. According to Kalma'r: 'It is quite likely that the number of subordinate clause types grew as narrative developed and accelerated with the advent of writing. Typical is the development of subordination in Greek, which hardly existed in Homer but was well developed in the classics (Goodwin 1912).' Mithun (1984) has made the same point in a Berkeley Linguistic Society paper. She undertook text counts on a number of languages with respect to the amount of subordination that one finds in discourses carried out in those languages. All languages manifest some subordination but there is a strong correlation between its rare use and the pre-literate status of their speakers. (Newmeyer 2002, 369)

In the language of mathematics, the semantic domain or lexicon consists primarily of precisely defined notations for numbers such as 0, 1, 2, 100, 1/2, 0.4, and the square root of 2; mathematical operations such as +, −, ×, and ÷; and logical relationships such as >, <, and =. The other semantic elements unique to mathematics are its definitions and axioms, such as those found in geometry, number theory, and other logical systems. The language of mathematics differs from natural language such as spoken English in that the semantic relationship between the signal – in this case, a visual sign like a numeral – and the phenomenon being represented, as an abstract number is totally unambiguous. In written languages, there are often ambiguities between the written signal and the spoken word being denoted. With the exception of totally phonetic languages such as Spanish and Finnish, there are also ambiguities of pronunciation. George Bernard Shaw's famous example (Stubbs 1980, 51) of using 'ghoti' to render the spoken word 'fish' – taking 'gh' from enough, 'o' from women, and 'ti' from nation – dramatically demonstrates the pronunciation ambiguities of the English alphabet.

The precision of the semantic conventions of mathematics extends to the syntactical domain. The basic syntax of the language of mathematics is that of logic. Mathematical syntax, unlike that of spoken or written language, again, is totally unambiguous. The rules of grammar that govern speech and writing are subject to conflicting interpretations, while those of mathematics are not. The language of mathematics introduces unique syntactical structures not found in natural languages, such as proofs, theorems, and lemmas.

The language of science includes the semantic elements of speech, writing, and mathematics, but it also introduces new semantic units unique unto itself. These include quantitative concepts like mass, force, velocity, mole; qualitative concepts like organic/inorganic, animate/inanimate, solid/liquid/gas, and intelligence; and theoretical concepts like inertia, entropy, valence, and natural selection. As is the case with the language of mathematics, the semantics of science is characterized by precise and unambiguous definitions even though much of the terminology that is employed corresponds to words that appear in everyday spoken language. In spoken English, mass can refer to either volume or weight. In physics mass is precisely defined in terms of its gravitational and inertial properties and a careful distinction is made between mass and weight. An object's mass is universal, but its weight depends upon what planet or in what gravitational field it finds itself. A traveller in outer space might experience weightlessness but never masslessness.

As was the case with semantics, the syntax of science includes the structure of speech, writing, and mathematics. Science also introduces its own syntactical elements, however. The three most important ones, the elements, which in a sense define the nature of science, are (1) the scientific method, (2) the classification of information or data (taxonomy), and (3) the organization of knowledge such as the grouping of scientific laws to form a scientific theory. The centrality of the classificatory and organizational structures is due to the fact that science is defined as organized knowledge. The scientific method, with its elements of observation, generalization, hypothesizing, experimental testing, and verification, is the key element that defines the character of science. It is the scientific method that qualifies science as a distinctive language rather than a carefully organized scholarly activity like history, which also makes use of organizational principles and other modes of language, namely, speech, writing, and mathematics.

The language of computing includes all of the semantic and syntactical elements of the earlier four modes of language. It also possesses its own semantic and syntactical elements by virtue of the activities of both its programmers and its end users. The semantics of the programming languages and end-user software programs specify computer inputs and outputs. The syntactical structures of programming languages and end-users' software formalize the procedures for transforming inputs into outputs. These syntactical structures are basically unambiguous algorithms for ensuring the accuracy and the reliability of the computer's output. The syntactical structures that arise in a programming language or a relational database differ from the other language modes so that the user can take advantage of the computer's rapid information-processing speeds.

Although the Internet and the World Wide Web incorporate all of the semantic and syntactical elements of computing, they also include their own unique elements in both categories. Perhaps we should clarify the relationship between the Web and the Net. The World Wide Web is one of many different elements of the Internet, which include its email facilities, listservs, chat rooms, ftp facilities, Telnet facilities, Web pages, Web sites, intranets, extranets, portal sites, and e-commerce sites. Each of these facilities represents the semantic elements of the sixth language of the Internet. Listservs are a way of distributing emails to a group of users who share an interest in a common topic, which allows an asynchronous email dialogue to take place. A chat room is a place on the Internet where people can meet online to discuss a topic in real time. The ftp facility allows files to be transferred from one computer to another through the medium of the Internet. The Telnet facility allows a user to access their server or home computer from anywhere in the world as long as they can find access to the Internet. Web pages are components of Web sites or intranets, which integrate text, graphics, video, and audio. Web sites are publicly accessible collections of Web pages that can be found using a URL or Internet address. Intranets are private Web pages that can only be accessed by qualified users. Extranets are a collection of Web sites that can be accessed from a single Internet address. An e-commerce site is a Web site that allows commercial transactions to take place using credit cards or digital money.

The Internet has a number of unique syntactical elements. One of the unique syntactical elements of the sixth language is hypertext, which makes it possible to link all of the Web sites and Web pages in cyberspace to form one huge global document. Another unique syntactical element is the Internet protocol, which allows all of the computers connected to the Internet to form one huge global network and makes the Web, ftp, and Telnet all possible. McLuhan's prediction of a global village has been realized. Still another unique syntactical element of the Internet are the search engines, which increase access to knowledge and information and, hence, provide an extra level of communication that the other forms of verbal language cannot match. The search engine also facilitates people finding each other and, hence, contributes to the creation of a global knowledge community.

This completes our description of how the five modes of notated language evolved from speech. Readers desiring more details are referred to Logan (2004b).

# 3 The Extended Mind Model
## of the Origin of Language

**The Emergence of Language as the Bifurcation
from Percepts to Concepts**

All media are active metaphors in their power to translate experience into new forms. The spoken word was the first technology by which man was able to let go of his environment in order to grasp it in a new way.

Marshall McLuhan, *Understanding Media*

The model of the evolution of notated language presented in chapter 2 started with spoken language as a given and showed how writing, mathematics, science, computing, and the Internet emerged in turn from speech. This approach gives rise to the question: How did the first form of language, speech, from which the other languages evolved, arise in the first place? It is from this consideration that I became interested in the origin of language problem and literature. My earlier work with the evolution of notated language was based on the premise that a new form of language evolved in response to the chaos resulting form the information overload associated with the previous forms of language. In light of this, we should anticipate that the origin of speech was a response to chaos and information overload.

As a starting point I assume that before the advent of speech hominid thought processes, as inherited from our earliest ancestors, were percept-based. Merlin Donald (1991, 226) makes a similar assumption about the perceptual basis of mimetic culture, the culture of hominids that existed just before the emergence of verbal language: 'The principle of similarity that links mimetic actions and their referents is perceptual, and the basic communicative device is best described as implementable action metaphor' (Donald 1998, 61).

Our earliest humanlike ancestors, whom we will refer to as hominids, emerged in the savannas of Africa, where they were an easy target for various predators. To defend themselves from this threat, as well as to increase their food supply, they acquired the new skills of tool-making, the control of fire, group foraging, and coordinated hunting. These activities resulted in a more complex form of social organization, which also increased the complexity of their lives. At first, this could be handled through more sophisticated percept-based responses, but at some point it became too great. Percept-based thought alone did not provide sufficient abstraction to deal with the increased complexity of hominid existence. The hominid mind could no longer cope with the richness of its life based solely on its perceptual sensorium. In the information overload and chaos that ensued, a new abstract level of order emerged in the form of verbal language and conceptual thinking.

This idea can be expressed in a slightly different way by making use of Ross Ashby's (1957) Law of Requisite Variety (LRV), which has been formulated in a number of different ways. I have chosen two that, in my opinion, are more appropriate for understanding language as a system that we use to represent or model the environment in which we live. One formulation of Ashby's LRV is 'a model system or controller can only model or control something to the extent that it has sufficient internal variety to represent it' (Heylighen and Joslyn 2001, n.p.). Another formulation of Ashby's LRV is 'for appropriate regulation the variety in the regulator must be equal to or greater than the variety in the system being regulated' (ibid.). By making use of these formulations of Ashby's LRV we are assuming that language is used by humans to regulate or control their social and physical environment.

When the complexity of hominid life became so great that perception and learned reactions to perceptions alone could not provide enough requisite variety to model or regulate the challenges of day-to-day life a new level of order emerged based on concepts. *Percepts* are the direct impressions of the external world that we apprehend with our senses. *Concepts* are abstract ideas that result from the generalization of particular examples. Concepts allow one to deal with things that are remote in both the space and time dimensions. If our first words were concepts, then language allowed us to represent things that are remote in both space and time and, hence, provided language with what Charles Hockett (1960) terms *displacement*. Concepts also increase the variety with which the brain can model the external world. Percepts are specialized, concrete, and tied to a single concrete event, but concepts are abstract and generative. They can be applied to many different situations or events. They can be combined with other concepts and percepts to increase variety in ways that percepts cannot.

What, we may ask, was the mechanism that allowed this transition to take place? Assuming that language is both a form of communication and an information-processing system, I came to the conclusion that the emergence of speech represented the actual transition from percept-based thought to concept-based thought. The spoken word, as we shall see, is the actual medium or mechanism by which concepts are expressed or represented. We must be very careful at this juncture to make sure that we do not formulate the relationship of spoken language and conceptual thought as a linear causal one. Language did not give rise to concepts, nor did concepts give rise to language, rather human speech and conceptualization emerged at exactly the same point in time creating the conditions for their mutual emergence.

My ideas regarding the relationship of words and concepts have been influenced by the work of Lev Vygotsky, in his seminal book *Thought and Language*, in which he reports on his investigation of the relationship between words and concepts in the following manner:

> Our investigation has shown that a concept is formed, not through the interplay of associations, but through an intellectual operation in which all elementary mental functions participate in a specific combination. This operation is guided by the use of words as the means of actively centering attention, of abstracting certain traits, synthesizing them, and symbolizing them by means of a sign.
>
> The process leading to concept formation develops along two main lines. The first is complex formation: The child unites diverse objects in groups under common 'family names'; this process passes through various stages. The second line of development is the formation of 'potential

concepts,' based on singling out certain common attributes. In both, the use of words is an integral part of the developing processes, and the word maintains its guiding function in the formation of genuine concepts, to which these processes lead. (1962, 81)

Concepts are absolutely essential for planning because they allow for abstraction and, in particular, for displacement in time. This explains why humans are the only animals capable of both conceptual language and planning: 'The available ethological evidence so far indicates that man is the only species with the ability to imagine future wishes and to plan and act accordingly' (Gärdenfors 2004). Vygotsky makes a similar point:

In addition to reorganizing the visual-spatial field, the child with the help of speech, creates a time field that is just as perceptible and real to him as the real one. The speaking child has the ability to direct his attention in a dynamic way. He can view changes in his immediate situation from the point of view of past activities, and he can act in the present from the viewpoint of the future.

For the ape, the task is unsolvable unless the goal and the object needed to reach it are both simultaneously in view. For the child, this gap is easily overcome by verbally controlling her attention and thereby reorganizing her perceptual field. The ape will perceive a stick one moment, but cease to pay attention to it after its visual field has changed and the goal comes into view. (1978, 36)

Language and conceptual thought are autocatalytic and the dynamically linked parts of a dynamic cognitive system, namely, the human mind. *Autocatalysis* is the mechanism that Stuart Kauffman uses to explain the emergence of life: 'A living organism is a system of chemicals that has the capacity to catalyze its own reproduction' (1995, 49). An autocatalytic set of chemicals is a group of organic molecules where the catalyst for the production (or really reproduction) of each member of the set is contained within the set itself. As a result of this the system can become a 'self-maintaining and self-reproducing metabolism,' that is, a living organism, in the presence of a source of energy and the basic atoms needed to build organic compounds. A key idea in Kauffman's approach is that the members of the autocatalytic set self-organize and, hence, bootstrap themselves into existence as a set with an identity different from the individual members that make up the set, and hence, represents an emergent phenomenon.

The autocatalytic process catalyzes itself into a positive feedback loop, so that once the process starts, even as a fluctuation, it begins to accelerate and build so that a new phenomenon emerges. The emergence of language and conceptual thought is an example of an autocatalytic process. A set of words work together to create a structure of meaning and thought. Each word shades the meaning of the next thought and the next words. Words and thoughts are both catalysts for and products of words and thoughts. Language and conceptual thought represent emergent phenomena, which bootstrap themselves into existence.

We will make use of a more generalized form of autocatalysis and suggest that any set of mechanisms or ideas that catalyze each other's existence is an autocatalytic set – an autocatalytic set of mechanisms or ideas. Language and conceptual thought form an autocatalytic set because language catalyzes conceptual thought and conceptual thought catalyzes language. We encountered another set of autocatalytic ideas when we examined the alphabet effect in chapter 2, where we postulated that the phonetic alphabet, codified law, monotheism, abstract science, and deductive logic are a set of ideas that are self-supporting. Later in our study we will return to Kauffman's idea of autocatalysis and its application to the origin of language and the notion of language as an organism.

## The Relationship of Percepts and Concepts

The use of a word transforms the brain from one state to another and replaces a set of percepts with a concept. A word is a strange attractor for all the percepts associated with the concept represented by that word. A word, therefore, packs a great deal of experience into a single utterance or sign. Millions of percepts of a linguistic community are boiled down by the language to a single word acting as a concept and a strange attractor for all those percepts.

I developed the notion that a concept and a word are equivalent when I first presented the Extended Mind Model back in 1997. Words represent concepts and concepts are represented by words. It is my belief that they emerged together so that words provided a medium by which concepts could be represented, manipulated, spoken about, and thought about. This differs dramatically from the position of many linguists, like Steven Pinker (2003), who claim that words emerged for the purpose of the communication of concepts that already existed before language emerged. There is no conflict with my view and Pinker's that words and concepts are connected. He suggested that a word is an arbitrary sign that is a connection between a signal and a concept. Where we differ is on the question of which came first the chicken (word) or the egg (the concept). For Pinker first comes the concept and then the word, whereas I believe that they co-emerged. The word gave substance to the concept and the concept was represented by the word. The word is more than a symbol or a sign that represents a thing or a concept. To my way of thinking, the word is the concept and the concept is wrapped in a word encased in a phonological utterance. To understand the origin of language and words, we have to understand the origin of concepts and why they emerged.

A concept in the form of a word links many percepts of an individual and, hence, extends the brain's capacity to remember. Words as concepts are a form of 'artificial memory' which creates 'artificial connections.' Words bring order to a chaotic mind filled with the memories of a myriad of experiences. Language is an emergent order.

Concepts are 'artificial or virtual percepts' – instead of bringing the mountain or the percept of the mountain directly to the mind, the word brings the mind to the mountain through the concept of the mountain. The concept of the mountain triggers instantaneously all of the mind's direct experiences of mountains, as well as instances where the word *mountain* was used in any discourses in which that mind participated either as a speaker or a listener. The word mountain acting as a concept and an attractor not only brings to mind all 'mountain' transactions, but its also provides a name or a handle for that attractor-concept, which makes it easier to access memories and share them with others. They speed up reaction time and, hence, confer a selective advantage for their users. And at the same time, those languages and those words within a language which most easily capture memories enjoy a selective advantage over alternative languages and words respectively.

At this point in my narrative I would like to introduce a personal note and acknowledge the debt I owe to Marshall McLuhan, who through the many conversations we had together introduced me to the idea that our mental life can be divided into percept-based and concept-based thinking. Long after developing my model based on language representing the transition from percept-based to concept-based thought I reencountered the following passage while rereading *Understanding Media*:

> All media are active metaphors in their power to translate experience into new forms. The spoken word was the first technology by which man was able to let go of his environment in order to grasp it in a new way. Words are a kind of information retrieval that can range over the total environment and experience at high speed. Words are complex systems of metaphors and symbols that translate experience into our uttered or outered senses. They are a technology of explicitness. By means of translation of immediate sense experience into vocal symbols the entire world can be evoked and retrieved at any instant. (McLuhan 1964, 56)

This passage, which I had read many years ago, before embarking on this project of trying to understand the origin of language, obviously stuck with me in the recesses of my mind. I am happy to acknowledge the role it must have played in the development of the ideas that I present here. It was striking to me that my idea that language speeds up thought processes was actually formulated by McLuhan many years ago.

In suggesting that the first words were the strange attractors of percepts, I did not mean to imply that all words arose in this fashion. I certainly believe that the first words to appear were the strange attractors of percepts, but once a simple lexicon of words and a primitive grammar came into being a new mental dynamic was established. The human mind was now capable of abstract thought and abstract concepts, which would need to be represented by new words. These new words would not have emerged as attractors of percepts, but rather as representations of abstract concepts in the form of grammatical relationships among words. The first words of this nature would have been, in all likelihood, associated with grammar and categorization. Examples of the former would be function words such as *he, she, this, that, and, or, but, if,* and examples of the words for categorization would be words such as *animals, people, birds, fish, insects, plants,* and *fruits.*

In proposing that human language began with the emergence of words acting as concepts, I am following a tradition known as the *lexical hypothesis*, which posits that 'the lexicon is at the center of the language system' (Donald 1991, 250). Language began with a lexicon, which then gave rise to phonological and syntactical structures. We will encounter advocates of this hypothesis as we travel through the narrative of this book and encounter the ideas of Merlin Donald (1991, 1998), Derek Bickerton (1990, 1995, 1998, 2000, 2003), Ray Jackendoff (2002), John Locke (1998), Willem Levelt (1989), and Richard Hudson (1984).

Syntactical structures are also concepts. They are concepts that encompass relationships between words, just as words are concepts that encompass relationships between percepts.

## The Complexity of Hominid Existence

We are still left with the question, however, of what developments in hominid evolution gave rise to the complexity, the information overload, and, hence, the chaos that led to the bifurcation from perception to conception – and the emergence of speech. No single development or breakthrough triggered this event, but rather the accumulation of developments that included the use of tools, the control of fire, the larger social settings that fire engendered, the social organization required for large group living, food sharing, group foraging, and coordinated large-scale hunting that resulted from the larger living groups, and the emergence of non-verbal mimetic communication, as has been described by Donald in *The Origin of the Modern Mind* (1991).

Terrence Deacon (1997) cites a similar set of hominid developments associated with the advent of speech. They include the provision of meat through hunting or scavenging, the use of stone tools for hunting and butchery, and social institutions or organizations such as marriage and ritual. Morten Christiansen (1994) and his co-workers (Christiansen and Devlin 1997; Christiansen, Dale, Ellefson, and Conway 2001; Christiansen and Ellefson 2002) cite another set of skills associated with the advent of speech, namely, sequential learning and processing. But since toolmaking and tooluse, social organization, and mimetic communication all involve sequential learning and processing, the hypotheses of Donald, Deacon, and Christiansen to my mind are similar. The aspects of hominid life that they allude to create new levels of complexity and result in new skill sets, which they assert served as pre-adaptations of language. In my model, language arises from this complexity, while for Donald, Deacon, and Christiansen the new skill sets act as pre-adaptations for language. There is nothing contradictory between my approach and theirs. Indeed, they reinforce each other. Both the skill sets acting as pre-adaptations and the bifurcation to a new level of order due to the increase to complexity complement each other, and each in its own way contributed to the emergence of language.

One thing is clear, however, percepts no longer had the richness or the variety with which to represent and model hominid experience once the new skills of hominids like toolmaking and social organization were acquired. It was in this climate that speech emerged and the transition or bifurcation from perceptual thinking to conceptual thinking occurred. The initial concepts were, in fact, the very first words of spoken language. Each word served as a metaphor and strange attractor uniting all of the pre-existing percepts associated with that word in terms of a single word and, hence, a single concept. All of one's experiences and perceptions of water, the water we drink, bathe with, cook with, swim in, that falls as rain, that melts from snow, were captured with a single word, *water*, which also represents the simple concept of water.

In my model, I assume that the human brain interacting with its environment, its memories of its past experiences in the form of percepts, its intention to communicate, and its social community is a non-linear dynamic system. A word operating as a concept acts as an attractor for all of the percepts associated with that word. An attractor is a trajectory in phase space towards which all of the trajectories of a non-linear dynamic system are attracted. The meaning of the word being uttered does not belong simply to the individual but to the community to which that individual belongs.

Furthermore, the meaning of the word at any given instance emerges from the context in which it is being used. The attractor is a strange attractor because the meaning of a word never exactly repeats itself. The trajectories of a strange attractor never meet, even though they come infinitesimally close to each other. It is the same with a word. The meaning of a word fluctuates about the strange attractor, but it is never exactly the same because the context in which the word is being used is always different. The context includes the other words in the utterance, who made the utterance, the social context in which the utterance was made, and the medium in which the utterance was made. Given that the medium is the message (as was explained above) the meaning of the word will be subtly affected according to whether the word was spoken, whispered, written, telephoned, telegraphed, emailed, or appeared on a Web site.

Our use of the word *utterance* in the above paragraph is an example of how context shifts meaning. Utterance usually refers to the oral production of language, but in the context we just used it utterance took on the meaning of the general construction of a sentence independent of the medium used to express it. Although in most cases a word moves around an attractor in the phase space of meaning, from time to time a word can bifurcate into two meanings. An example of this is the appropriation of the words *hot* and *cool* to refer to two different styles of jazz, namely, Dixieland and bebop respectively. The word cool used in jazz further bifurcated to add the meaning avant-garde, 'with,' or hip. *Hip* is another example of a word that bifurcated.

That we chose to identify words as strange attractors reflects the fact that words in the contexts of utterance have multiple, even ambiguous meanings or multiple simultaneous perspectives, to use the language of Michael Tomasello (1999, 8–9). Within the context of spoken language, the ambiguity is reduced because the prosody and accompanying gestures and hand movements add additional meanings to the words being spoken. Within the context of written language, without these extra-verbal signals, the ambiguity of a word is at its greatest. Within the context of mathematics and science, in which terminology is given precise definitions, the ambiguity of words is at a minimum. The attractors that represent mathematical and scientific terms approach fixed-point attractors, but they are not totally fixed-point attractors. There is always a bit of fuzziness about even mathematical and scientific terms, which can be attributed to the differences of opinions of mathematicians and scientists, and to Gödel's Theorem in the realm of mathematics, and Heisenberg's uncertainty principle in the realm of quantum physics.

Spoken language and abstract conceptual thinking emerged at exactly the same time as the bifurcation from the concrete percept-based thinking of prelingual hominids to conceptual-based spoken language and thinking. This transition, an example of punctuated equilibrium, I believe, was the defining moment for the emergence of the fully human species *Homo sapiens*. This discontinuous transition illustrates Prigogine's theory of far from equilibrium processes and the notion that a new level of order can suddenly emerge as a bifurcation from a chaotic non-linear dynamic system (Prigogine and Stengers 1984; Prigogine 1997).

Robin Dunbar has also made a link between the advent of language and the complexity of hominid existence, as measured by the size of the social group. He suggested that language replaced grooming as a way of creating social cohesion as the size and complexity of the social group increased: 'The principle function of language was (and is!) to enable the exchange of social information ("gossip") in order to facilitate bonding in larger, more dispersed social groups' (1998, 98).

### Three Preverbal Forms of Proto-language: Toolmaking, Social Intelligence, and Mimesis

The transition from percept-based thinking to concept-based thinking represented a major discontinuity in human thought. During this period, hominids developed the set of survival skills associated with toolmaking and tool use, the control of fire, cooperative social structures and organization, large-scale coordinated hunting and gathering, and mimetic communication (Donald 1991). Based on Donald's work I would interpret these major breakthroughs in hominid cognition as the emergence of three distinct percept-based preverbal proto-languages:

1  Manual praxic articulation (or toolmaking and use)
2  Social organization or the language of social interaction (which is sometimes characterized as social or emotional intelligence)
3  Preverbal communication, which entails the use of hand signals, mime, gesture, and *prosodic vocalization*, which Donald (1991) defines as mimetic communication.

Before proceeding with my analysis I have to comment on my use of the term proto-language, which Derek Bickerton (1990) coined, although without a hyphen, to describe a stage in the development of human language in which a lexicon of a small number of words existed without syntax, and utterances were confined to fewer than five words. I actually quite independently used the term *proto-language*, with a hyphen, before becoming acquainted with Bickerton's work (see Logan 1997) to describe what I am now referring to as the three percept-based preverbal proto-languages (listed above).

I believe that these three forms of preverbal activities, identified by Donald as elements of mimetic culture, are actually proto-languages, although Donald never spoke of them in these terms. As Bickerton has already co-opted the term *protolanguage* to describe the first stage of verbal language, I have altered my use of the term proto-language and will describe toolmaking, social organization, and mimetic communication as three percept-based preverbal proto-language forms. In a certain sense I regard these three forms of preverbal proto-language as more proto than Bickerton's protolanguage because they are earlier. To sum up I see an evolution from preverbal proto-language as identified by Donald to verbal Bickertonian protolanguage to full verbal language as the following time sequence indicates:

1 Toolmaking
2 Social intelligence
3 Mimetic communication (hand signal, gesture, body language, and vocalization)
4 Protolanguage (a limited verbal lexicon without syntax, as defined by Bickerton)
5 Full verbal language (with a lexicon and syntax).

I suggest that the first three breakthroughs in hominid cognitive development can be understood as three forms of percept-based preverbal proto-languages because they each represented a primitive form of communication and information processing, the two basic functions that I have used to define a language. *Mimesis*, according to Donald, 'establishes the fundamentals of intentional expression in hominids, without which language would not have had an opportunity to evolve such a sophisticated, high-speed communication system as modern language unless there was already a simpler slower one in place' (1998, 61).

The three preverbal proto-languages listed above were, according to Donald, the cognitive laboratory in which the skills of generativity, representation, and communication developed and, hence, were the source of the cognitive framework for speech. They also entail sequential learning and processing and, hence, following the ideas of Christiansen (1994), could have served as pre-adaptations for speech.

Justification for regarding the mimetic skill set that Donald (1998) identifies as preverbal proto-languages is that each one possesses its own unique primitive form of semantics and syntax – protosemantics and protosyntax, if you will. The protosemantics of manual praxis or toolmaking and tool use are the various components that go into making the tool, that is the materials and the procedures needed to create and use the tool. The tools themselves become protosemantic elements in the preverbal proto-language of tool use. The protosyntax of toolmaking and tool use is the order or sequence in which the procedures for making and using the tools are carried out. If the correct order or sequence is not adhered to, then the task to be completed will not be accomplished.

If, as postulated in *The Sixth Language* (Logan 2004b), a new language emerges when there is some form of information overload, then we should be able to identify the chaos or information overload that led to the emergence of the preverbal proto-language of toolmaking and tool use. Perhaps it was the flood of extra information that the earliest hominids had to deal with in order to survive as bipeds in the savanna where the protection of living in the tree tops was no longer available. Tools were created to deal with the new challenges of living at ground level where there were far more dangers than in the tree tops.

The skills associated with toolmaking presumably led to the control of fire and to transporting it from one site to another. The control of fire, in turn, contributed to new and more complex social structures, as nuclear families banded together to form clans to take advantage of the many benefits that fire offered such as warmth, protection from predators, tool sharpening, and cooking, which increased the number of plants that could be made edible, killed bacteria, and helped to preserve raw foods such as meat. These larger social structures bred a new form of information overload because of the increased complexities of social interactions and organization. In this environment, a new preverbal proto-language of social interactions emerged with its protosemantics of social transactions, which included greetings, grooming, mating, food sharing, and other forms of cooperation appropriate for clan living. The protosyntax of the social organization or intelligence included the proper ordering or sequencing of these transactions in such a way as to promote social harmony and avoid interpersonal conflict, and, hence, contribute to the survival and development of hominid culture. The overload of interacting with many people and carrying out more sophisticated activities led to the need for better communications to better coordinate social transactions and cooperative activities such as the sharing of fire, the maintenance of the hearth, food sharing, and large-scale coordinated hunting and foraging. From the chaos of this complexity emerged the preverbal proto-language of mimetic communication.

The protosemantics of mimetic communication, the third preverbal proto-language, consisted of the following elements: the variety of tones of non-verbal vocalization, facial gestures, hand signals, and miming actions (or body language). The protosyntax of this form of communication is the sequencing and coordination of these elements. Combining a gesture and a vocal tone would have a different meaning than the same tone followed by the gesture after some delay or the gesture followed by the tone. As the syntactical complexity of mimetic communication grew and became more sophisticated, it set the stage for the next development in hominid communication, namely, verbal language in the form of speech, which vestigially incorporates the elements of mimetic communication. It is not the literal meaning of words alone that convey the message of spoken language, but the tone of the words, the way they are inflected, as well as the facial gestures, hand motions, and body language that accompany them.

Embedded in the syntax of each of the three preverbal proto-languages of toolmaking, social intelligence, and mimetic communication are generative grammars that allow:

1 Different ways of articulating tools and manual praxis to carry out a variety of new tasks as new challenges arise
2 The creation of new forms of coordination and social cohesion to meet the infinite variety of challenges life presents including the navigation through different forms of social conflict, the variety of which is endless

3 The expression of a large number and shades of meaning and feelings through mimetic communication.

Starting with the manufacture and use of tools, hominids began to develop the capability of generativity that is essential for verbal language. Employing the correct syntax of the preverbal proto-languages, that is, doing things in the proper order or sequence served as the pre-adaptation for the generative grammar of verbal language. This model supports Chomsky's theory that humans possess a generative grammar that makes the rapid and universal acquisition of speech by young children possible. It also provides an alternative explanation to Chomsky's notion that the generative grammar is somehow magically hard-wired into the human brain.

Donald's work suggests that the generative grammars for the preverbal proto-languages of toolmaking (or manual articulation), social organization (or social intelligence), and mimetic communications served as a pre-adaptation for the generative grammar of spoken language:

> Mimetic skill represented a new level of cultural development, because it led to a variety of important new social structures, including a collectively held model of the society itself. It provided a new vehicle for social control and coordination, as well as the cognitive underpinnings of pedagogical skill and cultural innovation. In the brain of the individual, mimesis was partly the product of a new system of self-representation and mostly the product of a supramodular mimetic controller in which self-action may be employed to 'model' perceptual event representations. Many of the cognitive features usually identified exclusively with language were already present in mimesis: for instance, intentional communication, recursion, and differentiation of reference. (1991, 199–200)

My model for the emergence of language is based on Donald's work with the added twist that I believe that speech is concept-based and that it emerged as a bifurcation from the percept-based preverbal proto-languages just identified. My model for the origin of verbal language, which I have just outlined, was developed in 1997 and, for the most part, grew out of my previous work (1995, 2000) with the evolution of notated language plus my reading of Donald's *The Origin of the Modern Mind*.

I have since then become acquainted with Deacon's *The Symbolic Species*, in which he also suggests an association of the emergence of speech with toolmaking: 'The appearance of the first stone tools nearly 2.5 million years ago almost certainly correlates with a radical shift in foraging behaviour in order to gain access to meat. And this clearly marks the beginnings of the shift in selection pressures associated with changes in the brain relevant for symbolic communication' (1997, 386).

While Deacon does not make use of the concept of social organization or intelligence, he does introduce the notion that changes in the social dynamics of hominids led directly to symbolic communication and that marriage itself was one of the first forms of symbolic communication in which the parties to the marriage were themselves symbols:

> The near synchrony in human prehistory of the first increase in brain size, the first appearance of stone tools for hunting and butchery, and a considerable reduction in sexual dimorphism is not a coincidence. These changes are interdependent. All are symptoms of a fundamental restructuring of hominid adaptation, which resulted in a significant change in feeding ecology, a radical change in social structure, and an unprecedented (indeed, revolutionary) change in representational abilities. The very first symbol ever thought, or acted out, or uttered on the face of the earth grew out of this socio-economic dilemma, and so they might not have been very much like speech ... Marriage is not the same as mating, and not the same as a pair bond. Unlike what is found in the animal world, it is a symbolic relationship ... Symbolic culture was a response to a reproductive problem that only symbols could solve: the imperative of representing a social contract ... The symbol construction that occurs in these ceremonies is not just a matter of demonstrating certain symbolic relationships, but actually involves the use of the individuals and actions as symbol tokens. (1997, 400–1, 406)

While Donald speaks of speech emerging from mimetic communication, Deacon in a slightly different tack sees speech as assimilating these features and co-evolving with them: 'With the final achievement of fully articulate speech, possibly as recently as the appearance of anatomically modern Homo sapiens just 100,000 to 200,000 years ago, many early adaptations that once were essential to successful vocal communication would have lost their urgency. Vestiges of these once-critical supports likely now constitute the many near-universal gestural and prosodic companions to normal conversation' (1997, 364).

As to determining whether Deacon or Donald provide the most accurate model of the relationship between toolmaking, social organization, and mimetic communication and speech, there are no scientific criteria for making a choice. It is difficult if not impossible to falsify their propositions because data from the events they describe are so scarce. We must resort to the Kuhnian (1972) notion that the choice of rival descriptions will have to be based on what the reader finds most compelling. We shall return to this issue of the scientific basis of modelling the origin of speech in chapter 9.

# 4 A Grand Unification Theory of Human Thought and Culture

**From Preverbal Proto-language to Prototype:**
**The Origins of Technology, Commerce, and the Arts**

The three percept-based preverbal proto-languages identified in the last chapter gave rise to more than just spoken language and conceptual thinking. Transformed by verbal language and concept making that followed in their wake, they also served as the prototypes for three fundamental activities that form the core of modern human society, namely, technology which emerged from toolmaking; commerce which emerged from social organization and intelligence; and the art forms which emerged from mimetic communication. 'There is a vestigial mimetic culture embedded within our modern culture and a mimetic mind embedded within the overall architecture of the modern human mind' (Donald 1991, 162).

While it is true that the roots of technology, commerce, and the arts can be traced to mimetic culture, it is equally true that without the ability to conceptualize that language makes possible they would never have achieved the level of abstractness and sophistication that they did, a point underscored by Bickerton: 'Suppose that some single characteristic of humans turns out to be the antecedent of most or even all of the other characteristics that differentiate us even from our closest relatives among the apes ... Language is proposed as such a capacity' (1995, 7).

The hypothesis that is developed in this chapter that modern culture can be seen as the combination of mimetic culture with verbal language is highly speculative, but it may actually be true or at least partially true. It is presented as a probe to stimulate thought, dialogue, and debate.

**Manual Praxis: From Toolmaking to High Tech**

The generative tool makingskills that early hominids developed before the advent of speech are still very much a part of the repertoire of modern humans as is evidenced by the activity of today's craftsmen who work almost entirely with their hands and have little or no need of spoken language to pursue their craft. Generative manual praxis laid the foundation for the creation of human technology. However, with the advent of the verbal language of speech and the evolution of the notated forms of language, namely, writing, mathematics, science, computing, and the Internet, technology has evolved into progressively more sophisticated forms of high tech which are hybrid systems which combine percept-based manual praxis with language-based conceptualization. Vestiges of pure manual praxis remain in certain forms of traditional technology such as the knife and the ax whose design remains basically the same as that of early hominids and emerged over a long period of time from percept-based trial and error. A scientific analysis of these tools would reveal that they had achieved an optimum design long before the advent of modern engineering.

**Commerce as a Form of Social Organization and Emotional Intelligence**

Another example of a percept-based vestigial cognitive structure, which is still very much part of human intelligence, is social or emotional intelligence. The social intelligence that early hominids developed found some of its first applications in the maintenance of the hearth and in large-scale coordinated hunting and gathering. These skills eventually found their way into other forms of human commerce. Social or emotional intelligence is the basic building block of all forms of commerce. What is commerce after all? It is essentially the cooperative activities that a group engages in for the purposes of acquiring the necessities of life and ensuring the mutual survival of the group as a whole. Commercial transactions are entered into voluntarily by all the players involved because they benefit each of them. Any other transaction in which only one party benefits is not commerce but some form of exploitation such as theft, fraud, exploitation, or enslavement.

According to my definition *commerce* does not necessarily involve the use of money and should not be confused with the money economy. Commerce does not depend on money but is a system of cooperation for the gathering, production, and distribution of goods and services essential to survival. Commerce entails trade whose roots can be traced back to the earliest forms of social organization and food sharing when the specialization of tasks first emerged. The cooperation of individuals who performed specialized tasks for the good of the community laid the foundations of trade and commerce. This form of trade and commerce did not, however, entail a notion of a money-based market which requires the concept of monetary value to operate. Before speech and conceptualization there was no way of computing the value of the goods and services that were exchanged. No one counted or kept score. Those societies where individuals were generous had a better chance of survival than those whose members were selfish.

Before the advent of speech, the commerce of hominids was a percept-based activity based on hunting and gathering. Percept-based hunting and gathering was transformed over the years by the spoken word and conceptual thinking into a more sedentary form of commerce based on animal husbandry and/or agriculture.

The emergence of the industrial form of commerce can be traced to three developments that took place in Europe towards the end of the Middle Ages, namely, the evolution of agriculture into the manor system in which agricultural products were transformed in a systematic way to commodities, the rise of a market system for the distribution of these agricultural products and commodities, and the transformation of technology into a systematic form of engineering through the rise of the science of mechanics. The industrial system arose by combining new forms of social organization with the abstract conceptual skills of engineering, science, and mathematics.

The information age economy, another hybrid system of commerce, arose from the development of computing, which gave rise to new forms of social organization. We are on the threshold of a still newer form of commerce known as the knowledge economy, which differs from the information age economy in that the focus is on the sharing and management of knowledge rather than information. Information is structured or contextualized data, which gives them more meaning, but knowledge is the ability to exploit information to achieve one's objectives. The knowledge era will require greater cooperation, collaboration, and sharing than was the case in the information age or the industrial era, both of which were based on the hoarding of proprietary knowledge (Logan and Stokes 2004).

**The Fine Arts and Fine Motor Skills**

The roots of the fine arts can be traced to percept-based mimetic communication whose basic elements were prosody (the tones of vocalization), facial gesture, hand signals, and mime (or body language). The very first art forms were all non-verbal and grew out of mimetic communication, the third preverbal proto-language. They included music, painting, sculpture, and dance all of which were a part of ritual. Music can be traced to the variation of tone and rhythm and hence to prosody. Dance is basically a form of body language set to music. The first forms of painting were body and face painting, and the first forms of sculpture were masks and costumes which can be seen as attempts to enhance and intensify facial gesture and mime. With the advent of spoken language new hybrid forms of the arts emerged which combined mimetic communication with words to produce modern (postverbal) art forms such as poetry which include both words and prosody, songs which combine words and music, and theatre which combines words with mime and dance.

**A Grand Unification Model of Human Thought and Culture**

Spoken language gave rise to a number of concept-based cultural forms such as story telling or narrative, writing, mathematics, science, and computing. Speech also transformed a number of earlier forms of percept-based activities to generate new hybrid forms of human culture including science-based technology, agricultural, the arts, and industrial and computer-based forms of commerce. Our model for human cognition combines the three percept-based preverbal proto-languages of manual praxis, social intelligence, and mimetic communication with concept- and language-based skills associated with the six verbal languages of speech, writing, mathematics, science, computing, and the Internet. This approach provides a common link for activities that are often treated as quite independent of each other, namely, commerce, technology, the arts, and science and results in what we have playfully called a Grand Unification Theory of Human Thought and Culture.

## The Origin and Evolution of the Extended Mind

I have attempted to develop insights into the role that language has played in the development of human thought and culture by combining ideas on the nature and function of language, the concept of bifurcation from chaos theory, and Merlin Donald's (1991) notions of evolutionary psychology. Building on these ideas I would like to tackle the age-old question of the relationship of the human mind and the human brain. For some psychologists this is a non-problem as they believe that the brain and the mind are synonymous, just two different words to describe the same phenomena, one derived from biology, the other from philosophy. For others there is a difference. Some define the mind as the seat of consciousness, thought, feeling, and will. Those processes of which we are not conscious, such as the regulation of our vital organs, the reception of sense data, reflex actions, and motor control, on the other hand, are not activities of our mind but functions of our brain.

I believe that there is no objective way to resolve these two different points of view but that a useful distinction can be made between the mind and the brain based on our dynamic systems model of language as the bifurcation from concrete percept-based thought to abstract concept-based thought. I, therefore, assume that the mind came into being with the advent of verbal language and, hence, conceptual thought. This transition did not occur with the first emergence of words in the form of Bickertonian protolanguage, which contained a modest lexicon but no syntax. I believe this transition to the human mind took place with the emergence of syntax approximately fifty to a hundred thousand years ago, which allowed for full generativity and the ability of language to represent all aspects of the world.

Syntactilized verbal language extended the effectiveness of the human brain and created the mind. Language is a tool and all tools, according to McLuhan (1964), are extensions of the body that allow us to use our bodies more efficiently. I believe that language is a tool which extended the brain and made it more effective thus creating the human mind which I have termed the *extended mind*. I have expressed this idea in terms of the equation:

$$mind = brain + language.$$

The following passage from McLuhan's book *Understanding Media* inspired this hypothesis:

> It is the extension of man in speech that enables the intellect to detach itself from the vastly wider reality. Without language, Bergson suggests, human intelligence would have remained totally involved in the objects of its attention. Language does for intelligence what the wheel does for the feet and the body. It enables them to move from thing to thing with the greatest ease and speed and ever less involvement. Language extends and amplifies man but it also divides his faculties. His collective consciousness or intuitive awareness is diminished by this technical extension of consciousness that is speech. (1964, 79)

When I speak of language as extending the brain into a mind this occurred at the very initial emergence of language as speech. But as new forms of language evolved (as described in chapter 2) they too became extensions of the brain. Therefore writing, mathematics, science, computing, and the Internet, like the spoken word, are all part and parcel of our minds. A number of authors (McLuhan 1962, 1964; Havelock 1963, 1978; Ong 1982; Logan 2004a) have shown how the mind of the literate person differs from that of the non-literate person.

The human mind is the verbal extension of the brain, a bifurcation of the brain which vestigially retains the perceptual features of the hominid brain while at the same time becoming capable of abstract conceptual thought. Bickerton (1995, 150) reaches a similar conclusion and makes a distinction between a 'brain-state' and a 'mind-state.' Andy Clark, whose ideas are explored in greater detail in chapters 8 and 11, also developed the notion of 'the extended mind' (Clark 1997; Clark and Chalmers 2003).

The emergence of syntactilized language also represents, for me, the final bifurcation of hominids from the archaic form of Homo sapiens into the full-fledged human species, *Homo sapiens*. Tim Crow (2002, 93) reaches a similar conclusion. He points out that pictorial art demonstrating a capacity for representation, an essential element of human language, can be traced back to only ninety thousand years ago and was absent for both Neanderthal and Homo erectus. Citing Stringer and McKie (1996), Crow concludes, 'The parsimonious conclusion (because it links the distinctive characteristic of the species to its genetic origin) is that the origin of language coincided with the transition to modern Homo sapiens dated to somewhere between 100,00 and 150,000 years ago' (ibid.).

Humans are the only species to have developed verbal language and also to have experienced mind. This is not to deny that our ancestors, the earlier forms of hominids, experienced thought and consciousness. Their thought patterns, however, were largely percept-based and their brains functioned as percept-processing engines operating without the benefit of the abstract concepts which only words can create and language can process. It follows that animals have brains but no minds and that the gap between humans and animals is that only humans possess verbal language and mind.

In summary, the emergence of language represents three bifurcations: (1) from percepts to concepts, (2) from brain to mind, and (3) from archaic Homo sapiens to full fledged human beings, *Homo sapiens*.

These three bifurcations are not necessarily simultaneous. Bickerton claims (1990, 1995) that protolanguage, in which the first words were used symbolically, emerged with Homo erectus which means the first bifurcation can be dated to approximately two million years ago. The second and third transitions, on the other hand, can be dated to the emergence of fully syntactilized language, which occurred only 100 thousand to 150 thousand years ago and seems to be correlated with the explosion of human culture and technological progress of that time period (Bickerton 1995, 65).

This hypothesis or model provides a possible explanation of the fate of Neanderthals, who had a slightly larger brain than Homo sapiens but who, it seems, did not use spoken language. This conclusion, disputed by some, is based on the analysis of fossil remains which reveal that Neanderthal's vocal tracts were not as well developed as those of humans. Neanderthals who survived for over a hundred thousand years were dominated by their human rivals and disappeared in Europe after only ten thousand years of living side by side with humans. Obviously the mind, which combines the features of both the percept engine which is the brain and the concept generator of verbal language is a more powerful instrument of reasoning and thought than the brain alone. Once language emerged the size of the brain alone was no longer the sole determining factor in intelligence as had been the case for the evolution of the hominid brain.

Empirical data suggest that the size of the brain alone without language is not a particularly smarter brain. Bickerton points out that when the brain doubled in size, hominids did not get twice as smart. Artifact production and behavioural changes from Homo habilis to Neanderthal are insignificant compared to those found once our own species emerged, and unless there is no relationship whatsoever between intelligence and the products of intelligence (including tools and behaviour), an enlarged brain did not, in and of itself, significantly enhance the former' (2000, 271). What did enhance the former, in my opinion, was language.

Deacon has developed an alternative scenario to explain the demise of Neanderthals. He claims they perished as a result of a disease that the Homo sapiens arriving from Africa brought with them for which Neanderthals had no resistance in much the same way Amerinds perished from smallpox carried to North America by Europeans. While this is certainly a possibility, history has shown that even during the most virulent pandemics a certain percentage of the population always survived. In humans there are roughly thirty genes known as human leukocyte antigens, which vary wildly among people and allow a uniform population to survive a plague or an epidemic.

As the brain of hominids increased in size and complexity certain biological limits were reached. The head of an infant could only become so big and pass through the hips of a woman if humans were also to retain there capacity for mobility, an important factor for survival. One evolutionary strategy for packing more reasoning power into the small space of the head was the development of convolutions of the brain; another was the gender differentiation of the male and female anatomy and the specialization of gender tasks. The females had broader hips for childbearing large-headed babies and tended to spend more time attending to the tasks associated with the hearth, while the males remained narrow-hipped and roamed about as the hunters and defenders of the family from marauders.

Another reason for limits on the size of the brain comes from energy considerations: 'Brains are extraordinarily expensive organs to evolve and maintain. The average brain weighs about 2% of adult body weight, yet consumes something approaching 20% of the body's total energy intake ... Since brains do not come for free, some very powerful selection pressure is required to make it worth a species' while evolving them. Given this, having any space at all dedicated to language (or speech!) must add measurably to the costs incurred by the individual, and would be selected against unless countervailing selection pressure made language advantageous' (Dunbar 1998, 93).

According to the Extended Mind Model, language acting as an extension of the brain allowed human intelligence to increase without an increase in brain size: 'Language (whatever the value of its emergent properties) was not itself the driving force behind the evolution of the super large human brain. This would explain why the key language areas (Broca's, Wernicke's and associated areas) are significantly smaller in volume than those areas associated with social skills and theory-of-mind abilities (the prefrontal cortex)' (Dunbar 1998, 103). This observation by Dunbar supports our notion that language extends the brain into a mind which operates more efficiently because language accesses associations automatically and triggers memories more efficiently than the brain's neural nets would without the cues from language.

By making use of a facility to create abstract and symbolic thought at the conceptual level the effectiveness of the human mind was able to make a quantum leap forward without making large incremental energy demands. Our claim is that symbolic conceptual thinking is more efficient than concrete perceptual thinking and, hence, there was a selection pressure in favour of the emergence of language. Language extended the brain into a mind capable of symbolic thought. Dunbar concurs with our suggestion that the emergence of speech and the human race were concurrent: 'The evolution of language seems to correspond in time to the emergence of our own species, Homo sapiens' (1998, 104). Bickerton expresses a similar thought: 'It may be hypothesized that a larger number of the first type (those pushing at the boundaries of protolanguage) appeared in southern Africa, probably within the last two hundred thousand years, and that it was this chance agglomeration that launched our species' (2000, 276).

After all the physical mechanisms for increasing human intelligence by increasing head size and brain size had been exhausted, nature conspired through chaos theory to increase hominid intelligence with a software rather than a hardware stratagem. The software was verbal language from which emerged the human mind and conceptualization. Words encode basic concepts and, hence, allow for the more efficient processing of information and knowledge. Conceptualization allowed for the creation of more words and new metaphors to achieve still higher levels of conceptualization and representation. Concepts and words formed a dynamic systems bootstrap creating the conditions for their mutual and dynamic development. In other words, language and thought formed an autocatalytic system. A possible metaphor for the role language plays in enhancing brain function is the disk doubler or zip drive used to provide a microcomputer (an artificial brain) with a compact way to store and process data and information. Language is the brain's zip drive converting it into an extended mind. When we come to discuss the relationship of language and culture in chapter 12 we will discover that culture also acts as a zip drive storing the lessons learned by a society in the mind of each individual in a society or culture.

**Towards a Grand Unification Theory of Human Thought and Culture**

Within the framework of what I have playfully called the Grand Unification Theory I have proposed that the full gamut of human activities which includes technology, commerce, the arts, narrative, mathematics, science, and computing have a common thread, namely, they have all been influenced by the emergence of verbal language. The mind in our model is basically a system in which the vestigially retained percept system of the prehuman hominid brain interacts dynamically with the abstract analytic forms of reasoning associated with the verbal languages. We therefore need to understand these two different cognitive styles and the way they interact with each other. The problem is that most studies seem to focus on one or the other rather than examining the two together. Hopefully the metaphor of language that we have used to link these two forms of thought provides some insights into their dynamics.

As an extension of this approach we also need to examine the relationship of technology, cognition, and evolution and address the question of whether a new technology or language creates new cognitive structures and, hence, an evolution of the mind. Toolmaking generated a major shift in thinking that laid the foundation for spoken language and a number of other developments, hence, it should come as no surprise that new technologies and languages create new cognitive structures. With the emergence of a number of new digital media such as the Internet, virtual reality, and expert systems we have a perfect laboratory to study this question. This is an area worthy of the joint efforts of cognitive psychologists, linguists, and dynamic systems theorists.

I would like to propose that we can build a Grand Unification Theory of Human Thought and Culture based on a dynamic systems model of the human mind, its percept-based preverbal proto-languages, and its concept-based verbal languages. The evolutionary model of the development of the brain and the emergence of the human mind suggests that technology, commerce, the arts, literature, mathematics, and science form a dynamic system that needs to be studied holistically by making use of the ideas and tools of a number of disciplines integrated by a dynamic systems approach.

# PART 3

Comparison and Synthesis
of Other Approaches to
the Origin of Language

Although the emergence of language is a pluri-disciplinary field, my approach is a bit unusual in that I start with an analysis of notated language, and I employ the techniques of media ecology and exploit ideas from complexity theory and chaotics. In order to tie my ideas to the mainstream of those who study the origin of language, I have carefully studied the literature, attended conferences on the subject, and collaborated with a few researchers in the field. In what follows I would like to compare the different approaches one finds in the literature to my own. In reading the literature, I became torn between the many conflicting views, finding merit on both sides of opposing views. In numerous cases, however, I felt that the conflicts in the literature were artificial and were more a case of academic turf wars than anything substantive. To my mind, many of these conflicts could be resolved by resorting to a co-evolutionary approach which is implicit in my model and those of some other authors.

In reviewing the literature I have two objectives in mind. The first is to use my model and a co-evolutionary approach to address and attempt to resolve some outstanding issues and differences of opinion that exist in the field. The second is to attempt to synthesize my approach with four other approaches that I am particularly sympathetic to, namely, those of Merlin Donald (1991, 1998), Terrence Deacon (1997), Morten Christiansen (1994), and Michael Tomasello (1999). I have found a number of parallels with their approaches and my own, especially their notion and use of co-evolution. We share a similar belief that the mechanisms of speech, as well as the cognitive and the social-communicative functions of language have all co-evolved. There is also a parallel between my idea that language emerged as the bifurcation from percept-based thought to abstract conceptualization and Donald's proposal that mimetic culture was the springboard for the emergence of speech, Deacon's suggestion that language arose out of the ability of hominids for symbolic representation and thought, Christiansen's notion that sequential learning and processing were essential to the emergence of language, and Tomasello's notion that language acquisition is a result of cultural transmission and observation that young children are virtual 'imitation machines.'

Because there are so many aspects to the origin of language, my approach to examining the relevant issues of this field is to organize them along the lines of Tinbergen's Four Why's, namely, function, mechanisms, ontogeny, and phylogeny, which I will address in chapters 6 through 9. In part 4, chapter 10, I will attempt to synthesize the Extended Mind Model with the work of Donald, Deacon, Christiansen, and Tomasello. Then in chapter 11, we will compare the Extended Mind Model with Andy Clark's (1997) notion of embedded cognition and scaffolding and Ray Jackendoff's (2002) ideas on the emergence of a lexicon. We also explore the duality implicit in the notion that the brain and the human mind are distinct phenomena. But before embarking on these comparisons and syntheses, we will pause and consider the work of Noam Chomsky, who dominated the field of linguistics in the latter half of the twentieth century.

# 5 How Universal Is Universal Grammar? Chomsky's Generative Grammar

Even though Chomsky is a sceptic when it comes to trying to understand the origin of language in evolutionary terms, his work must be evaluated because of his dominance of the field of linguistics for the past half century. One cannot ignore his contribution when comparing different explanations of the origin of language, especially as the field divides rather neatly into Chomsky supporters and Chomsky detractors. Many members of the anti-Chomsky camp do not attempt to discredit the main thrust of Chomsky's work in describing the Universal Grammar (UG), but rather they are critical of some of his more extreme positions vis-à-vis the ontogeny and phylogeny of language. Perhaps the most contentious of all of these is his notion that the brain is hard-wired with a Language Acquisition Device (LAD), which is Chomsky's explanation of why children are able to learn languages with such ease. The hard-wiring of the LAD in the human brain also explains why all the languages of the world share the Universal Grammar (UG). While there is general agreement that the languages of the world share many similarities, not all linguists accept Chomsky's explanation of this regularity, and there is some debate as to just how universal UG is given his claim that it is hard-wired into the brain.

It is instructive to examine the roots of Chomsky's UG hypothesis and compare it with Newton's 'UG' hypothesis of universal gravity. Newton's theory of universal gravity arose from Newton's observations of the dynamics of mechanical systems and his application of his three laws of motion to planetary motion and the behaviour of objects in the earth's gravitational field near its surface. Not only did Newton's theory of universal gravity explain existing data, such as Kepler's Law of Planetary Motion and the constant rate of acceleration of all objects at the earth's surface independent of the value of their mass, but it also made precise mathematical predictions which experiments and empirical observations confirmed.

Chomsky's hypothesis of Universal Grammar was an a priori idea that explained existing linguistic data, according to his former student Ray Jackendoff:

> The term 'Universal Grammar' first appears in *Aspects* [*of the Theory of Syntax*] (Chomsky 1965, 5–6) in a 1788 quotation from James Beattie, where it is defined as those features that all languages have in common and that therefore do not need to be mentioned in grammars of particular languages. This usage apparently derives from the term grammaire generale of the 1660 Cartesian 'Port-Royal Grammar.' Soon afterwards in Chomsky's writings (1972b; 1975), 'Universal Grammar' comes to be used to denote the 'initial state' of the language learner; it thus is conceived of as the aspect of the human mind that causes language to have the features in common that they do. More precisely, Chomsky often uses this term to refer to the child's initial prespecification of the form of possible human grammars. He uses the term 'Language Acquisition Device' to refer to the child's strategy for constructing or 'inventing' a grammar based on primary linguistic data, using Universal Grammar as a starting point ... Chomsky's postulation of UG and the LAD is a priori and follows the rationalist tradition of Descartes, Leibniz and von Humboldt of an 'instinctive' cognitive structure underpinning the acquisition of knowledge. (2002, 70)

Another aspect of the way Chomsky developed his hypothesis that differs from Newton's development of his hypothesis is that Chomsky has continually refined his theory in a series of eleven books (see Table 5.1), published over more than four decades: 'Continued examination of more and more linguistic phenomena, with attention to not only what happens but also to what does not happen, has led to many reformulations of linguistic theory over the years, with concomitant rearticulation of the content of Universal Grammar' (Jackendoff 2002, 77). One expects a new theory to undergo a certain amount of revision at its onset. But the reformulation that Jackendoff alludes to seems to be an

Table 5.1
Chomsky's Major Publications, 1957 to 2000

| Year | Publication |
| --- | --- |
| 1957 | *Syntactic Structures* (The Hague: Mouton) |
| 1965 | *Aspects of the Theory of Syntax* (Cambridge: MIT Press) |
| 1966 | *Cartesian Linguistics* (New York: Harcourt, Brace and World) |
| 1972 | *Studies on Semantics in Generative Grammar* (The Hague: Mouton) |
| 1972 | *Language and Mind*, enlarged ed. (New York: Harcourt, Brace and World) |
| 1975 | *Reflections on Language* (New York: Pantheon) |
| 1980 | *Rules and Representation* (New York: Columbia University Press) |
| 1981 | *Lectures on Government and Binding* (Dordrecht: Foris) |
| 1986 | *Knowledge of Language* (New York: Praeger) |
| 1995 | *The Minimalist Program* (Cambridge.: MIT Press) |
| 2000 | *New Horizons in the Study of Language and Mind* (Cambridge: Cambridge University Press) |

ongoing process without end. Here are six examples of exceptions to UG taken from Jackendoff's (2002) book and, what I consider to be, ad hoc explanations of these exceptions:

1 It is proposed that, 'universally, NPs [noun phrases] are permitted in positions where they can be cased marked. In order for this proposal to be carried through consistently, it is necessary to claim that English too is relentlessly case marked, even though it makes no overt case distinctions except on pronouns (I/me, she/her, etc.)' (2002, 87). This seems like a totally ad hoc proposition to me. Even Jackendoff appears to have a reservation about this proposition, 'One might find it objectionable that this solution attributes a great deal of invisible structure to English, yet gets this structure in there via innate f-knowledge' (ibid.).

2 Jackendoff provides some examples of verbs without syntactic arguments and explains their absence in what seems to me to be an ad hoc manner: 'I conclude that the obligatoriness of syntactic arguments must be encoded as an idiosyncratic lexical property' (ibid., 134). The notion of an idiosyncratic lexical property is, in essence, an extra ad hoc variable that allows a linguist to wriggle out of any prediction that goes wrong. Languages as I will argue are regular in order to be easily learned, understood, and used and not because they are following

immutable rules that are genetically coded. From time to time irregularities emerge for one reason or another. These are then learned by mimesis or imitation as the exceptions, which prove the rule.

3 Jackendoff provides a number of other idiosyncratic violations of syntactical rules or regularities. He indicates that $5 in 'Fran's $5 bet with Phil that Mark wouldn't come' was an unexplained violation of the rule that 'all syntactic arguments of nouns are either genitive NPs (before the noun) or PPs [prepositional phrases] and clauses (after it)' (ibid., 137).

4 In his discussion of the dependence of syntactic argument structure on the semantical structure of a word Jackendoff asserts that 'a lot of syntactic behavior is predictable from meaning, but far from all; the syntax – semantics interface is highly constrained but not entirely rigid' (ibid., 138). He then provides a number of examples of violations of the generalization. 'With these exceptions as a caution [the] generalization [that] the number of syntactic arguments that a verb takes on any given occasion is equal to or fewer than the number of its semantic arguments, holds most of the time' (ibid., 140). This is typical of linguistic laws, which always seem to have exceptions. A physical law with exceptions is not a law. The law of gravity works all the time – there are no exceptions.

5 In discussing the order of multiple NPs Jackendoff indicates that the order often is as follows: agent, recipient, theme, location, predicate – but then offers the caveat: 'This does not account for all cases … partly because the semantic roles with verbs like last, cost and mean are not well understood – but it covers most of them' (ibid., 143).

6 'Many languages, e.g. Russian and Hebrew, have no present tense form of the verb *be*, so that *Beth is hungry* comes out *Beth hungry*. For the moment I will take the easy way out and say that the present tense *be*, the verb with the least bit of content, is expressed in these languages by a lexical item that lacks phonology but still appears in syntax' (ibid.).

I am almost certain that, by labelling these examples as ad hoc, I will be taken by the generative grammar linguistic community to be extremely naive and lacking an appreciation of the subtlety of their field, which I am more than willing to admit to. But perhaps naiveté is an advantage.

Consider the little boy who saw that the emperor's new clothes were non-existent and proclaimed that the emperor was naked. Chomskyan linguists are so used to squirming out of the inconsistencies of the UG that they cannot see the ad hocracy to which they subscribe. From my naive point of view, I do not see the necessity of explaining away these exceptions to the UG. For me it is amazing that languages show as much consistency between them as they do, and the times one finds exceptions to these mathematical rules it only demonstrates that language was an invention of humans and not gods or logicians.

I am not alone in characterizing the generative grammar approach as being ad hoc. Tomasello, an advocate of cognitive linguistics, takes issue with the propensity 'to simply designate some items and constructions of a language as irregular or idiomatic; they are then relegated to the lexicon ... More recently, it is also evident in ... Pinker (1999) and Clahsen (1999), in which all irregular aspects of a language are in the lexicon – and so must be learned by rote' (2003, 9). The question that arises is that if the LAD is not required for these idiomatic and idiosyncratic constructions, why would an LAD be required for the remainder of the language, which is regular and presumably easier to learn?

Are UG theorists providing ad hoc explanations of phenomena to keep their theory alive? The normal expectation with a scientific theory is that it makes a certain number of predictions that can be tested. Each time the UG has encountered a new linguistic phenomenon that it did not predict, it has been reformulated and oftentimes in different ways by different linguists. In other words, there is no agreement in the field of how to interpret and explain away anomalies. These remarks are not intended to say the UG is without merit. The UG has shown that the languages of the world have much that is in common and, for the most part, seem to follow, if not one, at least a small number of patterns.

If we compare the development of Chomsky's theory and his publication rate with that of Isaac Newton we see a world of difference. Newton published his hypothesis of mechanical dynamics and universal gravity only once in the *Principia Mathematica*. His theory stood the test of time, remaining unchallenged for over two hundred years. No other theory of dynamics and gravity was proposed until Einstein's theory of relativity, which did not negate Newton's work but only refined it for those instances where the velocity of objects approached the speed of light and

Table 5.2
Alternative Approaches to Chomsky's Formulation of Universal Grammar

| Approach | Author |
|---|---|
| Autolexical syntax | (Sadock 1991) |
| Case grammar | (Fillmore 1968) |
| Cognitive grammar | (Lakoff 1987; Langacker 1987) |
| Construction grammar | (Goldberg 1995; Langacker 1992) |
| Discourse representation theory | (Kamp and Reyle 1993) |
| Dynamic semantics | (Groenendijk, Stokhof and Veltman 1996) |
| File change semantics | (Heim 1989) |
| Head-driven phrase structure grammar | (Pollard and Sag 1994) |
| Lexical-functional grammar | (Bresnan 1982, 2001) |
| Relational grammar | (Perlmutter 1983; Perlmutter and Rosen 1984) |
| Role and reference grammar | (Van Valin and LaPolla 1997) |
| Stratification grammar | (Lamb 1966) |
| Tree-adjoining grammar | (Joshi 1987; Frank and Kroch 1995) |

where the gravitational field was unusually strong. Chomsky, however, has been challenged by a number of rival theories (see Table 5.2), which makes one ask, again, just how universal is the Universal Grammar?

The many different versions of Chomsky's theory represent his attempts (see Table 5.1) to rescue it as new data were uncovered that did not agree with his initial formulation of the UG. Even some of his own followers, who buy into the basic premise of the UG, are critical of the many revisions of the UG which they believe have betrayed its original promise. Jackendoff laments: 'It is my unfortunate impression that, over the years, Chomsky's articulation of the competence-performance distinction has moved from relatively soft ... to considerably harder as suggested by the flavor of passages like this one: "It has sometimes been argued that linguistic theory must meet the empirical condition that it account for the ease and rapidity of parsing. But parsing does not, in fact, have these properties ... In general, it is not the case that language is readily usable or *designed for use*" (Chomsky and Lasnik 1993, p. 18)' (2002, 33).

Jackendoff cites examples where inconsistencies in the way the UG deals with two different syntactic frames for essentially two sentences with the same meaning: 'How should the grammar account for the fact that many verbs expressing transfer (or intended transfer) appear in two possible syntactic frames? Beth gave a teapot to Nancy versus Beth gave Nancy a teapot. In early generative grammar, this alteration was accomplished by means of a derivational rule (often called Dative Shift) that optionally turned the underlying order into the surface order' (2002, 54).

But Jackendoff reports that most linguists have rejected this approach. Since linguists do not agree on this and many other points, how can one construe the UG to be universal?

There are different ways of modelling the regularities that occur in language. It is to Chomsky's credit that he pointed out these regularities. But it must be admitted that the regularities are not always consistent from one language to another or within the same language. Bart de Boer observes that 'if there are innate constraints it is not clear why there is still such huge variation between different languages' (2000, 178). Chomsky created a mathematical model of the grammar of human languages and its regularities, but none of his models were a unique solution for describing the regularities of the grammar. That he kept changing his model and refining it meant that he never made predictions that could falsify his theory. As soon as a contradiction emerged, Chomsky altered the theory, much as the Freudians and Marxists had done to prop up their theories. Later we will explore the notion that the existence of regularities in all of the world's languages does not require the existence of an LAD, but can be explained by the fact that to survive languages had to be easy to learn and, hence, evolved or emerged with these easy-to-learn regularities (Christiansen and Ellefson 2002).

Jackendoff, acknowledging the lack of consistency of UG, has suggested a softening of the term 'universal grammar': 'So the grammar acquiring capacity is what Chomsky claims is innate. If the child is not exposed to language, language will not develop. Perhaps the term "Universal Grammar" is misleading and Chomsky should have called it "metagrammar" or "the seeds of grammar"' (2002, 72).

During the late 1960s and early 1970s a dispute erupted, known as 'the linguistic wars' among the linguists, as to the connection between deep structure and meaning. The generative semantics approach posited that deep structure and meaning were identical, but made the syntactic structures much more complex, which was vigorously opposed by Chomsky and his followers:

> Chomsky emerged victorious – but with a theory, the so-called Extended Standard Theory, in which Deep Structure no longer had the privilege of determining meaning: rather, this role was shared by Deep and Surface Structure. And then he turned his interest away from meaning, to constraints on syntactic derivations. The reaction in the wider community was one of disillusionment ... Chomsky's theory turned out not to reveal meaning after all, at least in the sense that had been anticipated. The consequence was that many researchers felt as though they had been seriously misled by linguistics, and they lost all trust in the field. (Jackendoff 2002, 74)

Another dispute among linguists which split the community was centred on the relationship between words, lexical items, and morphemes. 'Looking at the tension between these theories (morpheme-based or item-and-arrangement theories versus lexeme-based or word-and-paradigm theories) from our present very concrete standpoint of storage in the brain, we arrive at the conclusion that both approaches are correct, but for different classes of words' (Jackendoff 2002, 162). This makes the non-linguist wonder about the universality of grammar. There is no doubt in my mind that there are regularities in the grammars of the world, but it is hard to accept that they are absolutely universal. Jackendoff, for example, has a different approach to constructional idioms than Chomsky: 'Derivational [i.e., Chomskyan] generative grammar has discouraged recognizing constructions as of any theoretical interest – for a principled reason ... By contrast, in the present approach, constructions turn out to be slightly unusual but perfectly respectable lexical items that combine with ordinary words according to ordinary procedures ... they are syntactically deviant ... but they are used all the time and must be learned by the child' (ibid., 178).

Jackendoff points out that verbs and nouns have the same argument structure in Classical Nahuatl but not English and then asks, 'Faced with this range of variation, what is the appropriate position to take on UG? Van Valin and LaPolla's (1997) position is that if a characteristic is not universal, it is not part of UG' (2002, 263). Jackendoff does not concur but suggests that 'the difficulty was that UG was being thought of ... as an indivisible "grammar box." Here we were able to resolve the paradox by saying that both make use of part but not all of modern UG' (ibid.).

It seems that the UG is a collection of all the rules (or tools if we are talking about language production) required to describe the languages of the world and, as suggested by Jackendoff, this is the 'UG toolkit.' It seems as though linguists, especially Chomsky and those that take his hypothesis as dogma, find it necessary to explain away all exceptions to this collection of rules which they take not to be optional tools that a language can make use of but rather to be hard and fast rules that languages must obey. Jackendoff appears to concur with the sentiment I just expressed when he writes: 'The overall conclusion is that grammar is not a single unified system, but a collection of simpler systems' (2002, 264). If the UG is a fixed single unified system how does one explain that the English language, a language with one of the richest lexicons, has been slowly sloughing off some of its grammatical complexities? English has dropped the use of the second person singular, thou, and its case structure only differentiates third person singular from all the other cases so that *he runs* but *they, you, we* or *I run.*

Jackendoff cites more exceptions to the UG vis-à-vis head constraints: 'The syntactic arguments and adjuncts in a phrase express the semantic arguments and modifiers of the phrase's head. The Head Constraint is subject to various sorts of exceptions ... Classical generative grammar maintained the Head Constraint as a universal by saying it applies in Deep Structure' (2002, 145). Deep structure and derivation rules are used in the UG program as a way of wriggling out of any inconsistencies and non-universalities of the UG. They play a role in Chomskyan linguistics similar to that of the subconscious for Freud or class structure for Marx. Where is the Karl Popper among linguists for the UG, who will suggest that perhaps the propositions of the proponents of the UG are not scientific statements because they cannot be falsified?

Early in his career as a social scientist, Karl Popper became acquainted with the theories of Karl Marx through his left-wing political activities and with the theories of Sigmund Freud as a result of his profession as a social worker engaged with socially disadvantaged youth. Popper became suspicious of the scientific nature of these latter two theories because they were always able to provide an ad hoc explanation when their predictions did not pan out. These two theories did not behave like the theories in the field of physics, in which experiments or empirical observation either corroborate a hypothesis or disprove or falsify it. By comparing these two domains Popper developed the criterion by which a system of propositions could be judged to be scientific or not, namely, the criterion of falsifiability. A theory could only be scientific if its propositions could be falsified. Popper concluded that the theories of Freud and Marx were not scientific because they were not falsifiable. One is forced to reach a similar conclusion regarding Chomsky is theory of generative grammar, as well as its many competitors, and that includes my own Extended Mind Model. The one hope I have, however, that I might be on the right track is that, I believe, Christiansen (1994), Deacon (1997), Donald (1991, 1998), Tomasello (1999), and I have come to similar conclusions from completely different starting points.

To conclude this chapter, we return to the question of how universal are the grammars of the world's languages. Can the UG be described by a simple 'syntactocentric grammar box' which is how Jackendoff characterizes the simplistic Chomsky approach to UG or is there more to the UG?

> Many other candidates suggest themselves as structural fragments that might act as UG 'attractors' for structural patterns of language ... The content of UG boiled down in large part to (a) architectural universals – what kind of structures there are in grammar and how they interface, and (b) what particular fragments of structure (or 'tricks') are prespecified to bias the child's acquisition of generalizations. These pieces did have to evolve in the history of the species; it is hoped that their evolution is more plausible than that of a standard syntactocentric 'grammar box' ...
>
> I must confess that at this point I hear linguists screaming: There's not enough machinery! How can this be constrained? He's sold out to the connectionists! And I hear the network modelers screaming: There's too much machinery! How can this be built in? Will those linguists ever learn? I can only respond that the position here is far from a weak kneed compromise: it is an attempt to make the most sense I can out of the genuine insights of

both sides. Both classes of objections indeed must be met; I take this as another challenge for future research. (Jackendoff 2002, 193)

Amen! Jackendoff displays a Solomon-like wisdom by not splitting the baby (the field of linguistics) in two. In the end, Jackendoff concludes that perhaps the UG is a bit overextended: 'The conviction has grown on me that the dominant view of Universal Grammar as a highly complex specification of all grammars – whether in terms of parameters or ranked constraints – is untenable. It does not allow enough room for the range of idiosyncrasy in language, as evidenced for instance by the variety of constructions in English. The present framework tentatively offers the possibility of seeing Universal Grammar as a much more limited (though hardly trivial) set of "attractor" structures that, through inheritance hierarchies, guide the course of the child's generalizations over the evidence. Jackendoff' (2002, 426).

## Cognitive Grammar

The critiques of Chomsky that we have been reviewing, like those of Jackendoff, come from people who do not reject Chomsky's ideas completely but try to salvage his approach from some of its more outlandish claims. There is a group of linguists, however, who do completely reject Chomsky's approach: Michael Tomasello is one of them. He regards 'Generative Grammar (as) nothing other than a form of mathematics' (1998, x) and goes on to level an even harsher critique: 'Chomskyan linguists distanced themselves from psychological experiments that attempted to translate the theory into performance models (perhaps because they yielded, to put it kindly, mixed results; Palermo 1978)' (ibid., ix).

Tomasello is less kind to generative grammar when citing the work of linguistic typologists: 'Linguists who are involved in detailed analysis of individual languages cross-linguistically – mostly known as linguistic typologists – now agree that there are very few if any specific grammatical constructions or markers that are universally present in all languages' (2003a, 5).

Tomasello shares Jackendoff's characterization of the UG as a 'syntactocentric grammar box': 'The most fundamental tenet of Generative

Grammar is that there is a level of linguistic description, namely syntax, that is independent of all other levels of linguistic description including semantics – and independent of all other aspects of cognition as well. This Autonomy of Syntax thesis is not an empirical discovery or even a hypothesis that is ever explicitly tested. It is a paradigm-defining definitional postulate that is a direct result of taking a mathematical approach to natural language' (1998, x).

Tomasello is critical of both the notion that the LAD is hard-wired as well as the notion that the UG is actually universal:

> Some linguists and psycholinguists believe that young children operate from the beginning with abstract, adult-like linguistic constructions – because they are born with certain innate linguistic principles. But this theory can work only if all languages work with the same basic linguistic principles, which they do not (for recent reviews documenting cross-linguistic variability much too great to be instantiated in an innate universal grammar, see Comrie, 1990; Givo´n, 1995; Dryer, 1997; Croft, 1998; van Valin and LaPolla, 1996; Slobin, 1997). The alternative is the view that early in ontogeny individual human beings learn to use their species-specific cognitive, social-cognitive, and cultural learning abilities to comprehend and acquire the linguistic constructions their particular cultures have created over historical time by processes of socio-genesis. (1999, 135)

Another critic of Chomsky, and someone who Tomasello draws upon in his work, is Ronald Langacker, who has proposed a kind of cognitive approach to linguistics that he defines as follows:

> The movement called *cognitive linguistics* belongs to the functionalist tradition. Although its concern with cognition hardly makes it unique, the label *cognitive* is not entirely arbitrary. Within functionalism, cognitive linguistics stands out by emphasizing the semiological function of language and the crucial role of conceptualization in social interaction. It contrasts with formalist approaches (like Chomsky's generative grammar) by viewing language as an integral facet of cognition (not as a separate 'module' or 'mental faculty'). Insofar as possible, linguistic structure is analyzed in terms of more basic systems and abilities (e.g., perception, attention, categorization) from which it cannot be dissociated. (1998, 1)

Langacker describes in great detail the differences between cognitive linguistics and generative grammar, pointing out that his approach is psychologically grounded. Tomasello formulates this approach by saying 'that the structures of language are taken directly from human cognition, and so linguistic communication, including its grammatical structure, should be studied in the same basic manner using the same basic theoretical constructs as all other cognitive skills' (1998, xx). He regards generative grammar as nothing more than a form of mathematics.

I agree with Langacker and Tomasello's characterization of cognitive grammar and generative grammar, but pitting one system against another is like pitting one coordinate system against another. It is not a question of whether rectilinear coordinates are better than polar coordinates, it is only a matter of picking the coordinate system that most simply describes the phenomenon under investigation. Chomsky and Langacker, with generative grammar and cognitive linguistics respectively, provide us with two different coordinate systems. It is not that one system is better than the other – each has something of value. The importance and value of cognitive linguistics, aside from its intrinsic value in tying language comprehension and production to psychology, is that it offers a critique of generative grammar which has, at times, overstated its virtues and has enjoyed an unearned hegemony in the past.

What pleases about Langacker's approach is the modesty of his position: 'Because the membership of certain classes (such as nouns and verbs) cannot be predicted, it has to be specifically learned and explicitly described by linguists. This does not by itself establish the autonomy of grammar, except in the weakest sense (acknowledged by every linguist) that functional considerations fail to fully and uniquely determine every detail of language structure – the specific patterns and distributions of a language are shaped by convention and acquired through social interaction' (1998, 23).

Langacker's approach is more in tune with the work of those who have analysed and compared the oral and literate traditions, such as McLuhan (1962, 1964) and Havelock (1963):

Because language is learned through usage, it ought not be surprising that the preponderance of linguistic knowledge consists of specific expressions and low-level patterns, many of which incorporate particular lexical items.

This is not to deny the existence and importance of general, productive patterns represented by high-level schemas. I would however suggest that fully general patterns fully constitute a distinct minority, that lower-level structures provide critical information and do much if not most of the work in speaking and understanding. Attempts to impose a strict boundary between structural regularity and idiosyncrasy – attributing them to distinct modules or processing systems (Chomsky 1965; Pinker and Bloom 1990) – are, I believe, both linguistically untenable and psychologically dubious. Instead I envision a dynamic, interactive process whereby structures at all levels of abstraction compete for activation and for the privilege of being invoked in producing and understanding utterances. (Langacker 1998, 25)

This is exactly what Eric Havelock found in his analysis of Homeric oral tradition, namely, that certain rhetorical expressions (i.e., low-level patterns) were used over and over again. The kind of language in which idiosyncratic structures are more prominent corresponds to written language, where the producer, of language have more time to compose and can edit and re-edit their text.

Although the cognitive linguists, like Langacker and Tomasello, are critical of Chomsky's notion of the UG, they do accept that there are universals associated with language but assert that they are due to the universality of human cognition. After listing a number of grammatical features that he claims are not universal, Tomasello writes: 'This does not mean that there are no language universals – there demonstrably are – but only that we must look for those universals in places besides particular linguistic items and constructions. One place to look is human cognition, and of course that is one of the central tenets of Cognitive Linguistics ... Along with plenty of idiosyncratic grammaticalization paths in individual languages, there would seem to be some universal, or nearly universal, grammaticalization and syntactization paths as well ... These happen separately in separate languages, presumably attesting to common processes of change based on universal principles of human cognition and linguistic communication' (2003, 5 and 7).

## Grammaticalization

Chomsky's view of grammar is that is that it is a fixed, static mathematical set of propositions, a view challenged by those who study grammaticalization. Joan Bybee expresses this dynamic appreciation of grammar succinctly as follows: 'Grammar is not a static, closed, or self-contained system, but is highly susceptible to change and highly affected by language use. The loss of grammar is generally acknowledged and often lamented by prescriptive grammarians, who mourn the loss of the distinction between who and whom but fail to rejoice in the creation of new grammar, such as the new future tense gonna. In fact, the creation of new grammatical morphemes and structures is as common as the loss of old ones' (2003, 145).

Grammaticalization is the process by which grammar emerges basically from the lexicon. It is the process whereby nouns that represent concrete objects and verbs that represent actions and relations among entities 'become prepositions, auxiliaries, and other grammatical forms ... Grammatical constructions and the concepts they represent become emancipated from the concrete and come to express purely abstract notions, such as tense, case relations, definiteness, and so on. It is important to note, however, that the sources for grammar are concepts and words drawn from the most concrete and basic aspects of human experience' (Bybee 2003, 145 and 152–3).

The notion that grammatical constructions emerge from the 'concepts and words' associated with concrete human experiences supports the extended mind hypothesis that language emerged from the conceptualization of our percepts. The extended mind hypothesis models the creation of the lexicon of nouns and verbs as strange attractors for our percepts, but it does not explain how grammatical constructions and grammar words emerge. Grammaticalization provides the mechanism how words operating as strange attractors for our percepts gave rise to grammar. The argument that the complexity of hominid existence gave rise to a new level of order in the form of words acting as concepts can be extended to grammaticalization. As the complexity of language increased through the growth of the lexicon, the information overload and complexity that resulted gave rise to a new level of order in the form of a grammaticalized grammar. According to this view, to reiterate, 'grammar is not a static, closed, or self-contained system, but is highly susceptible to change and highly affected by language use' (Bybee 2003, 153). This is in contrast to Chomsky's generative grammar which is fixed (hard-wired) and, hence, static. Grammaticalization is a diachronic approach to grammar, in contrast to Chomsky's synchronic approach.

Within the framework of grammaticalization the notion of universality of grammar changes. Rather than maintaining that all languages share a common grammatical structure synchronically, those that advocate the grammaticalization approach maintain that the processes by which new grammatical structures emerge are the universals (Bybee 2003, 146).

> All around the world, in languages that are not related genetically or geographically, we find analogous examples: definite articles developing from demonstratives, indefinite articles from the numeral 'one,' future tenses from verbs meaning 'want' or 'go to,' and auxiliaries indicating possibilities and permission from verbs meaning 'know' and 'be able.' (ibid., 148)
>
> In any language we look at, we find odd constructions that are near the end of ... a path, as well as new constructions that are just beginning their evolution and construction midway along. Grammar is constantly being created and lost along such specifiable and universal trajectories. (ibid., 150)

This new form of universality is explained in terms not of some accidental genetic mutation, which magically provided humans with the gift of language, but rather it is based on the universality of human cognition – something for which solid empirical evidence exists: 'Many of the very basic mechanisms that constitute the process of grammaticalization are cognitive processes that are not necessarily restricted to language' (Bybee 2003, 146).

Bybee concludes that grammaticalization refutes the notion that grammar is innate: 'Because all grammatical categories and constructions are derivable from experience with language, there is no reason to suppose they are innate. In fact, the notion of innate grammatical rules is incompatible with the gradual, usage-driven nature of grammatical change. Innate rules and categories would be unchangeable over time and over generations, or if change occurred, an abrupt shift from one discrete category to another would be required' (2003, 164–5).

### Hauser, Chomsky, and Fitch: A Neo-Chomskyan Perspective

The ever-flexible Noam Chomsky has recently surfaced together with two colleagues, Marc Hauser and Tecumseh Fitch, to offer still another approach to the emergence of the UG (Hauser, Chomsky, and Fitch 2002). A distinction is made between a faculty of language in the broad sense (FLB) and a faculty of language in the narrow sense (FLN), where the FLN is the computational mechanism for recursion and the FLB which includes the FLN also contains a sensory-motor system and a conceptual-intentional system. It is suggested that the latter two systems are capabilities that certain non-human animals possess and part of our genetic inheritance. The FLN, however, on the other hand is unique to humans in its application to language, but perhaps certain non-human animals evolved an ability for recursion 'to solve other computational problems such as navigation, number quantification or social relationships' (ibid., 1578).

The approach of Hauser et al. is rejected by two of Chomsky's former students, Steven Pinker and Ray Jackendoff, who 'find the hypothesis problematic [because] it ignores the many aspects of grammar that are not recursive, such as phonology, morphology, case, agreement, and many properties of words. It is inconsistent with the anatomy and neural control of the human vocal tract. And it is weakened by experiments suggesting that speech perception cannot be reduced to primate audition, that word learning cannot be reduced to fact learning, and that at least one gene involved in speech and language was evolutionarily selected in the human lineage but is not specific to recursion' (Pinker and Jackendoff 2004).

Having completed a review and critique of Chomsky's generative grammar and a brief description of the alternative approach of cognitive linguistics, we now turn to a survey and evaluation of the various approaches to understanding the origin of language making use of Tinbergen's Four Why's of the function, mechanisms, ontogeny, and phylogeny of language. We begin in the next chapter by examining the function of language.

# 6 Is the Primary Function of Language Social Communication or the Representation of Abstract Thought?

This computational role of language has been somewhat neglected (but not unnoticed, but not rigourously pursued either) in recent cognitive science, due perhaps to a (quite proper) fascination with and concentration upon, that other obvious dimension: the role of language as an instrument of interpersonal communication.

Andy Clark, *Being There*

Most linguists (Pinker and Bloom 1990; Barton 1996; Barton and Dunbar 1997; Byrne 1995; Byrne and Whiten 1988; Cheney and Seyfarth 1990; Dessalles 1998; Dunbar 1992, 1998; Jackendoff 2002; Knight 1998b; Locke 1998; Power 1998; Sawaguchi and Kudo 1990; Worden 1998) cite social communication as the principle function of language and believe it was this purpose that motivated the origin of speech. 'I assume that language arose primarily in the interest of enhancing communication, and only secondarily in the interest of enhancing thought' (Jackendoff 2002, 236).

There are those (Bickerton 1998; Ulbaek 1998), however, who hold that the principle function of language is the representation of abstract thought. Derek Bickerton (2003) points out that we are the only species that communicates with abstract symbolic language and we are also the only species that is so adaptive and creative. He suggests these two unique characteristics of our species cannot be coincidental.

We shall review the arguments presented by these two camps and argue that language serves both a communications and a cognitive function and that these two functions are mutually supportive and, hence, co-evolved. This position is similar to one advocated by Deacon (1997) and Tomasello (1999). Finally, we will review the work of Clark (1997) which represents a third approach in which he sees language as a tool for guiding our actions. We begin with those who attribute some form of a social communication function as the motivating factor for the emergence of speech.

## Social Communication as the Primary Function of Speech

Robin Dunbar suggests that because of the large energy cost of increasing the size of the brain to accommodate language there had to be a countervailing force which made language advantageous:

> The main thrust of most research in this area has favored the view that the required force was social, not environmental or technological ... Barton and Dunbar (1997) developed the 'social brain' hypothesis which emphasizes the claim that the primate brain (at least) is largely a social rather than an ecological tool. This view in turn rests on growing evidence that primates (in particular) are significantly more skilled at solving social problems than they are at solving ecological problems (Cheney and Seyfarth 1990) and that a significant component of these social skills involves what has become known as 'Machiavellian Intelligence' (Byrne and Whiten 1988). The strongest evidence to support this claim is provided by the finding that social group size correlates very closely with relative neocortex size in primates.' (1998, 94)

Another explanation for encephalization is offered by a number of researchers, as reported by Pinker and Bloom: 'Cooperation opens the door to advances in the ability of cheaters to fool people into believing that they have paid a cost or that they have not taken a benefit. This in turn puts pressure on the ability to detect subtle signs of such cheating, which puts pressure on the ability to cheat in less detectable ways, and so on. It has been noted that this sets the stage for a cognitive "arms race" (e.g., Tooby and Cosmides, 1990; Dawkins, 1976; Tooby and DeVore, 1987; Trivers, 1971) ... The unusually rapid enlargement of the human brain, especially the frontal lobes, has been attributed to such an arms race (Alexander, 1987; Rose, 1980)' (Pinker and Bloom 1990, 758).

Robert Worden attributes primate social skills to the development of human language. He proposes that 'language is an outgrowth of primate social intelligence' (1998, 148–9). One of his key hypotheses is that 'the internal representation of language meaning in the brain derives from the primate representation of social situations ... While some use of language is internal, for thought processes, this suggests strongly that it is an outgrowth of social intelligence' (ibid., 153).

Dunbar suggests that language was an effective solution to the social demands that arose with this increase in the size of social groups. First, it allowed more individuals to be groomed by substituting verbal grooming for physical grooming and, second, it allowed 'the direct exchange of information that [could] be used to build and service relationships without the need for direct physical contact ... Language is a consequence not a cause of group size evolution ... The need to evolve large groups drove brain size upwards, and this in turn eventually required the evolution of language as a more effective bonding device ... The function of language (as an activity) is to facilitate the management of social relationships' (1998, 96–7 and 105–7).

Dunbar further suggests that language was initially a 'bonding device' and only later was used to deceive by those possessed with 'Machiavellian Intelligence' which he claims is a 'very clear benchmark of advanced social skill' (1998, 107). I am of the opinion, however, that it takes greater social skills to achieve one's objectives by creating an environment of cooperation rather than relying on deception of one's fellow beings. Morality as far as I am concerned is the true 'benchmark of advanced social skills.' Perhaps my disagreement with Dunbar is a matter of values rather than a scientific hypothesis that can be objectively resolved, as there is no objective measure of what is an 'advanced social skill.' Social intelligence, the second preverbal proto-language in my Extended Mind Model, represents the emergence of hominid cooperation which eventually evolved into economic cooperation and human morality.

Dunbar's position is supported by Camilla Power: 'Dunbar argues that vocal signals were required to supplement and replace physical grooming as a mechanism of social bonding in increasingly complex groups. Compared with manual grooming, vocalization permitted greater efficiency in maintaining social relationships by reducing the time invested in servicing relationships, since multiple relationships could be serviced simultaneously ... It would [also] allow some saving in time budgets if foraging activities can continue while social contact is maintained' (1998, 111 and 113).

If this argument is valid, why didn't mimetic communication, as suggested by Donald (1991), which includes a vocalized component serve the same purpose as speech as a substitute for grooming? Why was it necessary for the vocalization to evolve an informatics component? Pure prosody would have been just as effective as speech for social grooming. Why not gesture, dance, hand signals viewed by many at once? Perhaps speech allowed more complex social structures to emerge rather than the other way around or perhaps the two phenomena, language and complex social structures, simply co-evolved.

Group size, according to Dunbar and Power, was the factor that seemed to drive hominid evolution: 'In human evolution we see a complex feedback process, driven ultimately by whatever caused the need for larger groups' (Power 1998, 112). It would seem larger groups were motivated by the need to share the many benefits of fire, to take advantage of the division of labour and food sharing, and to be able to conduct large-scale, efficient, coordinated hunting: 'Studies of baboons and gelada have also demonstrated a correlation between the amount of time a pair of animals spend grooming and their willingness to support each other in conflict' (ibid., 113). A similar conclusion can be reached concerning humans if we generalize our notion of grooming to include verbal exchanges and the sharing of ideas or concepts.

'The pressures on group cohesion in these circumstances (increase in group size) led to a new development in vocal communication, whereby spoken language facilitated exchange of information about third parties. This is the "gossip" hypothesis of language origins' (Power 1998, 114). Power claims that gossip contains an important feature of abstract human speech, namely, 'displaced reference.' Jean-Louis Dessalles supports the 'social brain' hypothesis, but introduces the notion of relevance – the need for an utterance to be socially appropriate – claiming that 'relevance is a requirement of language, which we only notice when some utterance does not comply with it ... If we see language as a tool for bringing out information and highlighting its relevance, the language may be considered in this context as an advertising device ... I have tried to show that the predictions of an altruistic model are not verified: conversational information is indeed valuable, but instead of being requested by listeners as is expected, it is generally put forward by speakers. To resolve this paradox, I proposed that linguistic behaviour is not altruistic, but rather is a form of trade: relevant information is given in exchange for status' (1998, 131, 142 and 146).

John Locke belongs to the school that sees the emergence of language as motivated by social needs: 'It is far more plausible that our ancestors had the means to express their feelings vocally and then discovered, over many generations, that this same modality could be manipulated to convey thought and co-ordinate action' (1998, 191). Locke distinguishes between two types of sound making: (1) talking to 'maintain cohesion with others, a socially oriented process that has little to do with thoughts, and it taps no more than the most superficial levels of language,' and (2) speaking which 'expresses unshared information.' 'My personal attraction to talking as the precursor to language in the species began with the observation that normally developing infants take vocal turns, use word-like sounds and sentence-like prosodies, and in some cultures talk on toy telephones long before they produce words and do anything grammatical ... It thus appears that humans have a mechanism in the brain that controls sound making, possibly operating in some isolation from other mechanisms that are needed for vocabulary acquisition or grammar' (ibid., 192–3).

Not only was the function of speech social communication, according to Chris Knight, but it also provided a mechanism that allowed speech to emerge: 'I treat speech as a revolutionary development made possible by the establishment of novel levels of social co-operation ... Speech has been co-operative from its inception' (1998b, 68 and 75). The mechanism for Knight that led to speech was ritual: 'Linguistic reference is not a direct mapping from linguistic terms either to perceptible things or to intentional states; the mapping is from linguistic terms to communal constructs – representations established in the universe of discourse' (1998b, 69). Knight summarizes by stating that speech is a special case of 'conspiratorial whispering' communicated among members of a ritual in-group.

## The Bias of Communication vis-à-vis the Origin of Speech

There is no doubt in my mind that the origin of speech was motivated in part by the need for social communication, and I find that all of the arguments presented in the last section have merit. However, the need for or the advantage of social communication was not the only factor that contributed to the origin of human language. The representation of abstract thought was of equal importance, and there is no conflict with the idea that communication and cognition co-evolved and catalyzed each other's development. What I find hard to understand is the bias some linguists have against the idea that speech arose to represent abstract ideas and thoughts. If, as they claim, language evolved strictly to meet the needs for social interaction, one must ask, as does Bickerton (1995), why our primate ancestors, who are highly social, did not also develop verbal language.

To support his position that the main function of language is social communication rather than an informatics tool for thought and to set a certain tone, Locke (1998, 190) quotes Malinowski (1923): 'It is only in certain very special uses among a civilized community and only in its highest uses that language is employed to frame and express thoughts.' The fallacy in Malinowski's position, and hence Locke's, is that most thoughts go uncommunicated and, hence, if one were to judge the frequency of the use of language for thought based on vocal communications, one would only be taking into account a small fraction of the times language is used to facilitate thought.

Locke's use of Malinowski is a mild attack on those who believe that the origin of language is tied to its cognitive functions as an informatics tool. Robin Dunbar is even more hostile to this idea: 'The past century of work in cognitive psychology and neuroscience has been directed down the wrong channel: all work in this area assumes that cognitive (and, hence, brain) function is concerned primarily with dealing with perceptual processing skills, but the "social brain" hypothesis suggests that our skills in these domains are all by products of the fact that the (primate) brain evolved to handle day-to-day social problems ... If our brain evolved to handle social problems, then the same is likely to be true of language. Both the functions of language and its modus operandi must be sought in the social rather than the physical world' (1998, 106).

Dunbar sets up a false dichotomy between the 'social' and 'physical' worlds. It is true that emotional or social intelligence has been traditionally discounted with respect to symbolic intelligence and that, until very recently, personal tacit knowledge has been devalued with respect to objective explicit knowledge. Dunbar's position is too extreme, however, and represents a swing of the pendulum in the opposite direction. Social and symbolic thinking and the use of language for social communication and the representation of abstract thought co-evolved iteratively, and the boundary between these two domains is not as sharp as Dunbar would have us believe. He writes, for example, that 'symbolic language (the language of metaphysics and religion, of science and instruction) would have emerged later as a form of software development (it embodies no new structural or cognitive features not already present in social language), probably at the time of the Upper Paleolithic Revolution some 50,000 years ago when we see the first unequivocal archaeological evidence for symbolism (including a dramatic improvement in the quality and form of tools, the possible use of ochre for decorative purposes, followed in short order by evidence of deliberate burials, art and non-functional jewelry)' (ibid., 105).

I can support Dunbar's position that social language was as sophisticated as metaphysical language, but what Dunbar is missing is that social language is just as abstract and symbolic as so-called metaphysical language. The concepts of I and thou, for example, are just as sophisticated and symbolic as the concepts of one and two and, in fact, possibly related.

Another group of linguists with a unifunctional view of language is Pinker and Bloom. While extolling the virtues of language for communication, they then run it down as a tool for thought: 'Natural languages are hopeless for (knowledge representation): they are needlessly serial, rife with ambiguity (usually harmless in conversational contexts, but unsuited for long term knowledge representation), complicated by alternations that are relevant only to discourse (e.g., topicalization), and cluttered with devices (such as phonology and much morphology) that make no contribution to reasoning. Similarly, the facts of grammar make it difficult to argue that language shows design for "the expression of thought" in any sense that is substantially distinct from "communication"' (1990, 728). At the same time (and on the same page) that they denigrate language for knowledge representation, they laud it for its powers of communication: 'Human language is a device capable of communicating exquisitely complex and subtle messages, from convoluted soap operas to theories of the origin of the universe' (ibid.).

Writing some thirteen years later, Pinker reiterates that there is a connection between language and concepts. He argues that a species that comes to depend on information and concepts would have no trouble developing language to communicate that information: 'Tooby and DeVore have pointed out that a species that has evolved to rely on information: should thus also evolve a means to exchange that information' (2003, 28). It seems as though Pinker is saying that concepts create words and not the other way around. Hurford holds to a similar position claiming that the capacity 'to form basic concepts' is a pre-adaptation for language (2003, 41). Pinker seems to waffle a bit on this position because later, in the same article from which the above quote is taken, he writes, 'Three key features of the distinctively human lifestyle – know-how, sociality, and language – coevolved, each constituting a selection pressure for the others' (2003, 29). There seems to be some confusion in Pinker's position.

One thing is clear, namely, that Pinker like many other linguists, regards language and thought as two separate activities. Hurford expresses this position in terms of two propositions in a recent article:

1 Much of the structure of language has no role in a system for the internal representation of thought.
2 Much of the structure of language has a role in systems for the external expression of thought, which includes communication. (2002, 312)

Hurford, Pinker, Bloom, and others hold to proposition (1), that language is the vehicle whereby thoughts are communicated and not the medium in which they (thoughts) are conceived. Needless to say, I hold the exact opposite view and subscribe to proposition (2). Our first concepts were the very first words of spoken language, and they are the medium for abstract concept-based thought. The confusion that arises over the notion that language and thought are distinct activities arises from the fact that there are two distinct forms of mental activity or thought, one percept-based and the other concept-based. It is true that there is not a complete overlap between language and thought because of the existence of percept-based thought which includes automatic reactions to certain stimuli or thinking in terms of images. But concept-based thought without language is not possible. Clark supports this notion that there exist two forms of thought, one verbally based and the other not: 'Sentential and non-sentential modes of thought thus co-evolve so as to complement, but not replicate, each other's special cognitive virtues' (1997, 211).

Bickerton also makes a distinction between concept-based and percept-based thinking, although he describes them as on-line and off-line thinking respectively:

> On-line thinking involves computations carried out only in terms of neural responses elicited by the presence of external objects, while off-line thinking involves computation carried out on more lasting internal representations of those objects. Such computations need not be initiated by external causes, nor need they initiate an immediate motor response. What differentiates human from nonhuman thought, and what has led many ... to deny thinking to other species, is that while all creatures above a pretty low level of brain organization can practice on-line thinking (to widely varying extents, I need hardly add), only humans can practice both on-line and off-line thinking. (1995)

I maintain that there is an exact overlap between concept-based abstract thought and verbal language and that one cannot exist without the other. The confusion regarding the relationship of language and thought arises because not enough of a distinction is made between abstract concept-based thinking, which arose with spoken language, and concrete percept-based thinking, which existed before speech and relied on mimetics for communication. Just as the mimetic elements of vocal tone, hand signals, facial gesture, and body language coexist with and have been incorporated into speech, so too, does abstract language based conceptual thinking co-exist with concrete percept-based thinking. We still think in images, have strong emotions, and experience pleasure and pain, all of which are part our mental life, but they are distinct from our conceptual thought in which language is the medium.

Donald maintains that 'symbols are a product of thought, not vice versa, and in their interpretation, symbols get their meaning from thought, not vice versa ... In every case thought is the arbiter, and language is the child of thought, invented in the service of thought, employed forever as the amplifier and mediator of thought' (2001, 276–7). To justify the primacy of thought over language, he then argues that 'humans can think without language. This can be seen in very young children. The same is true of aphasic patients who lose language altogether yet continue to be able to think in an artistic, musical, mechanical, social and spatial sense' (ibid.). But the fallacy in Donald's argument is that he does not distinguish between concrete-mimetic thought and abstract conceptual thought. The former is mimetic-based and the latter is language-based. Language is the medium that makes abstract conceptual thought possible, which is why I have argued that language acts as an extension of the brain creating the mind, just as physical tools are extensions of our body. Verbal language is the medium of abstract thought, just as notes are the medium of music and pigments the medium of paintings.

Bickerton makes a distinction between the concrete and the abstract levels of thought: 'Language is the only thing that frees our thoughts from the exigencies of the moment and to structure them into complex wholes ... Language is something added to what other creatures have in the way of intelligence. It doesn't take over the whole domain of thought. Humans like other creatures interact with their environment, and like other creatures they process the data from their sense organs to create a primary representation of the world' (1995, 100–1). The difference between us and animals, as Bickerton points out above, is that animals react to their environment, and humans not only react to their environment, but they also change it to suit their needs. The thesis being advanced here is that there existed a hominid mental life before the advent of language which changed radically with the emergence of speech.

We can find other examples of this kind of radical change or transformation of human thought if we follow the origin and evolution of the notated languages of writing, mathematics, science, computing, and the Internet. With the advent of the written word, new forms of human thought emerged including science, history, philosophy, and deductive logic (Havelock 1963; Logan 2004a, 2004b; McLuhan 1964; Stubbs 1980). Just as writing and mathematics required the existence of the spoken language and scientific thinking required the existence of the written and mathematical forms of language, abstract concept-based thinking required the existence of spoken language. In a similar manner, the language of computing required the existence of science, mathematics, and writing, and the language of the Internet required the existence of the language of computing. As we have argued earlier, speech, writing, mathematics, science, computing, and the Internet form an evolutionary chain of languages, each promoting a more abstract way of thinking and each serving as a medium for that thought. Similarly, the advent of verbal language through speech represented a transition to a more abstract form of thinking than the percept-based form of prehuman hominid thinking which Bickerton terms *on-line thinking*.

## Mentalese

Pinker and Bloom's diatribe against natural language, branding it as a 'hopeless' (1990, 28) medium for the representation of thought, arises because they fail to distinguish between spoken language and the notated languages of writing, mathematics, science, computing, and the Internet. Some of the weaknesses of spoken language as a medium for abstract thought have been overcome with the notated languages, each of which have their own unique semantics and syntax (Logan 1995, 2004b). There is a large overlap of semantics and syntax between these different forms of language, but never the less, they have each evolved their own peculiar lexicon and syntax to be able to carry out their particular functions. Each is a medium for the particular kind of thought that it generate, just as spoken language is an excellent medium for abstract thought and planning, as well as for ritual, story telling, social grooming, gossip, and the coordination of sundry tasks such as fire tending, hunting, gathering, planting, and harvesting.

Pinker and Bloom do not regard natural language as the medium of thought, but rather support a position of Fodor that there exists a special language just for thought: 'Human knowledge and reasoning, it has been argued, is couched in a "language of thought" that is distinct from external languages such as English or Japanese (Fodor, 1975) ... But while there may be a language-like representational medium – "the language of thought," or "mentalese" (Fodor, 1975) – it clearly cannot be English, Japanese, and so on' (1990, 714). The claim made by Pinker and Bloom in their statement here is not self-evident. If language is both a medium for thought and communication, then there is no reason that English or Japanese could not serve as 'mentalese.'

If we apply Occam's razor, there is no need to postulate a special language for thinking and another for communicating. If the language of mentalese exists, it is extremely difficult to identify. I know of no accounts of it, no description of its semantics or its syntax. I have, therefore, concluded that mentalese is an ad hoc concept, devised and supported by those who wish to believe that the sole function of language is communication and cannot recognize the obvious that it is both a communication medium and an informatics tool, a cognitive Swiss army knife if you will, with at least two blades. I would categorize 'mentalese' as one of those constructs that scientists create when they do not fully understand a process, and would liken it to the concept of the 'aether' that was postulated by the physicists of the late nineteenth century to describe the medium through which light presumably propagated. Einstein achieved his breakthrough theory of relativity and explained the negative result of the Michaelson-Morley experiment by simply assuming there was no aether. I suggest we follow Einstein's example and assume that mentalese does not exist.

Deacon provides a telling insight as to why the notion of 'mentalese' was conceived of in the first place and, hence, why it is not a very useful idea. He suggests that those who advocate a theory of the innate knowledge of language reflect 'an implicit analytic or top-down perspective on the nature of symbolic reference [which] ... leaves symbolic reference ungrounded and forces us to introduce additional top-down causal hypotheses, such as the existence of an ephemeral soul or the assumption that there can be forms of computation or mental language (mentalese) that are intrinsically meaningful, in order to fill in for this missing causal role in the explanation' (1997, 454–5).

The intrinsic weakness in the mentalese hypothesis for Deacon is the lack of representation between the symbolic tokens that make up mentalese and the objects outside the mind that exist in the real world: 'Symbolic reference does not derive from anything particularly special about the brain, but from a special sort of relationship that can be constructed by it' (1997, 447). Reframing Deacon's argument in my terminology, he is critiquing the lack of a bridge between the percepts or objects of preverbal thought and the words or concepts that arise with language. There is no mechanism to connect the words of mentalese with the percepts of the objects that they presumably represent. This leads Deacon to observe that 'even an algorithmic system that completely captures all possible syntactical relationships between tokens does not in itself provide any representation – only the potential for internal circular indexical association. This is why a self-sufficient mental language or mentalese is an impossibility' (ibid.).

Tomasello is another critic of the notion of mentalese as a language. He observes that some 'researchers characterize nonlinguistic cognition in terms of a kind of "language of thought," and thereby, in my opinion, miss the essential difference between nonsymbolic and symbolic forms of representation' (1999, 124).

In his most recent book *A Mind So Rare*, Merlin Donald develops an argument for the primacy of thought over language which smacks of the notion of mentalese without ever using the term. He contends that since humans at times are dissatisfied with the ability of their words to express their thoughts that this demonstrates that thoughts are primary and words their mere expression. Donald posits some 'deep semantic space' and a 'drive for clearer states of awareness' (2001, 278) which is served by symbolic language. But the only evidence he produces are examples of artists' dissatisfaction with their expression of their thoughts, using words citing Flaubert's remark: 'Language is like a cracked kettle on which we beat out tunes for bears to dance to, while all the while we long to move the stars to pity' (ibid.).

One could counter Donald's argument by citing the example of Shakespeare, who was not concerned with 'moving the stars to pity' but merely providing solid entertainment for Londoners and filling the Globe theatre, thereby protecting his financial investment. Yet Shakespeare succeeded in 'moving the stars to pity' and created a universe of ideas and enriched the vehicle of the English language, which has enabled others to express new ideas that would never have seen the light of day without the Bard's incredible contribution.

One more observation on mentalese is in order. There are those who claim that logic and the language of mentalese are closely related. This is an extremely Eurocentric position, as so-called rational thought based on deductive logic is not a universal way of thinking. This is not to suggest that other thought systems are illogical. They are not, but they tend to be inductive and/or analogical rather than deductive. Deductive logic originated in Western thought and, as I claimed in *The Alphabet Effect* (Logan 2004a), arose as a consequence of using a purely phonetic writing system, the phonetic alphabet. The use of the alphabet is based on analysis, coding, decoding, and classification, all of which are elements of deductive thinking. Alphabetic writing promotes analysis because each word must be analysed into its basic phonemes in order to be transcribed. When spoken language is transcribed, phonemes or sounds are coded with meaningless visual signs: the letters of the alphabet. And when written text is read those visual signs are decoded back into sounds. The alphabet is also a classification tool that allows a perfect ordering through alphabetization of all of the spoken words of any language transcribed with an alphabetic writing system. As previously mentioned, alphabetic writing and deductive logic are closely connected along with abstract science, monotheism, and codified law (ibid.).

### The Cognitive Function of Language

We may say that thinking is essentially the activity of operating with signs.

Ludwig Wittgenstein

We have no power of thinking without signs.

Charles Sanders Pierce

Only in terms of gestures as significant symbols is the existence of the mind or intelligence possible.

George Herbert Mead

Thought is not merely expressed in words; it comes into existence through them.

Lev Vygotsky

The above set of quotes collected by Tomasello (1999, 201) show that there is a long-standing tradition in Western thought that language and thought are intimately connected. Among linguists, however, there are two schools regarding what is the primary function of human language. Those that favour the 'social brain' hypothesis for the origin of language consider the primary function of language to be communication and that, among other things, it serves as a medium for the communication of thought. The second school, to which Bickerton belongs, sees the primary function of language as the production of abstract concept-based thought, 'I mean, quite simply and straightforwardly that human cognition came out of language' (1995, 160). Bickerton believes that the 'social brain' hypothesis arises out of a misunderstanding of the difference between animal communication and human language: 'The misunderstanding arises because animal communication systems, and all other things illegitimately described as languages, differ from language in that they can do nothing but communicate. Language has additional capabilities ... it is used to store information or carry out thought processes' (ibid., 11). Bickerton's definition of language justifies our identification of writing, mathematics, science, computing, and the Internet in chapter 2 as languages because they too are 'used to store information' and 'carry out thought processes' that differ from spoken language.

Although I find myself more in the Bickerton camp than the 'social brain' hypothesis camp, I believe that language, thought, and communication are intimately connected. Communication facilitates thinking and thinking facilitates communication. Dialogue and questions provoke new thoughts, new ideas, and new forms of language which require new vocabularies, and those new vocabularies then make new thoughts and insights possible. It is a never-ending cycle; the communicative and the cognitive interactions are an example of an autocatalytic system.

Vygotsky sees a similar to-ing and fro-ing between thought and language when he writes:

> The relation of thought to word is not a thing but a process, a continual back and forth from thought to word and word to thought. In that process the relation of thought to word undergoes changes which themselves may be regarded as development in the functional sense. Thought is not merely expressed in words; it comes into existence through them ... (1962, 125)
>
> The flow of thought is not accompanied by a simultaneous unfolding of speech. The two processes are not identical, and there is no rigid correspondence between the units of speech and thought ... (ibid., 149)
>
> Only a historical theory of inner speech can deal with this immense and complex problem. The relation between thought and word is a living process; thought is born through words. A word devoid of thought is a dead thing; and a thought unembodied in words remains a shadow. The connection between them, however, is not a performed and constant one. It emerges in the course of development, and itself evolves. (ibid., 153)

Another approach to the relationship of language as communication and language as a representation of abstract thought is to consider Gould and Lewontin's (1979) notions of a spandrel and an exaptation:

> Under the spandrel principle, you can have a structure that is fit, that works well, that is apt, but was not built by natural selection for its current utility. It may not have been built by natural selection at all. The spandrels are architectural by-products. They were not built by natural selection, but they are used in a wonderful way – to house the evangelists. But you can't say they were adapted to house evangelists; they weren't. That's why Elizabeth Vrba and I developed the term 'exaptation.' Exaptations are useful structures by virtue of having been co-opted – that's the 'ex-apt' – they're apt because of what they are for other reasons. They were not built by natural selection for their current role. (Gould 1996, 59)

Gould has suggested that language is a spandrel or exaptation of the mind as a multipurpose learning device. Pinker and Bloom point out that 'the main motivation for Gould's specific suggestion that language is a spandrel is his frequently-stated position that the mind is a single general-purpose computer. For example, as part of a critique of a theory of the origin of language, Gould (1979: 386) writes: "I don't doubt for a moment that the brain's enlargement in human evolution had an adaptive basis mediated by selection. But I would be more than mildly surprised if many of the specific things it now can do are the product of direct selection for that particular behavior"' (1990, 746).

Expanding on Gould's proposal, it is possible that language functioning as a medium for the representation of abstract thought is a spandrel or exaptation of language functioning as a communication medium. In other words, language might have originally been selected for its ability to facilitate communication and then, because it permitted abstract thinking, it was selected for its cognitive properties. I am not particularly advocating the idea that abstract thought emerged as a spandrel of language as a communication medium, but I offer it as a possibility. Personally, I like the idea of the two properties of language cognition and communication co-evolving.

Among the linguists who subscribe to the 'social brain' hypothesis Chris Knight acknowledges the importance of language for the representation of symbolic thought: 'Speech ... permits communication of information concerning a shared, conceptual environment – a world of intangibles independent of currently perceptible reality' (2000b, 99).

Knight asks: 'At what point and through which mechanisms did it become technically feasible to communicate details of conceptual thinking by exclusively vocal means?'(2000b, 101). The question posits that there was conceptual thinking to be communicated. Conceptual thought and the ability to communicate it emerged simultaneously. It is through the act of communicating using words, which act as concepts in and of themselves, that conceptual thinking, as opposed to prelingual perceptual thinking, takes place. Those who advocate that language began strictly as a social function or that language is primarily for communication fail to take into account the evolution within historical times of notated language in the form of writing, mathematical notation, science, computing, and the Internet. The primary lesson from studying this flowering and diversification of the format and function of language is the understanding that language is both a communication medium and an informatics tool.

I arrived at this conclusion through the study of the effects of the use of the various forms of notated language already listed. My views run contrary to those of traditional linguists, including de Saussure and Bloomfield (cited in chapter 2), who think of writing as merely a way of recording speech. This definition of writing reflects the position of de Sassure, Bloomfield, and many other linguists that the sole purpose of language is communication. They do not take into account the information-processing capabilities of language, as have Stubbs (1980), Hertzler (1965, 444), and Smith (1982, 204), who recognize the role of writing as an independent medium for developing abstract ideas.

Despite the efforts of these latter authors, this attitude persists in contemporary linguistics as evidenced by the following quote from Studdert-Kennedy: 'Writing is not an independent natural language, like sign language, that happens to use hand and eyes instead of mouth and ear. Rather, writing is parasitic on speech' (2000b, 172), The use of the term *parasite* is interesting in that writing does not weaken speech in the way a parasite weakens its host, but rather it strengthens language by allowing the addition of abstract terms, as pointed out in chapter 2 when we cited the work of Havelock (1963). Shakespeare, who composed in the written form, enriched the spoken English language with his plays and poetry.

Although written language is derived from spoken language, as we argued earlier, writing and speech may be regarded as two separate modes of language because they process information so differently. Despite a large semantic overlap, they nevertheless, have different and distinct vocabularies and their syntactical structures are quite different. Writing and speech have unique strategies for communicating, storing, retrieving, organizing, and processing information.

I find support for my position that cognition is one of the key functions of language in the work of Ib Ulbaek, Derek Bickerton, and Terrence Deacon. Ulbaek maintains that 'language evolved from animal cognition not from animal communication ... Language grew out of cognitive systems already in existence and working' (1998, 33). Ulbaek himself finds support from Sapir, Whorf, Wittgenstein, and de Saussure for his position that 'the hallmark of human rationality, thinking, is not only strongly influenced by language, but is even determined by language, or exists solely in language' (ibid.). He cites de Saussure, who wrote: 'Without language, thought is a vague, uncharted nebula. There are no pre-existing ideas, and nothing is distinct before the appearance of language' (1966, 112).

Although Bickerton acknowledges the importance of social communication and reciprocal altruism to the origin of language, he stresses the importance of the cognitive dimension of language: 'Language ... is not even primarily a means of communication. Rather it is a system of representation, a means of sorting and manipulating the plethora of information that deluges us throughout our waking life' (1990, 5). Bickerton suggests that protolanguage, with its limited lexicon and lack of syntax, 'arose directly from the requirements of group foraging, predator avoidance, and the instruction of the young, rather than from specifically social interactions between individuals (whether competitive or cooperative) ... As soon as protolanguage had achieved a critical mass ... it was undoubtedly co-opted for a variety of social purposes, which in turn contributed to its further expansion' (2002, 209).

Bickerton describes the first use of words in protolanguage as 'some kind of label to be attached to a small number of pre-existing concepts' (1990, 5). Where I differ from Bickerton is that I suggest that the concepts were not pre-existing, but came into existence as a result of the formulation of the word which acted as a strange attractor for all of the pre-existing percepts associated with that word and as such emerged as a concept. The differences in nuance of my notion of how the first words emerged and that of Bickerton's are not great. If I could persuade him to change one word in his just-quoted fragment so that 'pre-existing concepts' became 'pre-existing percepts,' there would be no difference in our positions.

In deed, despite Bickerton's use of the term *pre-existing concepts*, his position is not that far from mine based on the following quote from his 1995 book *Language and Human Behaviour* where he states: 'If it is to be of any use at all, a vocabulary cannot possibly mark all the particularities of objects that our senses reveal to us. If we are to think off-line in any general sort of way ... we have to boil down the Jamesian "buzzing, blooming confusion" of sensory experience into a much thinner gruel' (1995, 61). This statement, especially the notion of 'boiling down the complexity of sensory experience,' is equivalent to my idea that the word acting as a concept also acts as a strange attractor of all of our percepts associated with that word. Another remark of Bickerton's where he refers to a word as a 'convergence zone in which all their attributes are summarized' (ibid., 92), to my mind, supports my notion that words act as strange attractors of percepts.

Deacon sees cognition or symbolic thought, as he likes to describe it, as one of the main functions of speech: 'Language is not merely a mode of communication, it is also the outward expression of an unusual mode of thought – symbolic representation ... Symbolic thought does not come innately built in, but develops by internalizing the symbolic process that underlies language' (1997, 22).

## The Social Genesis and the Cognitive Function of Language

Language is a form of cognition; it is cognition packaged for purposes of inter-personal communication.

                                                      Michael Tomasello (1999)

So far we have reviewed two schools of thought on the question of the function of language – the social-communicative school versus the cognitive-symbolic school. I have tried to run a middle course by suggesting that language is both a medium of communication and an informatics tool. Michael Tomasello's (1999) approach to the question of language, communication, and cognition does not fit into either of these two schools of thought. He attributes a social genesis to language, but then shows its very strong impact on cognition. Rather than describe his approach, I will let him speak for himself with the following excerpt from *The Cultural Origins of Human Cognition*, with more to follow when we discuss ontogeny in chapter 8 and culture in chapter 12:

> The overall function of language is communication in the sense that language evolved for the purposes of communication phylogenetically, and it is learned for purposes of communication ontogenetically. (Tomasello 1999, xiv)
>
> Perhaps the reason that language is cognitively primary is that it is such a direct manifestation of the human symbolic ability, which itself derives so directly from the joint attentional and communicative activities that the understanding of others as intentional agents engenders. The point is thus that language is special, but not so special. And so my account for how a single human cognitive adaptation could result in all of the many differences in human and nonhuman primate cognition is that this single adaptation made possible an evolutionary new set of processes, that is, processes of sociogenesis (whereby something new is created through the social interaction of two or more individuals), that have done much of the work and on a much faster time scale then evolution. (ibid., 208–9)

Tomasello attributes the emergence of language and human cognition to sociogenesis. While I agree that sociogenesis and joint attentional interactions played a role in the birth of human language, I do not believe that social cognition alone can explain the emergence of language. Before verbal language emerged, mimetic communication had the power to express intentionality as well as create joint attention to objects, events, or persons outside the two communicating agents. Given this reality, the transition from mimetic to verbal communication had to satisfy some other need, as expressed in the

Extended Mind Model, was the need to conceptualize and move beyond percept-based thought so as to deal with the increasing complexity of hominid existence. To summarize, the social-communicative needs were a necessary but not sufficient motivator for the emergence of language. The other element that motivated the form of communication in terms of symbolic artifacts rather than mimetic elements was the need to create conceptual tools that increased the chance for survival.

While Tomasello overstates the role of sociogenesis by not giving enough credit to the need for conceptualization, his focus on the social-cultural aspect of language leads to some interesting insights into the nature of language. Because he regards words or linguistic symbols as cultural artifacts, Tomasello points out that language allows the child or any language user for that matter to 'categorize and construe' (1999, 8–9) the world in different ways. For example, a dog may be regarded also as 'an animal, a pet, or a pest':

> As the child masters the linguistic symbols of her culture she thereby acquires the ability to adopt multiple perspectives simultaneously on one and the same perceptual situation. As perspectively based cognitive representations, then, linguistic symbols are based not on the recording of direct sensory or motor experience, as are the cognitive representations of other animal species and human infants, but rather on the way in which individuals choose to construe things out of a number of other ways they might have construed them, as embodied in the other available linguistic symbols that they might have chosen, but did not. Linguistics symbols thus free human cognition from the immediate perceptual situation not simply by enabling reference to things outside this situation but rather by enabling multiple simultaneous representations of each and every, indeed all-possible, perceptual situations. (1999, 8–9)

> An important aspect of the role that language acquisition plays in cognitive development is thus the categories, relations, and conceptual perspectives embodied in conventional linguistic structures – from words to syntactic constructions to conventional metaphors – with which the young child must operate in normal discourse interactions. (ibid., 170)

## Language as a Scaffold for Human Action

Andy Clark, in his book *Being There*, proposes a function for language more closely associated with those who suggest a cognitive rather than a communicative function of language but which, nevertheless, is unique and deserves a section of its own. Clark proposes that 'the role of language is to guide and shape our own behavior – it is a tool for structuring and controlling action, not merely a medium of information transfer between agents' (1997, 195). This view emerges from his unique approach of 'embodied cognition':

> Carefully understood, the first moral of embodied cognition is thus to avoid excessive world modeling, and to gear such modeling as is required to the demands of real-time, behavior-producing systems ... We reduce the information processing load by sensitizing the system to particular aspects of the world ... In place of the intellectual engine cogitating in a realm of detailed inner models, we confront the embodied, embedded agent acting as an equal partner in adaptive responses which draw on the resources of mind, body, and world [such as an] external memory ... What emerges ... is a vision of the brain as a kind of associative engine, and of its environmental interactions as an iterated series of simple pattern-completing computations ... our behavior is often sculpted and sequenced by a special class of complex external structures: the linguistics and cultural artifacts that structure modern life including maps, texts, and written plans. (Clark 1997, 23, 24, 47, and 53)

Clark, citing the work of Carruthers (1996), posits a strong link between speech and introspective thought: 'It certainly often seems as if our very thoughts are composed of the words and sentences of public language. And the reason we have this impression is because it is true: Inner thinking is literally done in inner speech. By extension, Carruthers is able to view many intra-personal uses of language as less a matter of simple communication than of *public thinking* ... Carruthers suggests one does not first entertain a private thought and *then* write it down: rather, the thinking is the writing' (1998, 165).

Clark argues for a connection between language and thought that is slightly different from that of Carruthers and the other authors reviewed in this chapter: 'What is most important, I believe, is not to try to answer the question, do we actually think *in* words (to which the answer is in a way yes and in a way no!) but to try to see what computational benefits accrue to biological pattern-completing brains in virtue of their ability to manipulate and sometimes model external representational artifacts' (1998, 168).

Clark then lists 'six broad ways in which linguistic artifacts can complement the activity of the pattern-completing brain' (1998, 168). They are as follows:

1 Language is used to augment our memory as a medium for storing data.
2 Language acts as an aid to negotiate complex environments and learn abstract concepts.
3 Language is essential for planning, coordinating activities, and reducing the amount of 'on-line deliberation' needed to carry out activities on one's own or with others.
4 Language allows learning to be collective and to be easily passed from one generation to another (i.e., language is essential for the construction of human culture).
5 Language helps us 'to focus, monitor and control behavior' as suggested by the observations of Berk and Garvin (1984). By observing and recording the private speech of American children ages five to ten years old they found that the self-directed speech of these children helped them to master certain tasks, and those children who employed the most self-directed talk fared best at completing these tasks.
6 Written language provides us with the ability to store, organize, process, search, and edit data that would not be possible with speech alone and certainly not possible without verbal language.

This last point is reinforced by the remarks of Susan Sontag (2003), who modestly claimed that she is not really a great writer but by continually writing, editing, and rewriting her essays she has achieved a certain level of excellence.

Clark draws the following moral from his six points: 'The role of public language and text in human cognition is not limited to the preservation and communication of ideas. Instead, these external resources make available concepts, strategies, and learning trajectories which are simply not available to individual, un-augmented brains. Much of the true power of language lies in its underappreciated capacity to re-shape the computational spaces which confront intelligent agents' (1998).

Clark not only suggests an intimate connection between language and thought, but he also proposes a mechanism whereby language gives rise to reflection:

> By 'freezing' our thoughts in the memorable, context-resistant, modality-transcending format of a sentence, we thus create a special kind of mental object, – an object that is amenable to scrutiny from multiple cognitive angles, is not doomed to alter or change every time we are exposed to new inputs or information, and fixes the idea at a high level of abstraction from the idiosyncratic details of their proximal origin in input. Such a mental object is, I suggest, ideally suited to figure in the evaluative, critical, and tightly focused operations distinctive of second-order cognition ... The coding system of public language is thus especially apt to be co-opted for more private purposes of inner display, self-inspection, and self-criticism, exactly as predicted by [a] Vygotskian treatment. (1997, 210)

I shall give the last words of this chapter on the function of language and its relation to human thought to Andy Clark, who sums up the difficulty of disentangling thought from language: 'Finally, the sheer intimacy of the relations between human thought and the tools of public language bequeaths an interesting puzzle. For in this case, especially, it is a delicate matter to determine where the user ends and the tool begins' (1997, 194).

# 7 What Are the Mechanisms That Led to Spoken Language?

What is special to a grammatical utterance (i.e., to a linguistic event) is not that has meaning, expresses feeling, or calls for a relevant response – these are all common to many human activities – but that it is socially transmissible.

Zellig Harris, *Mathematical Structures of Language*

There are a number of mechanisms, physical and cognitive, that make spoken language possible and without which language as we know it would not have emerged. These mechanisms include:

1 Vocalization (the ability to make sounds)
2 Phonemic articulation (the ability to enunciate a full range of phonemes necessary for speech)
3 Phonemic generativity (the ability to combine phonemes to phonically create potentially an infinite number of words)
4 Syntax (the ability to combine words to create potentially an infinite number of propositions)
5 A theory of the mind (an understanding that there are other sentient beings who can understand one's utterances).

With the exception of vocalization which has been achieved by many animal species including our primate ancestors all of the other mechanisms are uniquely human and are not characteristic of any other form of animal communication. All linguists acknowledge that each of these mechanisms are required for human speech but opinions differ as to which of these mechanisms was the starting point for the emergence of language.

## Gesture versus Vocalization

There is debate as to whether human language was originally vocalized. 'There remains disagreement as to whether speech evolved from vocal or gestural antecedents' (Knight 1998a, 16). 'MacNielage (1998: 238) makes the strong claim that "the vocal-auditory modality of spoken language was the first and only output mechanism for language." This coincides with Robin Dunbar's (1996: 141) view that gesture was never necessary – "it can all be done by voice"' (Knight 2000b, 101). For Peter MacNielage, as for Michael Studdert-Kennedy, 'the one novel capacity, crucially distinguishing humans from other primates, is for vocal imitation, the basis of lexical acquisition' (Studdert-Kennedy 1998, 172). John Locke argues for the pre-eminence of the vocal mode, finding it 'a fundamental characteristic of all 6,000–8,000 normal human languages in the world – they are spoken; all of them' (1998, 190). In fact, there are sign languages, which are not spoken. Most of these have been derived from spoken languages. There are six known examples of indigenous sign languages, however, that are *not* derived from spoken languages that have been studied by Sonia Ragir (2002), so it is possible for a language to emerge without vocalization.

Steven Pinker and Paul Bloom sum up the arguments in favour of the vocal mode as the origin of language: 'The vocal-auditory channel has some desirable features as a medium of communication: it has a high bandwidth, its intensity can be modulated to conceal the speaker or to cover large distances, and it does not require light, proximity, a face-to-face orientation, or tying up the hands' (1990, 25).

'Donald, Power and Knight take a contrasting position (to Dunbar), locating early selection pressures for syntactical competence in a pre-linguistic protoculture of gesture, dance and song' (Knight, 1998a, 16). Chris Knight sees ritual as a mechanism that led to speech: 'Humans ... deceive collectively, recurrently establishing group identity in the process ... far from embodying self-evident truth, symbolic culture may be ... understood as a world of patent fictions held collectively to be true on some deeper level ... Utterances have force only through collusion with a wider system of ritual or ceremonial' (ibid., 75–6).

Merlin Donald claims that 'mimetic skill is the foundation for a variety of hominid achievements, including advances in toolmaking; co-ordinated collective endeavors such as fire use; sophisticated hunting and gathering; and the division of labour. This was a significant step away from the primate mainstream, without invoking anything so refined or powerful as (spoken) language' (1998, 60).

Michael Arbib (2003) has developed a model that parallels Donald's model (1991), in which gesture and pantomime are the seeds from which vocal language emerged. Arbib submits that the origin of language can be traced back to 'mirror neurons' which we inherited from the common ancestors of monkeys, apes, and humans. A set of premotor neurons fire when a monkey either goes to grasp something or sees another monkey (or an experimenter) grasping something. From such observations Arbib formulated the Mirror System Hypothesis (MSH): 'Broca's area in humans evolved from a basic mechanism not originally related to communication – the mirror system for grasping in the common ancestor of monkey and human. The mirror's system's capacity to generate and recognize a set of actions provides the evolutionary basis for language parity, in which an utterance means roughly the same for both speaker and hearer' (ibid., 190).

Arbib assumes that before vocal language prevocal intentional communication took place through pantomime. This process was controlled by 'mirror neurons' and that, with time, this 'proto-Broca's area gained primitive control of the vocal machinery' and as a result vocal communication emerged. What is interesting about Arbib's MSH is that it provides a neural mechanism for mimesis, as formulated by Donald (1991).

Michael Corballis (2003, 210) argues that mirror neurons play a key role in the origin of language, which was initially gestural in nature. Corballis reminds us that in the brain, Broca's area is involved in the gesturing that accompanies speech and sign language. He contends that this hypothesis can explain the predominance of human right-handedness and cites evidence that vocalization is predominantly a left-hemisphere phenomenon for most birds and animals, while mirror neurons do not display hemispheric asymmetry in monkeys: 'The mirror-neuron system gradually began to control vocalizations, previously subcortical and left-sided, and this had the effect of introducing a left-sided bias into manual as well as vocal action' (ibid., 211). Et voilà, human righted-handedness! Corballis posits that human language, which was originally manual, became voiced because of the many advantages of vocal language including that phonetic articulation allows many more signals to be produced and that one can communicate in the dark, while using one's hands to do other tasks, which would facilitate instruction of tasks that require manual articulation as pointed out by Pinker and Bloom.

While some claim that gesture and other mimetic forms of communication led to vocalization, others maintain that stone throwing and other forms of motor skills were the pre-adaptations for the motor control of the vocal apparatus: 'Lieberman (1973, 1975, 1984), Kimura (1976, 1979) and Calvin (1983) have suggested that human language might have originated in the serial-ordering capabilities of the primate motor system, coming from intentional control in hominids, and eventually generalizing this property to a more recently evolved hominid vocomotor system' (Donald 1998, 46). Not all linguists buy this argument, however. Pinker and Bloom, in commenting on 'Lieberman's claim that syntactic rules must be retooled motor programs, a putative case of preadaptation,' wrote: 'It may be right, but there is no reason to believe it. Lieberman's evidence is only that motor programs are hierarchically organized and serially ordered, and so is syntax' (1990, 770).

Lieberman's hypothesis of the association of human language with 'hierarchically organized and serially ordered' motor programs is supported by Greenfield, who asserts that 'during the first two years of life a common neural substrate (roughly Broca's area) underlies the hierarchical organization of elements in the development of speech as well as the capacity to combine objects manually, including tool use' (1991, 531). Christiansen, Dale, Ellefson, and Conway support Lieberman's hypothesis, citing empirical data from studies with aphasics, artificial learning experiments, non-human primate studies, and computational modelling: 'Several lines of evidence currently support the importance of sequential learning in language evolution ... acquisition and processing' (2002, 147).

Morten Christiansen offers evidence that the Broca's area of the brain first found in the Homo line with Homo habilis is associated not only with the use of language but also with toolmaking and sequential learning and processing. He therefore concluded that 'language might have originated with this hominid (Homo habilis) as a kind of systematic set of manual gestures' (manuscript in preparation, 16).

Each of the hypotheses reviewed in this section suggest that the first medium of language was either vocal or gestural but not both. One researcher who does not take this view is Terrence Deacon, who has argued that both the vocal and non-vocal channels played a role in the origin of speech and that the crucial step was not the physical medium of language but rather the advent of symbolic representation: 'The earliest forms of symbolic communication were therefore likely not speech-like or manual sign languages. They almost certainly included vocalizations along with conventional/ritual gestures, activities, and objects, all of which together formed a heterogeneous mélange of indices transformed to symbols, each systematically dependent on the other, and defining a closed set of possible types of relationships. Vocal symbolizing in the earliest stages would probably have played a minor role, owing to the lack of descending motor control until brain size increased. Probably not until Homo erectus were the equivalent of words available' (1997, 407).

Deacon goes on to speculate that the transition to a purely vocal form of speech augmented with manual gesticulation came about because 'physical object symbols are constrained to highly specific uses and contexts – e.g., use as physical icons or markers – and tend to keep complex performance symbols confined to use in specialized ritual contexts. The manipulation of vocalizations and hand gestures would have been far less constrained' (1997, 407). He concludes that 'gesture and speech have co-evolved complex interrelationships throughout their long and changing partnership' (ibid., 355–6). While gesture and prosody were initially essential for vocal communication, they now only play a supplementary role. The existence of written communication for which gesture and prosody are totally absent suggests that human language has managed to wean itself of mimetic communication and is used primarily to embellish oral communication and to express emotions.

Derek Bickerton also holds that both vocal and hand signals played a role in the origin of languages: 'If our ancestors were already trying to interpret the behaviour of their conspecifics, even perhaps to the extent of reading meaning where none was intended, they surely wouldn't have taken long to recognize intentional meanings. It also neatly solves the problem of whether language began as sign or speech. The answer is that it probably began as both – a mixture of anything that might serve to convey meaning' (2003, 80–1).

## Which Came First: Phonology, Semantics, or Syntax?

If we accept the popular view that speech began as vocalizations, but leave open the possibility that there might have been some non-vocal

pre-adaptation for speech, we are still left with the puzzle of phonological and syntactical generativity. For Andrew Carstairs-McCarthy 'two
aspects of human language remain mysterious: its lexical elaboration
and its syntactical structure' (1998, 290). He points out that the lowering of the larynx created a problem in that humans swallow food and
breathe at the same time. The cost of this disadvantage of possibly chok-
ing was obviously compensated for because the lowering of the larynx
allowed so many more sounds to be made, the sounds characteristic of
human phonology which made language possible. The ability to articulate many different sounds would not have been sufficient to create
language unless there was a syntactical structure to enable words to be
strung together to form propositions: 'Grammars for spoken language
must map propositional structures onto a serial channel, minimizing
ambiguity in context, under the further constraints that the encoding
and decoding be done rapidly, by creatures with limited short-term
memories, according to a code that is shared by an entire community of
potential communicants' (Pinker and Bloom 1990, 725).

The question then arises as to which came first: the lexicon or the
grammar? Bickerton attempted to answer this question with a theory in
which he claims that the first emergence of speech was in the form of
what he terms protolanguage which is a vocal system with a substantial
lexicon but no syntax (1998, 342). Utterances consisted of three or four
spoken words without any particular order in the way they were strung
together. Bickerton claims his approach is very much like Lieberman's
(1991, 1992) because:

> both accounts emphasize preadaptation, with modern language resulting
> from the operations of a task-specific neural circuit formed relatively late
> (possibly being itself the speciation event that produced Homo sapiens).
> The account differs only in the relative importance they place on syntax
> and phonology, and in the conclusion they draw with respect to the innate-
> ness and autonomy of the language faculty. To Lieberman, phonology is
> primary, and syntax results automatically from pre-existing motor processes
> once there is an adequate vocal channel in place. To me [Bickerton], syntax
> is primary, and the birth of syntax as we know it was precisely what selected,
> very rapidly and efficiently for an improved voice apparatus even at the
> cost of maladaptive effects on ingestion. (1998, 342)

Bickerton makes an argument for the emergence of the lexicon before syntax and phonology, based on the fact that bonobos (Savage-Rumbaugh 1986) are capable of rudimentary symbolic communication within a laboratory setting but they are not capable of syntax (2003, 82). He concludes that the 'genetic and neural substrates' for symbolization and syntax are quite different and that symbolization preceded syntax by quite a long time. While we are on the topic of the bonobo's use of symbols it is worth mentioning, as pointed out by Donald, that 'he [Kanzi] still cannot invent symbols ... [and] has never tried to describe his own experiences or feelings, using symbols' (2001, 121).

For Deacon the relationship of phonology, semantics, and syntax is one of co-evolution, all of them the consequences of symbolic communication:

> The structure of syntax often only vaguely conceals its pragmatic roots in pointing gestures, manipulation and the exchange of physical objects, spatial and temporal relationships, and so on ... we can nevertheless observe a progressive assimilation of nonverbal language supports to more flexible and efficient vocal forms as their language abilities develop ... It well may be that with the advent of modern vocal abilities, languages for the first time fully assimilated many functions that were previously supported by nonvocal counterparts. With the added power of increased distinctiveness and more rapid articulation, more information could be packed into the short-term memory time bins, and the full range of pragmatic functions, previously supported by links to other simultaneous communications, was finally encoded as a series of syntactic operations. The one class of paralinguistic functions which probably has the longest co-evolutionary relationship with language is speech prosody ... The evolution of this system of indices must also have been tightly linked to the evolution of speaking abilities because they are effectively opposite sides of the same neurological coin. (1997, 354 and 364)

While Deacon suggests that phonology, semantics, and syntax co-evolved, Kazuo Okanoya proposes 'that the symbolic and syntactical aspects of human language evolved independently' (2002, 58–9). This suggestion was based on his work with Bengalese finches, where Okanoya found that 'syntactical complexity is grounded to sexual selection ... and bears no survival basis' (ibid.). He then generalized his result to humans and concluded that 'as in the Bengalese finch songs, in humans too, the rudiment of syntax might have also evolved through sexual selection; in this case, mutual sexual display using song and dance involving males and females was a pre-adaptation for syntax' (ibid.).

If ontogeny is any guide to how language might have first emerged, then Michael Tomasello's observation that children learn words and syntactical structures in the same manner might argue for the simultaneous emergence of semantics and syntax: 'At the same time they are acquiring their first words children are also acquiring more complex linguistic constructions as kind of linguistic gestalts ... Fundamentally, the way the child learns a concrete linguistic construction – composed of specific linguistic items is the way she learns words ... and so general processes of cultural learning, specifically imitative learning, are sufficient to account for the acquisition process' (1999, 134 and 143–4).

In still another view, Peter Gärdenfors proposes a fixed ordering for semantics and syntax, giving first priority to pragmatics where *pragmatics* can be roughly defined as how context influences the interpretation of meaning: 'Syntax is required only for the subtlest of communication – pragmatic and semantic features are more fundamental' (2004, 247). He argues that Chomsky and company consider the study of syntax as the primary focus of linguistics and when they cannot explain things with syntax they revert to semantics and then pragmatics as the last resort. Gärdenfors, however, makes the opposing argument, namely, 'that when the goal is to develop a theory of the evolution of communication the converse order – pragmatics before semantics before syntax – is more appropriate' (2004, 247).

## Particulate Principle

Vocalization is not unique to humans but speech is, because it requires the ability to articulate as many different sounds as there are words. Studdert-Kennedy points out that human speech is able to represent 'an unbounded set of objects, events and their relations as specified in simple propositions, by means of a finite set of discrete signals' (1998b, 205). In order for the system to work for phonology, the discrete signals, namely, the phonemes are themselves meaningless. This parallels the way in which the alphabet is able to represent spoken language visually. Each discrete element of the alphabet, namely, each letter, is a meaningless sign representing a phoneme. The construction of words from phonemes or phonemic generativity is the first level of generativity of human speech. But the process, according to Studdert-Kennedy, does not stop there, otherwise human language would require a new word for all 'objects, events and propositions concerning their relations' which would place 'a prohibitive tax on creative phonetic invention and memory' (ibid., 206).

The solution is the emergence of syntax which allows propositions to be generated from the words built by combining phonemes. The syntax of ordering words into propositions represents a second level of generativity of human language which, to paraphrase Studdert-Kennedy, allows an unbounded set of propositions to be created from a finite set of words. The syntactical generativity differs from phonemic generativity in that the elements that are permuted in phonology are meaningless, namely, the phonemes, while in syntax the elements that are permuted are meaningful, namely, the words of the proposition. Syntactical generativity also goes by the name of *compositionality* (see Kirby 2000a, 304), a term that Cann (1993, 4) defined by suggesting that the meaning of a proposition is a function of the meaning of its components and the order in which they are presented.

The double level of generativity, phonemic and syntactical, of human speech distinguishes it from animal signals which 'directly express a sender's needs or emotions and directly elicit a receiver's response' (Cann 1993, 4). Human speech is abstract in that it 'disassociates signal from meaning, and thereby sets up a cognitive preadaptation, perhaps, for its evolution into a system free from stimulus control' (ibid.).

The emergence of speech not only entails a transition at the functional level from perceptual thinking to conceptual thinking, as was pointed out in Chapter 3; it also entails at the mechanical/phonological level a transition from analogue representation to a representation by coding. After the emergence of phonologically produced and conceptually based speech the next step in the development of human language was the emergence of syntax or grammar. The emergence of syntax must have taken place at the conceptual/symbolic level since syntax allows a higher order level of meaning to be created from the basic lexical units of words each of which represents a basic concept. This argument supports Bickerton's protolanguage hypothesis (1990) of the emergence of a 'primitive and unstructured' human language consisting simply of words devoid of syntax before the emergence of modern fully grammaticalized language.

Michael Studdert-Kennedy explains the origins of language generativity by making use of a formalism devised by von Humboldt (1836/1972) which exploits 'what Abler (1989) called "the particulate principle of self-diversifying systems." According to this principle, elements drawn from a finite set (e.g., in spoken language: phonemes, words) are repeatedly permuted and combined to yield larger units (words, sentences) higher in a hierarchy, and more diverse in structure and function than their constituents' (1998b, 203). The emergence of full language or speech entailed phonemic generativity generating words and syntactical generativity generating sentences or propositions.

**The Third Level of Generativity**

In the last section the particulate principle was shown to lead to two forms of linguistic generativity, namely, phonological and syntactic generativity leading respectively to words and sentences. In this section we use the particulate principle to introduce a third level of generativity, namely, narrative generativity. The propositions of spoken language generated by syntax become the building blocks to which the particulate principle is applied to generate narratives. These narratives can be oral narratives like Homer's, written narratives like an essay or a story, mathematical narratives, scientific narratives, computing narratives, or Internet narratives like a Web site.

According to the hypothesis that I presented in chapters 3 and 4 (see also Logan 2004b), language continued to evolve after the emergence of speech with the appearance of writing, mathematics, science, computing, and the Internet. Re-examining this hypothesis in terms of the von Humboldt-Abler particulate principle of self-diversifying systems provides an interesting insight into the emergence of this evolutionary chain of languages. We may regard the emergence of each of the notated languages to be an application of the von Humboldt particulate principle to a finite set of words and sentences from spoken language.

Paraphrasing the emphasized part of the Studdert-Kennedy quote above, and if we substitute some of his words with those that here are underlined, we may extend the particulate principle as follows: 'According to this principle, elements drawn from a finite set (e.g., in spoken language: *words, sentences*) are repeatedly permuted and combined to yield larger units (*sentences, notated narratives, including writing, mathematics, science, computing, and the Internet*) higher in a hierarchy, and more diverse in structure and function than their constituents.' The notated narratives are also more analytic, more organized, and more formal than the utterances of spoken language, and they are structured according to the syntax of the particular language be it writing, mathematics, science, computing, or the Internet.

The application of the particulate principle to words and sentences to generate the notated narratives represents a third level of generativity, narrative generativity, which is a recursion of the first two levels of generativity, namely, the phonological and syntactical. The type of narrative obtained using the particulate principle depends on what elements, that is, types of sentences, from spoken language are repeatedly permuted and combined. The application of the particulate principle to qualitative analytic sentences led to prose, applied to qualitative prosodic sentences it led to poetry, and applied to quantitative analytic sentences or propositions it led to mathematics. The language of science represents the application of the particulate principle to the propositions of writing and mathematics rather than just to the syntax of spoken language to generate propositions that can be empirically tested and possibly falsified. Computing, the fifth language, emerges from applying the particulate principle to the propositions of all the languages that preceded it making use of the computer medium. The sixth language, the Internet, emerges from applying the particulate principle to all the propositions that can be generated with the language of computing making use of hypertext and the Internet protocol.

That all of the subsequent forms of language that evolved from speech were notated follows from the fact that to achieve the third level of generativity it was necessary to have a notation system since the memory capacity of the human brain could no longer handle a higher level of generativity. Words that are committed to memory can be easily recalled to generate syntactically correct sentences using easily memorized formulae of grammar. Maintaining a set of sentences in a generative fashion could not be achieved given that short-term memory can only deal with seven plus or minus two items at a time. This explains why orally composed sentences rarely contain more than seven to nine words. It is only sentences that are written out that will contain large numbers of words with the exception of certain erudite lecturers who compose written prose in their head or read them from a prepared text. Such a speaking style often puts its listeners to sleep because they are unable to keep track of such long sentences.

There is one exception to the rule that narratives are always notated. These are the epic poems of oral societies like the poems of Homer and other preliterate bards who made use of mnemonic devices such as prosody, rhyme, meter, formulae, characters, and plot to compose and memorize their narratives. Eric Havelock, in *Preface to Plato* (1963), has described this technique. He characterizes Homer's tales as a tribal encyclopedia whose poetic epics were meant to preserve the history of a culture as well as other vital cultural information. Although the epics achieved their objective of cultural preservation they cannot be considered truly generative as they were limited as to what they could express: 'The poetic conventions and standardized imagery that were essential to the memorization of the myths and sagas had the hidden effect of severely limiting the kinds of things that the culture could transmit and, hence, could think about' (Logan 2004a, 102). It was only with written prose that an analytic style of narrative developed that allowed authors to express themselves freely and create narrative generatively in the same way that we can create spoken sentence generatively using the syntax of spoken language.

**Theory of Mind**

The phonological mechanisms that make speech possible are a mixture of physical and cognitive skills whereas syntax is a purely cognitive mechanism. 'Syntax is a computational mechanism' (Bickerton 1998, 346). Another mechanism without which speech would not have been possible is a theory of mind which is also a purely cognitive skill. Dunbar defines a theory of mind as 'the ability to understand another's individual mental state' (1998, 102) without which, he claims, 'there would be no language in the form we know it ... Language requires more than the mere coding and deciphering of well-formed grammatical statements. Indeed, as has been often pointed out, many everyday conversations are conspicuous by their lack of grammatical structure (Gumperz 1982). However, important formal grammar may be in the precision of information transfer, it is surely the intentionality of speech that is the most demanding feature for both speaker and listener' (ibid., 101).

Worden supports Dunbar's position in arguing that 'social intelligence and a theory of mind are vital pre-requisites for language. I propose that language is not just a new mental faculty which uses these two, but is a direct application of them ... I propose that primate social intelligence was incrementally extended to include a working theory of mind (initially much simpler than today's adult human version). This theory of mind was an essential pre-requisite for language use, and the computational ingredients of the theory of mind were co-opted for language. By proposing that language evolved from a pre-existing theory of mind, we minimize the amount of new cognitive design' (1998, 149 and 154–5).

Robbins Burling has proposed a theory of the origin of language which parallels the theory of mind approach. His model is based on two simple and self-evident observations: 'The first ... is that all of us, humans and animals alike, are always able to understand more than they can say. Comprehension runs consistently ahead of production. The second observation extends the first; both humans and animals are sometimes able to interpret another's instrumental behavior even when that other individual had no intention at all to communicate' (2000, 27). A dog raises its lips when about to attack and the snarl becomes associated with an imminent attack. Soon the snarl becomes enough to scare off the target of the dog's aggression: 'Word-like signs could have had an origin that is quite similar to that of animal signals like the snarl, but there is one crucial difference. Almost all animal signals have been ritualized by the long process of natural selection. Early word-like signs, on the other hand, could have been conventionalized within the lifetime of a single individual ... Like language, but unlike gesture-calls, the conventionalized signs are learned, conventional and discrete. These characteristics make them a much more promising source for early language than is any part of a gesture-call system' (ibid., 31 and 37).

There is no doubt that a theory of mind is an essential mechanism for the full flowering and development of language as we now know it. The question that arises is which mechanisms came first: the lexicon, the syntax or the theory of mind? To my way of thinking a theory of mind could not occur without conceptualization which in turn I have attributed to the emergence of the first spoken words. Does a theory of mind depend on the existence of words such as I and thou? The notion of a relationship between language and a theory of mind also suggests that there is a relationship between language and consciousness. Without the concept of you and me how can one have a theory of mind and how can one have a concept of you and me without the words to represent these notions? These are all compelling and fascinating questions which perhaps are not susceptible to scientific analysis but rather belong to the domain of philosophy. A theory of mind, consciousness, language, and the concept of I and thou emerged together as a autocatalytic set of mental states. Each of these mental states creates an environment which is mutually conducive to the emergence of the other states.

Deacon sees a theory of mind more as a consequence of speech rather than a causative agent: 'Without symbolic representations at their disposal, it seems unlikely that other species could behave according to a theory of others' minds, much less share representations of others' experiences ... If I am correct about the social-reproductive dilemma that served as the initial impetus for symbol evolution, then the ability mentally to represent other minds is one of the primary functions of symbolization' (1977, 428).

Bickerton also associates the emergence of consciousness with language: 'The creation of human consciousness depended on the creation of areas of the brain from which the workings of animal consciousness could be objectively perceived. And, as we saw in the previous chapter, only the emergence of language could have created such areas of the brain' (1995, 130).

Before closing this discussion of a theory of mind we need to mention the work of Michael Tomasello for whom the theory of mind is an essential part of how children acquire language and how language itself emerged. We will leave a full discussion of the role of the theory of mind in Tomasello's work when we come to discuss his model of ontogeny and the child's acquisition of language in the next chapter.

# 8  Ontogeny and Language

One of the mysteries of language, aside from how it originated, is the ease with which it is acquired by young children. It is truly miraculous how children do not need to be taught how to speak. All that is required is that they be exposed to a language and within two or three years they are masters of that language. They acquire both the syntax and the complete vocabulary of commonly used words. If while they are young they are exposed to two or possibly three languages, they will learn each of these languages and speak them without an accent. Their language learning is almost automatic. What is even more mysterious is that they achieve this mastery of language without being taught the rules of grammar. This lack of instruction is known as the poverty of stimulus.

Adding to the mystery is the fact that an adult will have a great deal of difficulty learning a second language past a critical age usually somewhere during adolescence. If they do master a second language before this critical period they will always speak it with an accent. In the few documented cases where children were deprived of language altogether past that critical age they remained alingual their entire life (Itard 1962).

This evidence clearly indicates that the ontogeny of language acquisition is clearly biological, and at the same time it is also cultural in that its success depends on the exposure to a language. A language does not belong to an individual but to a community or a culture. Richard Dawkins has argued that Darwinian principles apply with the same validity to cultural replicators (memes) as they do to biological replicators (genes): 'Just as genes propagate themselves in the gene pool by leaping from body to body via sperm or eggs, so memes propagate themselves in the meme pool by leaping from brain to brain via a process which, in the broad sense, can be called imitation' (1989, 192).

It is also true that cultural phenomena are as much governed by plectic processes as by biological ones. So when we entertain the question of ontogeny taking into account both the biological and the cultural dimension of the problem we may still retain our Darwinian-plectic model of language. However, it is best to state up front that there does not exist a satisfactory explanation of this phenomenon nor do we promise to provide one here. Instead we will survey the current models for language acquisition corresponding to the various theories for the origin of language we have reviewed. We will also attempt to provide our explanation of language acquisition based on the Extended Mind model presented in chapters 3 and 4.

We have already encountered how Chomsky deals with this problem. 'To learn a language, then, the child must have a method for devising an appropriate grammar, given primary linguistic data. As a precondition for language learning, he must possess, first, a linguistic theory that specifies the form of the grammar of a possible human language, and second, a strategy for selecting a grammar of the appropriate form that is compatible with the primary linguistic data' (1965, 25). Chomsky assumes that the human brain is biologically endowed with an innate Language Acquisition Device (LAD) and the Universal Grammar (UG) which provides the same basic structure to all human languages and explains the automatic acquisition of language by the young. Chomsky makes no attempt to connect the existence of this cognitive endowment with the origin of speech or any other cognitive ability for that matter. Rather than embracing a Darwinian explanation of the Universal Grammar he disavows himself of such an explanation and merely suggests that this facility arose or emerged as a consequence of so many brain cells being packed into the small space of the human skull.

To my mind Chomsky has merely sidestepped the issue and offers no real explanation of the automatic acquisition of language. This opinion is shared by Deacon, who refers to Chomsky's Universal Grammar as 'a "hopeful monster" theory of human language: the evolutionary theorist's counterpart to divine intervention, in which a freak mutation just happens to produce a radically different and serendipitously better-equipped organism ... The accidental language organ theory politely begs us to ignore the messy details of language origins ... It rephrases the problem by giving it a new name' (1997, 35–7).

Tomasello also criticizes Chomsky on the grounds that he provides no explanation for the UG other than a lucky genetic mutation: 'There is no question that acquiring and using a natural language contributes to, even transforms, the nature of human cognition ... But language did not come out of nowhere ... nor despite the views of some contemporary scholars such as Chomsky, did it arise as some bizarre genetic mutation unrelated to other aspects of human cognition and social life ... natural language is a symbolically embodied social institution that arose historically from previously existing social-communicative activities' (1999, 94).

Not only are we asked to accept the notion that the UG was a random mutation, but to boot that it somehow evolved genetically with a set of parameters that children could somehow set to accommodate the language(s) to which they are exposed and thereby be able to install that particular grammar in their brain. Even Jackendoff, a proponent of the UG, has expressed a concern with this model: 'It is hard to imagine all this structure emerging in the brain prior to experience, much less being coded genetically ... [when] few of the actual parameters determining differences among languages, have been successfully worked out, despite nearly twenty years of intensive research' (2002, 190). Another cogent argument has been made by Peter Culicover (1999) to the effect that if children have enough knowledge of the language to which they are exposed to set the correct parameter of the UG, they would not need the form of the UG they are supposed to trigger.

Another problem with the idea of an innate UG is that the grammar of literate cultures, on the whole, differs from the grammar of preliterate cultures: 'Some grammatical features are more characteristic of literate than pre-literate societies. Givo´n (1979), for example, suggests that the use of referential indefinite subjects is such a case. More importantly Givo´n and many others have suggested that the use of subordinate clauses increases dramatically with literacy' (Newmeyer 2003, 73).

For those children who learn two or even three languages simultaneously there is the additional challenge of having two or possibly three sets of parameters simultaneously operating in their LAD. Do these children have multiple LADs or a LAD with two or three separate compartments and an interface device which channels their mind to the correct compartment of the LAD every time they are spoken to or wish to speak? As we have already suggested a more satisfying and less grandiose explanation of the observed phenomena is to ascribe the regularity of language to the idea that in order to be easily learned through mimesis or imitation languages must have certain internal consistencies or regularities which Noam Chomsky was able to detect and formulate as the UG.

The poverty of stimulus argument can be traced back to Chomsky's (1965) original formulation of the UG in *Aspects of the Theory of Syntax* in which he points out children acquire language(s) automatically without instruction. And they do this on the basis of observing speech 'fragments and deviant expressions of a variety of sorts.' Chomsky concludes that 'thus it seems that a child must have the ability to "invent" a generative grammar that defines well-formedness and assigns interpretations to sentences even though the primary linguistic data that he uses as a basis for this act of theory construction may, from the point of view of the theory he constructs, be deficient in various respects' (1965, 200–1).

I have no quarrel with the Chomsky's position in the excerpt quoted above except with the one word he wrapped in quotation marks, namely, 'invent.' I submit that children do not 'invent' a generative grammar but merely 'imitate' the generative grammar that they hear or observe. The child learns words first, then how to order or structure them. A child's first utterances consist of a single word. It is only after children have acquired a sizable vocabulary that they begin to construct multiple word utterances. Their language development follows Bickerton's two-step model of language origin consisting of protolanguage followed by fully syntactilized language.

That languages incorporate a generative grammar can be attributed to mimesis. If a structure or syntax with an initial set of words serves the purpose or intention of the communication and the representation of thought, then as the vocabulary of that language grows that initial structure or syntax will be imitated and reused. Those of us old enough to remember the introduction of facsimile transmission or fax observed that the noun fax, as in 'I sent a fax,' evolved into the verb to fax, as in 'I will fax that document to you.' The pattern continued as fax became a regular verb: I/you/we/they fax, but he faxes; I faxed for past tense; I will be faxing for future tense. The new noun and verb email also exhibits the same mimetic pattern.

Merlin Donald (1991), the scholar who claimed that mimesis foreshadowed verbal language, offers an important hint as to the direction in which we should proceed to gain an insight into the mystery of language acquisition. He suggests that a solution will require a consideration of more than just the human brain and genetics and that there is an important social and cultural dimension to the problem: 'The language brain does not act like a preprogrammed capacity in one very important way ... it does not automatically self-install or self-trigger. This can be seen in people who are linguistically isolated from birth, such as the nonsigning deaf ... Without extensive cultural programming the mind does not suspect the possibility of language, not even of inner language ... languages are inherently collective and consensual communication systems ... This implies that much of the replicative information needed to perpetuate language is stored in culture, not in the genes' (1998, 49).

Donald's position is in direct opposition to that of Pinker and Bloom (1990, 2), who assert on the basis of listing a number of the somatic aspects of speech (Pinker 1989a) that the ability to use a natural language belongs more to the study of human biology than human culture; it is a topic like 'echolocation in bats' or 'stereopsis in monkeys,' not like writing or the wheel.

How does one resolve this conflict between such prominent scholars? I suggest the conflict is only one of degree and that both sides would agree that language is both a biological-genetic phenomenon as well as a cultural-collective one. I must take issue with the Pinker and Bloom assertion that the 'ability to use a natural language' is like echolocation not like writing. We have demonstrated in chapters 2 and 3 that speech and writing are both part of the same evolutionary chain of languages and, hence, are similar phenomena. Both speech and writing, unlike echolocation and stereopsis, have profound cognitive impacts which lead in the case of speech to conceptualization and in the case of writing to an even deeper level of conceptual thought that includes among other things analytic thought, mathematics, and science.

### The Pinker-Bloom and Jackendoff Arguments for
### Chomsky's Hypothesis of the Hard-wiring of the Universal Grammar

Pinker and Bloom support Chomsky's contention that the Universal Grammar is hard-wired by citing evidence from the way in which language is acquired by children. They claim that 'from the very start of language acquisition, children obey grammatical constraints that afford them no immediate communicative advantage.' They suggest that it is because it is difficult to acquire the Universal Grammar that it must be hard-wired into the human brain as innate constraints: 'The requirement for the standardization of communication protocols dictates that it is better for nature to build a language acquisition device that picks up the code of the ambient language than one that invents a code that is useful from a child's eye view. Acquiring such a code from examples is no mean feat, and so many grammatical principles and constraints must be hardwired into the device ... No mortal computer user can induce an entire communications protocol or programming language from examples; that's why we have manuals ... The child has no manual to consult, and presumably that is why he or she needs innate constraints' (Pinker and Bloom 1990, 46).

This argument is called the 'poverty of stimulus', according to which children do not receive enough information from the examples of speech that they sample to construct the rules of grammar yet seem to acquire this capacity effortlessly. By suggesting that children have no manual to guide their use of oral language, Pinker and Bloom reveal a lack of understanding of the way narrative is stored in the oral tradition. As Havelock (1963) has pointed out oral information is stored as a result of context, meter, prosody, plot, and so forth. The same applies to children learning language who also make use of similar cues. Parents make an effort to use the prosody of 'motherese' and repetitive context to teach their children to speak.

There is disagreement among linguists and psychologists of just how impoverished is the stimulus that infants receive as they are learning language. Jackendoff cites some evidence that learning can also be an important part of how language is acquired by children, criticizing Chomsky for ignoring this possibility: 'Opponents of Universal Grammar have argued that the child has much more evidence than Chomsky thinks: among other things, special modes of speech by parents ("Motherese") that make linguistic distinctions clearer to the child (Newport et al. 1977; Fernald 1984), understanding of context, including social context (Bruner 1974/5; Bates and MacWhinney 1982), and statistical distribution of phonemic transitions (Saffran et al. 1996) and of word occurrence (Plunkett and Marchman 1991). All these kinds of evidence are indeed available to the child, and they do help' (2002, 82).

Despite citing this evidence Jackendoff still maintains that the 'poverty of stimulus' problem needs to be addressed, but he reformulates 'the problem of learning more starkly in terms of what [he] like[s] to call the Paradox of Language Acquisition: The community of linguists, collaborating over many decades, has so far failed to come up with an adequate description of a speaker's f-knowledge of his or her native language ... Yet every normal child manages to acquire this f-knowledge by the age of ten or so ... How is it that in some sense every single normal child is smarter that the whole community of linguists?' (2002, 83).

My response to the question Jackendoff poses is that to be able to do something and to describe it are two different matters. A child can learn to ride a bicycle without much difficulty, but this does not mean she can describe the way in which the physics of bike riding works. One does not have to be a rocket scientist or a theoretical physicist to ride a bike. One might ask how does a child acquire the ability of bike riding despite the 'poverty of bike riding stimulus'? Is there perhaps an innate, pre-specified Bike Riding Acquisition Device? Probably not, but all that is required to master bike riding is a sense of balance that evolved with bipedal mobility and a little practice: 'It is worth pointing out that the Paradox of Language Acquisition finds parallels in every cognitive domain. All normal children learn to see, navigate, manipulate objects, and engage in rich social interactions; but we are far from being able to describe the f-mental process that constitutes these abilities, and even farther from being able to specify a simple learning process that leads to these abilities without support from a rather richly specified initial state. There seems no reason why language should be singled out for different treatment' (Jackendoff 2002, 84).

If this is indeed the case, as Jackendoff purports, then are there innate acquisition devices for seeing, navigating, manipulating objects, and engaging in rich social interaction?

There is a major difference that Jackendoff overlooks when comparing language with seeing, navigating, manipulating objects, and engaging in rich social interactions which is that language is the basis of conceptual and abstract thinking and the emergence of the human mind. To see, navigate, manipulate objects, and engage in rich social interactions are still part of the percept-based activities of the brain and hence are a lot simpler than the use of language and conceptual thinking. If what Jackendoff claims is true, then this would explain the universality of seeing, navigating, manipulating objects, and engaging in rich social interaction. The latter is of particular interest to me because it foreshadows the possibility of Universal Culture, a theme I will return to in chapter 14.

Using the 'poverty of stimulus' and the 'Paradox of Language Acquisition' arguments respectively Pinker-Bloom and Jackendoff justify the claim that the rules of grammar are hard-wired into the brain of the human child as an innate constraint which allows him to acquire the rules of the Universal Grammar and apply them to the mother tongue to which he is exposed: 'Language learning is not programming: parents provide their children with sentences of English, not the rules of English. We suggest that natural selection was the programmer' (Pinker and Bloom 1990, 747). The point that they (Pinker-Bloom, Jackendoff, and by inference, Chomsky) are missing is that children learn language by imitation or mimesis and that this applies to the rules of grammar as well as to the vocabulary.

An alternative to the Pinker-Bloom argument for a Language Acquisition Device is that, since the transmission of language is cultural, the specific mechanism for the actual transmission could be mimesis. If, as Donald (1991) has suggested, verbal language emerged from mimetic communication, then the mechanism of mimesis could account for the child's acquisition of grammar and vocabulary by imitation. Children recognize structures in the language to which they are exposed and then they imitate those structures without any need for a theory. That children generalize the rules to create past tenses such as hitted and cutted can be understood in terms of mimesis. They are merely imitating the way in which past tenses are created for regular verbs for the irregular verbs. The errors they make with the irregular verbs do not have to be corrected by their parents because, with time and enough exposure to hearing hit and cut used for the past tense as well as the present tense, they will finally come around to adopting the rules for the irregular verbs. Once again mimesis will become the mechanism whereby they learn the grammatical rules of their mother tongue. It is only when they learn a second language in school that children need to be taught grammar by rote rather than by mimesis. Even children who are bilingual will learn the grammar of the mother tongue spoken in their home and the grammar of the second language they hear from their friends outside the home.

While Pinker and Bloom are attempting to find a Darwinian explanation for the evolution of the Universal Grammar it is puzzling why they suggest that 'so many grammatical principles and constraints must be hardwired.' Darwinian evolution is achieved by tinkering not by engineering a clean new design, as was pointed out by Jacob (1977). Given that the ability for imitation or mimesis already existed in the primate and hominid lines long before the advent of speech one would expect nature to take advantage of this existing competency in engineering verbal language and its acquisition. It would have been more economical to make use of the innate ability to imitate to pass the rules of grammar along than to code them genetically. We know that the semantics or lexicon of language is not coded genetically but is preserved in the environment of the culture and passed from one generation to the next by mimesis, as noted by Pinker and Bloom: 'Once a mechanism for learning sound-meaning pairs is in place, the information for acquiring any particular pair, such as dog for dogs, is readily available from the speech of the community. Thus the genome can store the vocabulary in the environment, as Tooby and Cosmides (1989) have put it' (1990, 733).

Why would nature choose one mechanism of transmission for semantics (sound-meaning pairs) and another for syntax (hard-wiring)? As was already mentioned, children are able to imitate grammatical structures with great logical precision, as can be observed in their construction of the past tense by adding the morpheme 'ed' to the present tense of a verb which they do inappropriately with verbs like hit and cut which become 'hitted' and 'cutted.' Pinker and Bloom try to use the fact that children eventually conform to the adult form of the past tense for irregular verbs like hit and cut to support their argument that the child's grammar is programmed: 'When children say hitted and cutted, they are distinguishing between past and nonpast forms in a manner that is unavailable to adults, who must use hit and cut across the board. Why do children eventually abandon this simple, logical, expressive system? They must be programmed so that the mere requirement of conformity to the adult code, as subtle and arbitrary as it is, wins over other desiderata' (1990, 733). A much simpler explanation is that eventually children conform to the adult form of creating the past tense of the irregular verbs because of mimesis, they eventually imitate their parents' form of speech.

One other example that Pinker and Bloom present to bolster their argument for an innate grammar can also be explained in terms of mimesis: 'They claim that 1– and 2–year-olds acquiring English obey a formal constraint on phrase structure configurations concerning the distinction between lexical categories and phrasal categories and as a result avoid placing determiners and adjectives before pronouns and proper names. They will use phrases like big dog to express the belief that a particular dog is big, but they will never use phrases like big Fred or big he to express the belief that a particular person is big (Bloom, in press). Children respect this constraint despite the limits it puts on their expressive range' (1990, 727). This phenomenon can be easily explained as mimesis. Since children hear terms like *big dog* or *big house* they will imitate these constructions and use them, and since they never hear terms like *big Fred* or *big he* they do not make use of these forms of expression. Indeed, if someone has the nickname Big Fred, you can be sure children will also call this person Big Fred. We will return to the role of mimesis in language acquisition later in the chapter when we examine Tomasello's (1999) hypothesis that children's ability to identify with conspecifics allows them to easily imitate the vocabulary and syntactical structures to which they are exposed.

### Is It Possible that the UG Is Soft-Wired and the LAD Is Weak? – Reconciling the Approaches of Chomsky and His Critics

Jackendoff wonders how genomes are able to code innate behaviour or instincts (2002, 90–1). Obviously they do, as all humans develop their perceptual capabilities such as seeing and tactility without being taught anything. The same is true for many aspects of language such as the automatic babbling of babies. The question is to what extent is the language capacity innate? It is possible that the level or degree of innateness of the language capacity is not total, as is suggested by the hard wired UG hypothesis. Rather the human genome is coded with sequential learning and processing capabilities (Christiansen 1994) or perhaps symbolic representation (Deacon 1997) or conceptualization (Logan 2000) which provides the human mind with enough capacity to learn a language despite the so-called poverty of stimulus. We must distinguish between criticism of the mechanism of hard-wiring and the criticism of the UG, for there are two distinct issues at stake: hard-wiring and the UG. There is not much dispute about the existence of a lowercase universal grammar, that is, the proposition that the languages of the world share many common features; however, like many others, I am critical of the uppercase Universal Grammar which carries with it the notion that this grammar is genetically hard-wired with an LAD and all of the details of UG, including a mechanism to pick out the particular language to which the child is exposed.

Some in the Chomsky camp, like Pinker and Bloom, are ardent supporters of hard-wiring. Others, like Jackendoff, are open-minded about just how much of the UG is hard-wired and take the criticisms of the 'connectionists' seriously: 'Jeffrey Elman et al. (1996) and, following them, Terrence Deacon (1997) have mounted a series of important arguments against a detailed innate language-learning capacity' (2002, 90). This remark, together with some of the other excerpts that follow, demonstrate Jackendoff's ability to consider the ideas of others who do not agree with his point of view; he does not suffer from the hubris that characterizes the behaviour of Chomsky and some of his followers. Jackendoff points out that 'on the whole, linguists have taken more interest in establishing universals than in reducing them to more general cognitive capacities ... This is an area where sympathetic cooperation with researchers in other areas of perception and cognition would be extremely helpful: an attempt to find detailed functional parallels to linguistic phenomena is usually beyond the professional competence of either an unaided linguist or an unaided non-linguist' (ibid., 80–1).

Because of Jackendoff's openness to the ideas of Deacon and the connectionists my own position of initial opposition to hard-wiring has softened. I have been persuaded that perhaps a weak LAD exists and that it is possible to reconcile the position of the Chomskyites and the connectionists. The weak LAD I have in mind does not contain as much detail as the proponents of strong UG/LAD would suggest. Rather I would propose that the weak LAD consists of the sequential learning and processing skills (as suggested by Christiansen 1994) or the capacity for symbolic representation (as suggested by Deacon 1997) or conceptualization – as I suggested in the Extended Mind Model. The skill sets identified by Christiansen, Deacon, and the Extended Mind Model are basically equivalent, and any one of them could serve as the effective LAD which, in turn, could give rise to the universality or uniformity of the grammars of the world's languages originally identified by Chomsky as UG. One can, then, accept the existence of the UG which approximates to a certain degree all the grammars of the world without accepting that all of the details of the UG are hard-wired. What is wired is just enough to explain the ease of language acquisition by children and just enough to generate the regularities of the grammars of the world's languages. If I had to give a name to this position I would call it *soft-wiring*.

The idea remains that there has to be some form of wiring, whether hard or soft, even if one accepts the hypothesis that languages evolved so that they could be easily learned. This can be explained by the simultaneous co-evolution of language and the human genome. Evolution has been a thorn in the side of linguistics. Consider that because of hubris or stubbornness Chomsky has not been able to accept the idea that natural selection could have anything to do with the origin of language. His disciples, Pinker and Bloom, opened the door to natural selection but lurched to the other extreme by suggesting that UG is an exclusive product of the Darwinian evolution of the human genome. Neither they nor Jackendoff, who is open to connectionist ideas, can conceive of language as evolving: 'But what can it mean for a language to evolve by "itself"? The noises are not subject to natural selection, only the organism is' (Jackendoff 2002, 94). This is a most peculiar conclusion for someone open to Darwinian evolution, given that Darwin discussed the evolution of language and found that it bore an analogy to the evolution of biological species as the following excepts from chapter 3 of *The Descent of Man* (1871) attest:

> The formation of different languages and of distinct species, and the proofs that both have been developed through a gradual process, are curiously parallel. (See the very interesting parallelism between the development of species and languages, given by Sir C. Lyell in The Geological Evidences of the Antiquity of Man, 1863, chap. xxiii.) But we can trace the formation of many words further back than that of species, for we can perceive how they actually arose from the imitation of various sounds. We find in distinct languages striking homologies due to community of descent, and analogies due to a similar process of formation. The manner in which certain letters or sounds change when others change is very like correlated growth. We have in both cases the re-duplication of parts, the effects of long-continued use, and so forth. The frequent presence of rudiments, both in languages and in species, is still more remarkable. The letter m in the word am, means I; so that in the expression I am, a superfluous and useless rudiment has been retained. In the spelling also of words, letters often remain as the rudiments of ancient forms of pronunciation.
>
> Languages, like organic beings, can be classed in groups under groups; and they can be classed either naturally according to descent, or artificially by other characters. Dominant languages and dialects spread widely, and lead to the gradual extinction of other tongues. A language, like a species, when once extinct, never, as Sir C. Lyell remarks, reappears. The same language never has two birth-places. Distinct languages may be crossed or blended together. (See remarks to this effect by the Rev. F.W. Farrar, in an interesting article, entitled Philology and Darwinism, in Nature, March 24, 1870, p. 528.) We see variability in every tongue, and new words are continually cropping up; but as there is a limit to the powers of the memory, single words, like whole languages, gradually become extinct. As Max Müller (Nature, January 6, 1870, p. 257.) has well remarked: 'A struggle for life is constantly going on amongst the words and grammatical forms in each language. The better, the shorter, the easier forms are constantly gaining the upper hand, and they owe their success to their own inherent virtue.' To these more important causes of the survival of certain words, mere novelty and fashion may be added; for there is in the mind of man a strong love for

slight changes in all things. The survival or preservation of certain favoured words in the struggle for existence is natural selection.

In two passages in chapters 4 and 21 respectively of *The Descent of Man*, Darwin again proffers his opinion that language is the product of evolution: 'The half-art, half-instinct of language still bears the stamp of its gradual evolution.' Furthermore, 'no philologist now supposes that any language has been deliberately invented; it has been slowly and unconsciously developed by many steps.'

The bridge of co-evolution was built from both sides of the river, a product of the genetic evolution of the human brain and the memetic evolution of language. One advantage of the soft-wiring approach is that it neutralizes the argument against the creation of the UG by solely genetic means given the extreme complexity of linguistic structures, a fact underscored by Jackendoff (2002, 83). A model for the emergence of language begins first with the emergence of mimetic communication, as suggested by Donald (1991). This development was followed by the emergence of Bickertonian protolanguage as the cognitive capabilities of phonological structure, conceptual structure or semantics, and syntactic structure co-evolved (Jackendoff 2002, chapter 5).

Although I have provided a reasonable argument as to how children learn the grammar of their language and how the structure or syntax of a language is applied to new vocabulary items as they emerge, this does not necessarily negate Chomsky's hypothesis that a UG exists – only his notion that the UG is hard-wired. Both approaches provide an explanation of known facts. The one trump card that I would play now to argue for the mimetic approach as opposed to the hard-wired UG approach is Occam's razor whereby one should describe things as simply as possible eliminating unnecessary structures. Or, as Einstein said, a theory should be simple but not too simple. Even Jackendoff concurs with the need for simplicity: 'It is of course a scientific desideratum that this grammar be as simple as possible, consistent with the facts. The need for simplicity is driven not only by an apriori desire for elegance, but also by the need for the learner to acquire the grammar' (2002, 101).

Mimesis or the ability of humans to imitate structures eliminates the need for assuming that children come bundled with UG built into them. This is not to say that I challenge the existence of a universal grammar, far from it, I accept the idea. I just want to apply Occam's Razor and suggest that the human infant comes bundled only with what we have called the weak LAD. We may wish to label this weak LAD as a mimetic acquisition device, following Donald; or a linear sequential acquisition device, following Christiansen; or a symbolic representation acquisition device, following Deacon; or a concept acquisition device, following the Extended Mind Model.

### Demystifying Language Acquisition: Do Languages Evolve to Be More Learnable?

The 'hardwired language acquisition device,' posited by Chomsky and supported by Pinker and Bloom, might be the solution to a problem that does not exist. Deacon does 'not think that children's grammatical abilities are the crucial mystery of language' (1997, 39). He and a number of others, including Newport (1990, 1991) and Elman (1991, 1993), are of the opinion that language evolved in such a way that it could be easily learned and acquired. Elman (1993) has shown through a computer simulation of a neural net that it was possible for a net that was exposed to grammatically correct sentences to identify by induction other sentences that were grammatically correct as well. Newport (1990, 1991) suggests rather than possessing the hard-wiring of an innate LAD, children are able to acquire a language at a very early age due to two factors: (1) languages evolved in such a way as to accommodate the learning biases of the young in order to insure their (the languages') survival, and (2) the young child's limited memory capacity and ability to deal with details is an actual advantage, as it allows the child to better see the overall structure of the language she is learning, that is, 'more is less.'

A number of researchers (including Christiansen 1994; Batali 1998; and Kirby 1998, 2000a, 2000b) have been testing Newport's conjecture by making use of computer simulations and artificial language learning (ALL) experiments:

> More recently an alternative perspective is gaining ground, advocating a refocus in thinking about language evolution. Rather than concentrating on biological changes to accommodate language, this approach stresses the adaptation of linguistic structures to the biological substrate of the

human brain. Languages are viewed as dynamic systems of communication, subject to selection pressures arising from limitations on human learning and processing. (Christiansen and Ellefson 2002, 336)

It is important to distinguish between the evolution of language itself – in particular the emergence, modification, and enrichment of grammatical resources in human languages – and the biological evolution of articulate hominids. (Batali 1998, 406)

Languages evolve historically to be optimal communicative systems, and the innately specified human language learning mechanisms have evolved in order to learn these systems more efficiently. (Kirby 1998, 360)

Perhaps the purest expression of these ideas comes from Christiansen's (1994) notion of 'language as an organism':

Languages exists only because humans can learn, produce, and process them. Without humans there would be no language. It therefore makes sense to construe languages as organisms that have had to adapt themselves through natural selection to fit a particular ecological niche: the human brain. In order for languages to 'survive,' they must adapt to the properties of the human learning and processing mechanisms. This is not to say that having a language does not confer selective advantages onto humans. It seems clear that humans with superior language abilities are likely to have a selective advantage over other humans (and other organisms) with lesser communicative powers. This is an uncontroversial point, forming the basic premise of many of the adaptationist theories of language evolution. However, what is often not appreciated is that the selection forces working on language to fit humans are significantly stronger than the selection pressures on humans to be able to use language. In the case of the former, a language can only survive if it is learnable and processable by humans. On the other hand, adaptation toward language use is merely one out of many selective pressures working on humans (such as, for example, being able to avoid predators and find food). Whereas humans can survive without language, the opposite is not the case. Thus, language is more likely to have adapted itself to its human hosts than the other way around. Languages that are hard for humans to

learn simply die out, or more likely, do not come into existence at all.
(Christiansen, Dale, Ellefson, and Conway 2002, 144–5)

The results of the computational simulations and artificial language learning show that it is possible that languages evolved to match hominid cognitive abilities rather than the other way around. Kirby, reporting on one of his studies, wrote: 'I show, using a computational model, that compositional syntax is an inevitable outcome of the dynamic of observationally learned communication systems. In a simulated population of individuals, language develops from a simple idiosyncratic vocabulary with little expressive power, to a compositional system with high expressivity, nouns, verbs, and word order expressing meaning distinctions' (2000a, 303).

While indicating that the deployment of ALL techniques is still in its infancy Christiansen, Dale, Ellefson, and Conway, nevertheless, report that their experiments 'illuminate the importance of complexity and consistency in learning artificial languages' and that these 'experiments suggest that languages have evolved these and other properties to facilitate learning. Over time this process of linguistic adaptation has resulted in the structural constraints on language use that we observe today' (2002, 161). That is, Universal Grammar.

Clark from the context of his notions of embedded cognition and scaffolding also argues for the possibility that languages evolved to be easily learned: 'Suppose (just suppose) that language ... is an artifact that has in part evolved so as to be easily acquired and used by beings like us' (1997, 212).

An independent piece of information supporting the hypothesis that languages evolved to be more easily learned and used is the observation of Zipf (1935) that common words tend to be shorter than uncommon ones, which he related to the principle of 'least effort' (Corballis 2003, 212).

The notion that languages evolve so as to be easily learned explains how home sign languages and pidgins might have arisen with a UG-like structure without having to resort to the proposition that the brain is hard-wired with the UG. Jackendoff tries to justify the UG by arguing that the home sign languages created by deaf children with non-signing parents 'display certain rudiments of grammatical structure: consistent word order and incipient morphological marking. Where can the consistent structuring of these systems come from, if not the child's f-expectations of what linguistic communication is suppose to be like?' (2002, 99). The answer to Jackendoff's question is simple: only a language with a consistent word order would be functional and hence emerge. The idea of an f-expectation is simply another example of ad hoc reasoning.

A further example of an ad hoc argument is the following used by Jackendoff to explain the grammatical structure of creole languages: 'Thus, Bickerton's argument goes, creole grammar must have come from the expectations of what a language has to look like – i.e. Universal Grammar – and they built these expectations into their linguistic output' (2002, 100).

## Catalytic Closure

Stuart Kauffman, whose ideas we have already encountered, makes use of the notion of catalytic closure or autocatalysis to explain the origin of life. If one embraces Christiansen's notion of language as an organism, some of Kauffman's ideas can be applied to our understanding of the origin of language: 'Life at its roots, lies in the property of catalytic closure among a collection of molecular species' (1995, 50). It is appropriate to borrow Kauffman's idea of catalytic closure and apply it to language as a living organism. The words of a language acting as concepts and symbolic tokens form an autocatalytic set from which the grammar of the language emerges which is consistent with Kauffman's idea that 'catalytic closure insures that the whole exists by means of the parts, and they are present both because of and in order to sustain the whole. Autocatalytic sets exhibit the emergent property of holism' (ibid., 69). If one accepts the contention that language emerged through autocatalytic closure, it supports the claim of Deacon (1997) and others that language emerged whole with both a primitive lexicon and a rudimentary grammar.

Kauffman also asserts that 'if life began with collectively autocatalytic sets, they deserve awed respect, for the flowering of the biosphere rests on the creative power they unleashed on the globe – awed respect and wonder, but not mysticism. Most of all, if this is true, life is vastly more probable than we have supposed. Not only are we at home in the universe but we are far more likely to share it with as yet unknown companions' (1995, 69).

Kauffman contends that autocatalysis as a principle should give rise to life forms throughout the universe. This notion is consistent with the idea that language emerged as a living entity not in some far-flung corner of the universe (although that certainly is a possibility) but right here on earth as a 'nonobligate symbiant' with humans. Language and culture are each self-replicating life forms that grow, reproduce, and evolve just like biological entities or species.

### Supracriticality

Kauffman introduces the notion of supracriticality which we can apply to languages operating as organisms:

> Some guess that the number of species in the biosphere is on the order of 100 million species ... [and] on the order of 10 million different organic molecular structures ... Chemicals can be catalysts that act on other chemical substrates to create still further chemical products. Those novel chemical products can catalyze still further reactions involving themselves and all the original molecules to create still further molecules. These additional new molecules afford still further new reactions with themselves and all the older molecules as substrates, and all the molecules around may serve as catalysts for any of these newly available reactions ... This explosion of molecular species is what I mean by supracritical behavior. (1995, 116)

Something similar happens with language as a word operating as a concept acts as a catalyst for new concepts and, hence, new words. Words take on nuances of meaning as they are used metaphorically until new meanings emerge and the word in some instances takes on a new morphological and/or phonemic form (eg., slide into sled or strip into stripe). Let us consider the word *sense* which derives from the French *sens* which in turn derives from the Latin *sentire*, to feel. This word in English gives rise to many (at least seventy-five) words: sensed, sensing, senseless, common sense, sense organ, sense perception, sensation, sensational, sensationalism, sensationalist, sensibility, sensible, sensibly, sensitive, sensitivity, sensitivity group, sensitivity training, sensitize, sensitization, sensitometer, sensorium, sensory, sensual, sensualism, sensualist, sensualistic, sensuality, sensuous, sentient, sentiency, sentiment, sentimental, sentimentalist, sentimentality, sentimentalize, sentinel, sentry; absent, absence, absent-minded, absentee, absently; consent, consensual, consensus, consentient; dissent, dissenter, dissentient, dissension; insensate, insensible, insensibility, insensibly, insensitivity, insentient; presence, presence of mind, present, presentation, presentational, presentationism, presentient, presentiment, presentive, presently, presentment; represent, representation, representational, representative, resent, resentment, and resentful.

## The Language Used by Each Speaker Is an Organism

Another Kauffman idea that we can apply to language operating as an organism is the catalysis of reproduction: 'A living organism is a system of chemicals that has the capacity to catalyze its own reproduction' (1995, 49). Let us generalize Kauffman's definition to apply it the idea of language operating as an organism. A language operating as a living organism is a system of words and grammatical structures that has the capacity to catalyze its own reproduction. If we consider the language produced and comprehended by each individual speaker to be an organism, then we may regard language reproducing itself each time a child acquires the language of her parents and other linguistic conspecifics.

By defining the language of each individual in the society as an organism, we not only meet Kauffman's criterion that an organism catalyzes its own reproduction, but we are able to consider the evolution of this organism using Darwin's simple one-line definition of evolution, namely, 'descent with modification.' By *descent* Darwin meant reproduction. The only way we can speak of a language reproducing itself is by considering the language of each individual in the society as an organism. In which case the inheritance or descent is not by diploidy but the polyploidy of parents, siblings, peers, teachers, relatives, and society in general. One can now apply the concept of natural selection to the language organism of each individual in a society.

But what are we to make of the language of the society as a whole? It is not an organism because it cannot reproduce itself. The solution to this dilemma is simple. The language of the society is not an organism, but a species whose member conspecifics are the languages of the individuals comprising the society. The language of society was denoted by de

Saussure as *langue*, whereas the practice of a language by an individual was denoted as *parole*. In our scheme, *langue* is the species and *parole* is the organism. Just as the conspecifics of a biological species are able to reproduce among themselves, the conspecifics of a linguistic species are able to communicate with each other. So English and French are linguistics species. American, Canadian, and British English are subspecies, as are the many dialects of English in these three countries. They may be regarded as subspecies in that they are distinct in some ways but their members can intercommunicate just as members of biological subspecies are distinct but can interbreed.

The linguistic competence of each individual represents an organism with its own unique language which can communicate only with members of the same language species. The language possessed by each individual is, in Christiansen's words, 'a kind of beneficial parasite – a nonobligate symbiant – that confers some selective advantage onto its human hosts without whom it cannot survive' (Christiansen and Ellefson 2002, 339). The way in which the language that belongs to the community rather than the individual evolves is through the mutations that arise in the idiosyncratic use of the language by individuals. Those idiosyncratic mutations can then be reproduced by being incorporated into the individual languages of other individual members of the linguistic community.

A person may possess more than one language, more than one nonobligate symbiant. In Europe most people possess their village language or dialect and the national language not to mention that many can speak the languages of their neighbouring countries. Individuals who are members of more than one linguistic community can act as cross-pollinators between languages as they borrow an expression from one language and use it in another. An example of a language that has experienced a great deal of cross-pollination is Yiddish which originated from old middle German but contains loan words from Hebrew and most of the languages of eastern Europe. English is another example of a language with many loan words as a result of successive migrations and conquests of England as well as the fact that England was a maritime power that created a world empire upon which 'the sun never set.' As a result of which English mariners and colonists came into contact with many different languages.

From this perspective there are two meanings to *language*. The language of the individual speaker or user and the common language of the linguistic community. The linguistic community can be a nation state or a tiny village or even an extended family. National languages are regarded as national cultural heritages which are often protected from change by an academy which tries to define the 'proper' or 'correct' usage of the language. Then there is the language of the street or the village, often referred to as a dialect, so as to confer a lower status upon it. But dialects are often more expressive of day-to-day affairs even though they might lack some of the technical sophistication of the national languages. For some observers loan words enrich a language, while for others they are cultural pollutants. As the Latin expression goes one cannot dispute taste: *De Gustibus non disputatum est.*

Catalytic closure, which Kauffman (1995, 50) has suggested is at the heart of the origin of life, might also provide a mechanism for the way in which language is reproduced from parents to children despite the 'poverty of stimulus' barrier that some have suggested exists. I do not deny that there is a poverty of stimulus but I am not certain that it is a barrier, and perhaps its effect has been somewhat exaggerated as a way of justifying the UG approach and the concept of a LAD. If language exhibits the property of catalytic closure then the reproduction of some elements of the language catalyze the reproduction of others. By reproduction of the language we are talking about the 'individual' language of each speaker and the process whereby young children are able to acquire the language of their parents with great ease. The biological capacity to imitate, which hominids and humans acquired through selection plays the role of the analogue of autocatalytic chemical reactions which create more of the same products. Catalytic closure is possibly the mechanism that allows acquisition of language to proceed so rapidly.

If we can accept the hypothesis that language is an organism that arises from catalytic closure, we have another possible alternative to Chomsky's contention that the UG is hard-wired. At the root autocatalysis is self-organization or what Kauffman calls 'order for free': 'We have seen that the origin of collective autocatalysis, the origin of life itself, comes because of what I call 'order for free' – self-organization that arises naturally' (1995, 71). If language emerged through a process of self-organization, it comes with its UG already in place; the UG does not sit hard-wired in the brains of its users, but rather it is an emergent property of the language itself which replicates itself every time the non-obligate symbiant language of the parent or caregiver reproduces itself as a nonobligate symbiant language of the child. Kauffman's 'order for free' translates into 'grammar for free,' the self-organization of the language itself: 'Biologists divide cells and organisms into the genotype (the genetic information) and the phenotype (the enzymes and other proteins as well as the organs and morphology that make up the body). With autocatalytic sets, there is no separation between genotype and phenotype. The system serves as its own genome' (ibid., 73). This idea translates for language into the notion that the lexicon that first emerged did so with its own intrinsic grammar. Applying Kauffman's remark above to language, we may regard the phenotype as the lexicon and the genotype as the grammar. According to this notion the lexicon automatically possesses a grammar as soon as it emerges, as has been suggested by Deacon (1997) and proponents of the lexical hypothesis.

## Language Acquisition, Ontogeny, and a Theory of Mind

Tomasello rejects Chomsky's approach to language acquisition and the notion of a poverty of stimulus: 'The most general point about acquisition is that the categories and schemas of a language are not given to children innately, as is demanded by the mathematical approach of Generative Grammar, but rather they are generalizations that children make on the basis of their own categorization skills working on the language they hear' (1998, xix). Tomasello invokes genetic evolution to explain joint attentional interactions and then assumes cultural transmission due to these joint attentional interactions to explain language acquisition. My specific hypothesis is that human cognition has the species-unique qualities it does because:

- Phylogenetically: modern human beings evolved the ability to 'identify' with conspecifics, which led to an understanding of them as intentional and mental beings like the self.
- Historically: this enabled new forms of cultural learning and sociogenesis, which led to cultural artifacts and behavioral traditions that accumulate modifications over time.

- Ontogenetically: human children grow up in the midst of these socially and historically constituted artifacts and traditions, which enable them to (a) benefit from the accumulated knowledge and skills of their social group; (b) acquire and use perspectivally based cognitive representations in the form of linguistic symbols (and analogies and metaphors constructed from these symbols); and (c) internalize certain types of discourse interactions into skills of metacognition, representational redescription, and dialogic thinking. (1999, 10)

Tomasello suggests that 'infants' early understanding of other persons as 'like me' is indeed the result of a uniquely human biological adaptation' which gave them the ability to identify with conspecifics; this, in turn, gave rise to 'many, if not all, of the most distinctive and important cognitive processes of the species Homo sapiens' (1999, 11 and 71).

The strength of Tomasello's (1999, 11) approach in contrast to those of others who try to explain language acquisition is his prodigious use of empirical data based on studies and observations that he and others have made of children's linguistic and cognitive development. The central element in his model of language acquisition by children is that they ontogenetically develop a theory of mind, which, Tomasello suggests, is part of a series of cognitive developments, the first stage of which is the realization that there is a difference between animate and inanimate objects. This he claims is part of the human cognitive inheritance from our primate ancestors. The second stage kicks in at about nine months when 'infants begin to engage in joint attentional interactions when they begin to understand other persons as intentional agents like the self' (1999, 68). Tomasello suggests that this development is 'the result of a uniquely human biological adaptation' and hypothesizes that 'when the infant comes to a new understanding of their [sic] own intentional actions, they then use their "like me" stance to understand the behavior of other persons in the same way' (ibid., 72). Children, once they achieve this cognitive ability, are able to tap into their cultural and linguistic inheritance and learn through other persons with whom they can now identify: 'If they do not understand others as intentional agents ... then they will not be able to take advantage of the cognitive skills and knowledge of conspecifics that is manifest in [their] cultural milieu' (ibid., 78).

To empirically establish that joint attention capability correlates with emerging linguistic skills, Tomasello pointed out that 'a number of measures of children's nonsocial cognitive development – mostly involving their knowledge of objects and space – emerged in an uncorrelated fashion with language and other joint attentional activities' and their 'ability to engage in nonlinguistic mediated joint attentional activities with adults at around one year of age is integrally related to their newly emerging linguistics skills' (1999, 111).

Perhaps the most important culture-based cognitive skill that a child acquires is language: 'The ability to see the self as one participant among others in an interaction is the social-cognitive basis for the infant's ability to comprehend kinds of socially shared events that constitute the basic joint attentional formats for the acquisition of language and other types of communicative conventions' (ibid., 92). One of the consequences of this ability of youngsters to learn from their culture is that 'one of the most significant dimensions of human culture is ... the way in which adults actively instruct youngsters' (ibid., 80). Tomasello points out that children are allowed to pick up some information and cultural skills such as language on their own but that other skills or pieces of knowledge are taught explicitly by adults because of their importance to their culture.

The third stage in the child's development of a theory of mind commences when the child begins to develop a sense of morality and comes when the child realizes that others have thoughts and beliefs like themselves. Tomasello suggests that this aspect of the theory of mind that children develop at about four years of age emerges from the conflicts that emerge in discussions with their peers: 'In their linguistic discourse with others young children experience myriad conflicting beliefs and points of view about things, a process which is almost certainly an essential ingredient in their coming to see other persons as beings with minds similar to, but different from, their own' (1999, 189). It is as a result of this experience and understanding of others that the child gradually becomes capable of 'moral reasoning' (ibid., 174 and 182).

One of the aspects of Tomasello's model that makes it so compelling is the stress he places, based on solid experimental data, on imitation in his explanation of the child's acquisition of language production, which obviates the need for a nativist explanation. Tomasello's emphasis on the role of imitation is consistent with Donald's (1991) emphasis on mimesis, discussed earlier in this chapter:

> It is also important that in children's acquisition of complex linguistic constructions they are initially so conservative, in the sense that they generally imitate exactly the relational structure of the constructions they are learning from mature language users. The importance of this observation is simply that the human adaptation for cultural learning is a very strong tendency, even in a domain – the acquisition of complex linguistic constructions – where it has classically been thought to play a minor role.
>
> The human adaptation for cultural learning is a very strong tendency … [which] is perfectly consistent with children's imitative tendencies in (a) tool use tasks – especially two-year-olds as in the study of Nagell et al.; (b) word learning tasks – again especially two-year-olds [the Tomasello et al. studies reviewed here in Chapter 4]; and (c) object manipulation and symbolic play tasks – again especially two-year-olds [see Tomasello et al. reviewed here in chapter 3]. The overall conclusion is thus that during the period from one to three years old, young children are virtual 'imitation machines' as they seek to appropriate the cultural skills and behaviors of the mature members of their social groups.
>
> This imitative tendency is not all-pervasive, of course, as children do some creative things with cultural artifacts and linguistic conventions from early in development, and it is certainly a tendency that recedes in influence in later cognitive development as children do various kinds of novel things with the cultural tools they have mastered. But initially – in the period in which they first begin to acquire the artifacts and conventions of their culture between the ages of one and four years – human children have a very strong imitative tendency. (Tomasello 1999, 159–60)

Tomasello's approach to language acquisition is based on cognitive functional grammar in which it is posited that language skills are cognitive skills. Tomasello holds that hominids came equipped with certain basic primate cognitive skills, that the cognitive skill of joint attention then evolved genetically which gave rise to verbal language, and after that new cognitive skills arose as the result of language use and development. Although to my knowledge Tomasello does not speak of the co-evolution of language and the cognitive skills associated with language, my interpretation of his model is that of co-evolution, which the following three excerpts from his work would seem to support:

> Acquiring language thus leads children to conceptualize, categorize, and schematize events in much more complex ways than they would if they were not engaged in learning a conventional language, and these kinds of event representations and schematizations add great complexity and flexibility to human cognition. (1999, 159)
>
> Social and cultural processes during ontogeny do not create basic cognitive skills. What they do is turn basic cognitive skills into extremely complex and sophisticated cognitive skills. (Ibid., 189)
>
> I will argue that engaging with others minds dialogically via symbols and discourse over a several-year period works to transform one- to two-year old children's cognitive skills, which differ in only a few important ways from those of other primates, into cognitive skills and forms of cognitive representation that differ in myriad ways from those of other primates. (ibid., 174)

My one quibble here is with Tomasello's last-quoted point. One important way in which the young human being's cognitive skills differ from those of other primates, and which should be mentioned is this context, is through the ability to conceptualize, a skill absent in other primates. With the exception of this one minor point I can buy into Tomasello's model of language ontogeny, which I find completely compatible with the Extended Mind Model.

### The Memetic Evolution of Language

Most of the focus on the evolution of language is actually on the emergence of language. In this section we will focus on the way in which language changes once it has emerged. We have examined the notion that language can be treated as an organism which evolved so that it could be easily acquired. Robert Worden (2000), in an attempt to understand how language changes, thinks of language as an ecology populated by words which are memes and at the same time behave like species which interact with other species (other words) in the ecology (of language).

I was intrigued by Worden's idea that all words are memes and extended it by hypothesizing that every word and every grammatical construction of spoken and written language as well as every semantic element and syntactical structure of mathematics, science, computing, and the Internet are memes just like the other elements of culture. If a new word is used to refer to a new experience or a new or syntactical structure is used to refer to a new relationship, and it is copied by a listener and replicated, that word or syntactical structure becomes a meme. Words and syntactical structures evolve; they compete; they are adaptations; and they contain vestigial structures. They are living entities if they are part of a living language, and they are like biological systems which also evolve and compete. They are different in that they are information rather than a living thing that occupies physical space and is made up of atoms, but one can also think of living systems as information or organization that propagates itself.

Dawkins considers verbal language as a cultural replicator that evolves: 'Language seems to "evolve" by non-genetic means, and at a rate which is orders of magnitude faster than genetic evolution' (1996, 81). As we have already demonstrated, speech is part of an evolutionary chain of languages which includes writing, mathematics, science, computing, and the Internet, all of which serve as cultural replicators or propagators of organization. All cultural artifacts, institutions, belief systems, and manifestations are also memes that evolve and, hence, are cultural replicators – cultural replicators evolve and things that evolve are cultural replicators. In all systems, whether biological or cultural, some form of information is passed on. In the case of living biological systems the information is passed on by genes. In the cases of both the instruction for the manufacture or use of tangible physical artifacts and of intangible semiotic cultural artifacts information is passed on through mimetic and/or verbal communication.

Language is a growing living phenomenon which changes in many different ways. Not only does the lexicon and syntactical structures of language change but the media by which language is transmitted also changes. The emergence of a written notation for speech represents a major form of punctuated equilibrium of language. The evolution of the notated languages of writing, speech, mathematics, science, computing, and the Internet have all taken place within approximately the past five thousand years (computing and the Internet actually in the past sixty years), a time frame in which the biological evolution of

*Homo sapiens* would have been insignificant. The evolution of notated language was clearly cultural, and therefore, we can expect that the same is at least partially true for the origin and evolution of spoken language.

Technology changes the evolutionary course of language, contrary to the claim of Pinker and Bloom that 'all languages are complex computational systems employing the same basic kinds of rules and representations, with no notable correlation with technological progress: the grammars of industrial societies are no more complex than the grammars of hunter-gatherers; Modern English is not an advance over Old English' (1990, 708).

Language is not a passive container or medium of human thought whose only function is to transmit and communicate our ideas and sentiments from one person to another. Language embodies 'living vortices of power' (Innis 1972, v, McLuhan's foreword) that shape and transform our thinking. Language is both a system of communication and an informatics tool. Language is a dynamic living organism which is constantly growing and evolving. Not only does spoken language grow in terms of its increased semantics and new syntactical forms, it also evolves into new forms of presentation and expression.

Writing, mathematics, science, computing, and the Internet represent the evolution of language in ways directly correlated with 'technological progress,' as we showed in chapter 2. The primary technological breakthrough that permitted the emergence of these languages was notation which extended human memory and objectified knowledge. In the case of writing and mathematics the technologies deployed at first were a stylus and clay, followed by parchment and ink, paper and ink, the printing press, the typewriter and in recent years, the computer.

Science, a phenomenon restricted to literate societies, required the notation systems of writing and mathematics. It was with the printing press, however, that modern science finally emerged (Logan 2004a, 193–209). The language of computing obviously would not have been possible without electronics, and the Internet arose as a result of computers and telephony. In addition to the shifts in syntax that accompanied technological progress it is worth noting that a major increase in semantics accompanied every breakthrough in technology. This is a rather trivial observation if we just restrict ourselves to the new terminology required to describe the new technologies, but the correlation between technological progress and an increase of the lexicon is more profound than that. For example, with the advent of writing the syntax of expression became more analytic and a much more abstract vocabulary suddenly appeared (Havelock 1963):

> Under the influence of alphabetic literacy, Greek writers created the vocabulary of abstract thought that is still in use to this day, notions such as body, matter, essence, space, translation, time, motion, permanence, change, flux, quality, quantity, combination and ratio. These terms and concepts became the language of philosophy. A rational approach to solving problems logically and finding solutions to them developed. Ideas such as truth, beauty, justice, and reason took on new meanings and became the subject of a new type of discourse. Havelock (1963, p. 180) notes that the way in which statements of knowledge are made in the oral and literate traditions are quite different. Statements in the oral tradition must be made in the context of real space and real time. It is only with alphabetic literacy that timeless analytic statements emerge that can express universal truths independent of the context in which they occur. (Logan 2004a, 105)

Tooby and Cosmides (1989) describe language as the ability of the genome to store vocabulary in the environment. This idea parallels our contention that language extends the brain into a mind that can tap the resources of the culture to which that brain has been exposed. The notated languages of writing, mathematics, science, computing, and the Internet allow the genome to store even more knowledge and to access it faster and in a greater quantity than could be achieved straight from human memory.

One of the ideas I promote in the Extended Mind Model is that human cognitive evolution sped up with the advent of language: 'A theory of language evolution should be consistent with the neo-Darwinian theory of evolution. In this framework, there is a proven limit on the speed of (genetic) evolution (Worden, 1995) which places powerful constraints on the evolution of language. This is a limit on the rate at which new design information in the brain can be created by natural selection' (Worden 1998, 150). The evolution of language is not biological however, as Worden suggests and, as a result, the rate of evolution was much faster. The same is true of the evolution of technology which is not biological but cultural.

## The Evolution of Words

When Worden suggests that words behave like species in the ecology of language, he is claiming that Darwin's principle of natural selection should apply to words, but this poses the following questions: 'What is in a word package and what is not? What is the mechanism of reproduction and what information can it propagate? Such a theory is like the theory of Darwinian evolution before the discovery of DNA replication – it is quite plausible, but fundamental questions remain about how it really works. Until we find the answers to these questions the idea remains an appealing story rather than a predictive theory' (2000, 354–5).

I was intrigued by the Worden's challenge and came up with the following thoughts about a possible mechanism to explain the evolution of words acting as species in the ecology of language. I start with his suggestion that words are memes, and as such they are replicated through cultural transmission in a population. In the Darwinian evolution of biological systems there are sometimes errors in the transmission of genes, and the resulting mistake might be a gene which possesses a selective advantage giving rise to a change in the species. The analogue with words is that from time to time a word is used metaphorically in a new way and in a new context and that metaphorical use of the word has a selective advantage.

The metaphor that is created might even survive longer than the original use of the word, resulting in a dead metaphor. In most cases, however, the original use of the word and the metaphorical use both survive and the richness of the word increases. An example of the first type or a dead metaphor is the word *gay* which originally meant merry but now is almost exclusively used to represent something pertaining to homosexuality. The term *bug*, which originally denoted an insect, but now can also be used to represent a germ, a computer software error, a covert listening device for spying, or the verb to bother or annoy someone as in 'don't bug me.' All these meanings convey the notion of a small thing that is usually unwanted and/or unpleasant.

If we want to use the creation of metaphors as the mechanism by which a spoken language evolves, then we should have some explanation of how metaphors are created. Books have been written on this subject but I will confine myself to a mechanism for the emergence of metaphors based on the Extended Mind Model. A word acts as an attractor for all the percepts one associates with that word. Consider a new situation or experience where one does not yet have a word or concept to represent it but it reminds one of a similar situation or experience for which a word already does exist. One is able to 'move across' the meaning of the existing word to describe, represent or, more literally, to re-present the new situation or experience. The term *metaphor* is derived from the Greek work *metaphorein* where 'meta' means across and 'phorein' means to move. The meaning of metaphorein really hit home for me one day in Toronto, one of the most multicultural cities in the world, where I saw a moving van operated by a Greek fellow with the word Metaphorein blazoned across the side of his van.

When a word is used metaphorically both the use of the word in its original context and in its new metaphorical context become part of a newly minted attractor attracting an even richer set of percepts than the original word. Let us illustrate this idea with the word *bug*, used originally to denote an insect. The meaning of the word bug splits into multiple meanings because the use of the metaphor bug becomes a concept with many different attributes, one being annoying, and another being small or petty. When the mind is searching for a way to describe a situation in which a small and annoying thing such as a computer software glitch the word bug as in insect or germ leaps to mind and a new metaphor is born.

There is a story told of how the word bug became associated with a computer glitch. In the early days of vacuum tube computers, one of the experimental computers was not performing as expected and after an exhaustive search it was discovered that a bug in the form of an insect was causing an interruption in the flow of electricity. The success of the use of the word bug to describe a computer glitch does not depend on whether or not the story is true, but rather on how well the term describes the annoyance created by a computer glitch.

The way in which metaphors arise and subtly change the meaning of a word can be likened to the accidental way in which a gene of a biological species changes either by a mistake in the reproduction of a chromosome or by the accidental hit of radiation which randomly changes the structure of the gene. The use of a word to create a metaphor is accidental and depends solely on the creativity and mindset of the creator of the

metaphor. Once this happens, however, the word changes and its meaning even in its original context changes. Worden describes a word as
'represented in the brain by a package of information that embodies
that word's sound, syntax and meaning' (2000, 354). As a word is used
metaphorically to describe a new situation it adds a new context in
which it can be used and, hence, its meaning changes. Each of the
meanings of a word may be thought of as a facet of that word. Although
only one facet of a word is used in a sentence the other meanings of the
word, that is, the other facets, interact with the primary facet being
used and enrich that word and slightly change the meaning of the
sentence. Poets are masters of making use of the multiple meanings of
words in the lines that they compose just as the Impressionists were
masters of juxtaposing colours beside each other and thereby changing
their effect.

The metaphoric use of words and the way in which their various
meaning interact can be likened to the web of symbol-symbol relationships that Deacon (1997, 136) introduced to describe syntax. But the
web of symbol-symbol relationships between different meanings of the
same word creates a semantic web of sorts which I suggest is the mechanism that Worden was asking for in his quest to understand the evolution of words and the way language as an ecological system changes.

Another example of the way in which the metaphoric use of words
expands and changes the language is the way that nouns become verbs
(telephones, televise, radio), or verbs become nouns (sleep, run, walk,
eats) or the noun orient (east) becomes the verb (orients) becomes the
noun orientation becomes the verb orientate (perhaps not grammatically correct by some standards but gaining in common use so that
many native speakers will accept it as correct). And finally there is the
example of supracriticality with words that we gave above in which the
Latin words *sentire*, the French word *sens*, and the English word *sense*
expanded into at least seventy-five different words.

Worden's metaphor of language as an ecology has some interesting
implications worthy of pursuit. Let me recapitulate his original statements: 'Language change can be regarded as a form of evolution – not
the evolution of language itself, but of the individual words which constitutes the language … Each language is an ecology, and each word is
one species in the ecology' (2000, 353). I presume by this excerpt that

Worden meant by a language, one of the many world languages such as English, German, Yiddish, or Sanskrit. But I believe an additional meaning is possible in that the language used by carpenters or the language of physicists or that of brain surgeons, rocket scientists, painters, baseball players, or politicians is each a separate ecology, so that a language like English is an ecology of ecologies.

# 9 Phylogeny or the Evolutionary History of Language

In this chapter we will focus on Tinbergen's fourth 'why,' namely, the evolutionary history of language. This discussion will entail a recapitulation of some of the points we covered when we addressed the first three 'why's' of function, mechanism, and ontogeny. We will review a number of approaches and identify areas of contention where the different models clash in significant ways. We will attempt to resolve some of these issues within the linguistic community by making use of the Extended Mind Model for the evolution of notated language, as was presented in chapter 3. The major issues to be addressed are contained in the following seven questions:

1 Was the origin and evolution of language a purely Darwinian process governed by natural selection acting on the human genome?
2 How have co-evolutionary processes affected the emergence and evolution of language?
3 Was the evolution of language strictly a genetic phenomenon or did it include cultural evolution or memetics as well?
4 In what order did the mechanisms of speech – phonology, phonemics, auditory analysis, lexicography, and syntax – appear?
5 Did the emergence and evolution of language occur gradually or catastrophically, and if language is an organism, what role did autocatalysis play in its emergence and origin?
6 What role, if any, did emergence theory or complexity play in the origin of language?

7  Are the questions related to the origin of language subject to scientific inquiry as defined by Popper in that one can formulate propositions that can be falsified?

## Question 1:
**Was the origin and evolution of language a purely Darwinian process governed by natural selection acting on the human genome?**

There is no uniform answer to this question within the linguistic community. There are almost as many models of how language originated and evolved as there are scholars addressing this question. Some linguists are highly sceptical of a Darwinian explanation of the origin of language while some are extremely supportive of the idea and believe that all of the features of language, including the Universal Grammar postulated by Chomsky, can be explained in terms of biological natural selection operating on the hominid genome.

Then there is a middle ground, in which I place myself, of those who take the position that biological natural selection played an important, perhaps even a dominant, role in the origin of language but that this alone does not (or cannot) explain all aspects of the phenomenon. Even Darwin admitted the possibilities of other mechanisms when he wrote, 'I am convinced that natural selection has been the main but not the exclusive means of modification, (1859/1968, 69). Those in the middle group which we encountered in the last chapter accept natural selection as the mechanism responsible for the emergence of language but maintain that there were two forms of natural selection operating, one biological acting on the hominid genome and the other cultural operating on language itself. We will examine their approaches in the question immediately following this one when we examine the role of co-evolution in the origin and evolution of language, but for now we turn to those who debate the role of biological natural selection.

Perhaps the most prominent sceptic of the natural selection approach is Noam Chomsky, who maintains that natural selection can explain certain things but not the origin of speech: 'Evolutionary theory appears to have very little to say about speciation, or about any kind of innovation.

It can explain how you get a different distribution of qualities that are already present, but does not say much about how new qualities can emerge' (1982, 23).

Sharing Chomsky's scepticism vis-à-vis a Darwinian explanation of language is David Premack, who notes that 'It is not easy to picture the scenario that would confer selective fitness on, specifically, syntactic classes and structure-dependent rules ... I challenge the reader to reconstruct the scenario that would confer selective fitness on recursiveness ... Human language is an embarrassment for evolutionary theory because it is vastly more powerful than one can account for in terms of selective fitness' (1986, 132–3).

Pinker and Bloom, of the Chomsky school of linguistics, are nevertheless, strong supporters of the notion that the emergence of the Universal Grammar can be explained in terms of biological natural selection: 'Human language, like other specialized biological systems, evolved by natural selection. Our conclusion is based on two facts that we would think would be entirely uncontroversial: language shows signs of complex design for the communication of propositional structures, and the only explanation for the organs with complex design is the process of natural selection' I completely agree with their first 'fact,' but the second 'fact' seems to contain a priori their conclusion and, hence, to my mind is circular. The whole crux of the matter comes down to whether or not the second 'fact' is true. Pinker and Bloom seem to hedge their bet a bit, but in the end they conclude the emergence of language is a Darwinian process: 'While there are no doubt aspects of the system that can only be explained by historical, developmental, or random processes, the most likely explanation for the complex structure of the language faculty is that it is a design imposed on neural circuitry as a response to evolutionary pressures' (1990, 48).

Pinker and Bloom's assumption that language is an organ or a module in the brain has been criticized by Deacon and Tomasello:

In summary, images of the working brain doing language tasks show a hierarchical organization, which correlates both with time and with the hierarchic-segmental organization of sentences, and a segregation with respect to the physical form, presentation, or manipulation of the signal. They also show that the classic language areas are not unitary modules, but

rather complicated clusters of areas, each with different component functions. This is not consistent with the view that there is one self-contained
'language organ' in the brain, even one dedicated only to grammar. If
language had evolved as a consequence of the addition of a language module in the human brain, we should not expect such an extensive distribution of linguistics processes in diverse cerebral cortical areas. If a grammar
module exists, it is not localized to one cortical region, since subfunctions
associated with grammatical and syntactic processes are found in both the
anterior and the posterior regions. (Deacon 1997, 97–8)

The basic problem with genetically based modularity approaches – especially when they address uniquely human and socially constituted artifacts
and social practices – is that they tend to skip from the first page of the
story, genetics, to the last page of the story, current human cognition, without going through any of the intervening pages. These theorists are thus in
many cases leaving out of account formative elements in both historical
and ontogenetic time that intervene between the human genotype and
phenotype. (Tomasello 1999, 204)

Another challenge to the notion that the whole of language including
syntax is a result of natural selection of the human genome is made by
Alison Wray, who argues that the 'grammar we have ... misaligns with
our communication needs, giving us grammatical sentences that are
incomprehensible (e.g. centre-embedded ones) [and] ungrammatical
sentences that are perfectly comprehensible (e.g. many of those violat-
ing PRO-drop, subjacency, etc.)' (2000, 290–1).

Wray submits that 'plausible explanations for the origin of grammar'
include the notion that 'word-sized concepts and referentiality emerged
as a means of organising creative thought and planning, the hierarchical
structured grammar evolved as a way of better marshaling thought ...
[and] grammatical language was first used not for interpersonal communication but for "talking to oneself"' as a way of depositing 'information
during complex thought' (ibid., 291). Her arguments parallel those of
the Extended Mind Model, as well as those of Deacon (1997).

Despite Pinker and Bloom's conviction and enthusiasm for a Darwinian explanation of language, which is shared by many other linguists,
this hypothesis is still an open question. As Knight points out, 'Modern

Darwinism seeks to harmonize research into human life with the rest of scientific knowledge. This project depends, however, on accounting for the emergence of symbolic culture, including speech, a system of communication unparalleled elsewhere in biology. While Darwinians confidently expect an explanation, it has to be admitted, that to date, no compelling account has been advanced' (Knight 1998b, 68).

Bickerton presents a third option, based on Baldwinian evolution (1896), of how some of the properties of language might have become incorporated in the human genome which is different than the mechanisms proposed by Pinker and Bloom and those that make use of complexity or emergence theory. The mechanism by which language could effect genetic evolution is through the Baldwin effect by which certain biological changes are selected for as a result of behavioural changes. If language capability has a selective advantage then language capabilities will improve over time genetically, as those adapting successfully to their environment will have more prodigy: 'Baldwin suggested that learning and behavioral flexibility can play a role in amplifying and biasing natural selection because these abilities enable individuals to modify the context of natural selection that affects their future kin. Behavioral flexibility enables organisms to move into niches that differ from those their ancestors occupied, with the consequence that succeeding generations will face a new set of selection pressures' (Deacon 1997, 322).

Bickerton uses the Baldwin effect to argue that as hominids' behaviour changed as a result of the use of protolanguage it 'unleashed a cascade of consequences including the development of grammatical morphology and parsing algorithms that were incorporated into the human genome by Baldwinian evolution' (2000, 282). Bickerton then suggests that Baldwinian evolution would have instantiated similar algorithms in the human nervous system. Thus, Bickerton has developed a hypothesis for the natural selection of UG via Baldwinian evolution as desearched by Deacon: 'Baldwin's theory explains how behaviors can affect evolution, but without the necessity of claiming that responses to environmental demands acquired during one's lifetime could be passed directly on to one's offspring (a discredited mechanism for evolutionary change proposed by the early nineteenth century French naturalist Jean Baptiste Lamarck)' (1997, 322).

While 'no compelling accounts have been advanced' (including my own) to explain the origin of language, there are still many fascinating models which will, no doubt, contribute to our final understanding of the origin of language and, hence, are worthy of serious consideration. We will review these proposals and critique and compare them with the Extended Mind Model of chapter 3 as we address the other questions in this chapter. We next consider the role of co-evolution.

## Question 2:
## How have co-evolutionary processes affected the emergence and evolution of language?

Biological systems are intrinsically non-linear, and as a consequence evolutionary processes are intrinsically co-evolutionary as no system can evolve in a vacuum. As an organism evolves and interacts with its environment, the other organisms respond in kind with their own changes and co-evolve with the organism under consideration. The same kind of process takes place among the various organs and components of an organism which also undergo a process of co-evolution. Bipedalism, for instance, led to many other anatomical and cognitive changes in the hominid line. Both forms of co-evolution – inter-organism and intra-organism – have affected the origin and development of human speech. The notion of co-evolution, as we will see, helps to resolve many of the controversies and dichotomies that characterize this field of study.

*The Co-evolution of the Human Capacity for Language and Language per se*

The idea of the co-evolution of the human genome with language arises from the notion that human language may be regarded as an organism with its own evolutionary dynamic, an idea that dates all the way back to Darwin (1871) and has more recently been explicitly advocated by Deacon (1997) and Christiansen (1994). 'Following Darwin, I propose to view natural language as a kind of beneficial parasite – i.e. a nonobligate symbiant – that confers some selective advantage onto its human hosts without whom it cannot survive.' Darwin's expression of the co-evolution of language and the intellectual power of humans can be found in chapters 3 and 21 respectively of *The Descent of Man* (1871), from which the following are excerpts:

> As the voice was used more and more, the vocal organs would have been strengthened and perfected through the principle of the inherited effects

of use; and this would have reacted on the power of speech. But the relation between the continued use of language and the development of the brain has no doubt been far more important. The mental powers in some early progenitor of man must have been more highly developed than in any existing ape, before even the most imperfect form of speech could have come into use; but we may confidently believe that the continued use and advancement of this power would have reacted on the mind itself, by enabling and encouraging it to carry on long trains of thought. A complex train of thought can no more be carried on without the aid of words, whether spoken or silent, than a long calculation without the use of figures or algebra.

A great stride in the development of the intellect will have followed, as soon as the half-art and half-instinct of language came into use; for the continued use of language will have reacted on the brain and produced an inherited effect; and this again will have reacted on the improvement of language. As Mr Chauncey Wright ('On the Limits of Natural Selection,' in the North American Review, Oct., 1870, p. 295) has well remarked, the largeness of the brain in man relatively to his body, compared with the lower animals, may be attributed in chief part to the early use of some simple forms of language, that wonderful engine which affixes signs to all sorts of objects and qualities, and excites trains of thought which would never arise from the mere impression of the senses, or if they did arise could not be followed out. The higher intellectual powers of man, such as those of ratiocination, abstraction, self-consciousness, &c., probably follow from the continued improvement and exercise of the other mental faculties.

In chapter 8 we reviewed how the idea that language could be treated as an independent organism has been used to explain that human language evolved in such a way as to make it easy for children to acquire language at a very early stage in their cognitive development. Christiansen (1994) has also used this notion to explain the mystery of why it is that of all the possible forms that the syntax of human language could have taken that the actual set that emerged took the characteristics of the Universal Grammar. The Chomsky school claims that the characteristics of UG are an innate part of our genetic inheritance and the particular choice was arbitrary: 'In the evolution of the language faculty many "arbitrary" constraints may have been selected simply because they defined parts of a standardized communicative code in the brains of some critical mass of speakers ... To be sure, some combination of historical accidents, epiphenomena of other cognitive processes, and neurodevelopmental constraints must have played a large role in the breaking of symmetry that was needed to get the fixation process running away in one direction or another. But it still must have been selection that resulted in the convention then becoming innately entrenched' (Pinker and Bloom 1990, 722).

A fellow Chomskyite, Ray Jackendoff, is cognizant of what a large leap Pinker and Bloom made by proposing that UG evolved solely in the human genome: 'Sometimes it is objected that positing an innate basis for language acquisition is a counsel of despair or resignation, just pushing the problem downstairs into the genes. But one might justifiably have said the same of the theory of gravitation in Newton's time: it postulated an occult, invisible, inexplicable force that physicists are still trying to explain' (2002, 84).

The effects of gravity can be observed directly, measured, and precise predictions can be made. One example was the prediction of the existence of the planet Pluto before it was observed directly by telescope. Unfortunately, the UG and LAD hypotheses have not made any dramatic predictions, and as we saw in chapter 5, there are many exceptions to UG which led us to question just how universal is UG. Rather than comparing UG and the LAD to gravity which can be directly measured and observed, the UG and LAD would be better characterized as more like quarks or the strings of String Theory. Quarks have been posited to explain the symmetries in the behaviour of elementary particles, but according to the theory one can never observe an isolated quark because quarks only come bundled together with other quarks within the elementary particles of which they are the constituent parts. The theory, therefore, uses quarks to explain certain regularities, but does not permit an empirical detection of them directly. Strings are even more removed from phenomena and are pure theoretical constructs, as are UG and the LAD.

There are a number of alternatives to the Pinker-Bloom hypothesis that UG is a result of the biological evolution of the human genome. Christiansen (Ms. in preparation, 9) explains the universality of the characteristics of human language by simply applying natural selection to language and treating language as an organism which in order to survive had to evolve in such a way as 'to fit the human learning and processing mechanism.' Deacon develops a position very similar to that of Christiansen: 'Languages are far more like living organisms than like mathematical proofs. The most basic principle guiding their design is not communicative utility but reproduction – theirs and ours. So, the proper tool for analyzing language structures may not be to discover how best to model them as axiomatic rule systems but rather to study them the way we study organism structure: in evolutionary terms. Languages are social and cultural entities that have evolved with respect to the forces of selection imposed by human users' (1997, 110).

### The Co-evolution of the Functions and Mechanisms of Language

When we speak of the co-evolution of the functions and mechanisms of language we are talking about the intra-organism co-evolution of different aspects of language development. As has been pointed out by Michael Studdert-Kennedy, this use of the term *co-evolution* is somewhat misleading because 'coevolution properly refers to the evolutionary matching of independent genetic systems – clover and bumble-bee, pinon jay and pine nut, cheetah and gazelle. We do not refer to the coevolution of seeing and the eye or of hearing and the ear because, like language and its physiology, they are not independent: they are directly related as function to structure' (2000a, 128).

Having been duly warned of this distinction I will nevertheless continue to make use of the term co-evolution in the context of discussing the role of functions and mechanisms in the evolution of language. The emergence of language, as we have already suggested, can be thought of as the co-evolution of two organisms, the human host and natural language, where Christiansen (1994) identifies natural language as a 'beneficial parasite, a nonobligate symbiant.' Having clarified this point I do not believe the reader will confuse 'the relation between two aspects of a single process, between morphology and behavior, structure and function,' which was Studdert-Kennedy's (2000a, 128) concern with the use of the term of co-evolution which I will be making use of in this section.

There are three aspects of intra-organism co-evolution of language that we have already alluded to in the course of this study: (1) The co-evolution of the set of functions of language and the set of mecha-nisms that make language possible; (2) the co-evolution of the various mechanism that make language possible; and (3) the co-evolution of the cognitive and communicative functions of language.

## THE CO-EVOLUTION OF THE FUNCTIONALITY
## AND MECHANISMS OF LANGUAGE

As has already been pointed out, language would never have emerged unless it served some function, and yet there had to have been some available mechanism language for it to have emerged in the first place. The mechanism might not have been originally intended to serve as a medium for language, but once this process began improvements and enlargements of the mechanism(s) would have been selected for which, in turn, increased the range of the function of language. In other words, the set of functions and the set of mechanisms bootstrapped each other into existence and began the process of the co-evolution of the func-tions and mechanisms of language.

## THE CO-EVOLUTION OF THE MECHANISMS OF LANGUAGE

I prefer to consider the co-evolution of the mechanisms of language when we address Question 4 which deals with the order in which the mechanisms of language appeared, and where I hope to be able to dem-onstrate that the mechanisms that make language possible co-evolved and bootstrapped each other into existence.

## THE CO-EVOLUTION OF THE COMMUNICATIVE
## AND COGNITIVE FUNCTIONALITY OF LANGUAGE

It is almost axiomatic to assert that one of the intentions of language is communication, but what about the role of language in thought and thought in language? We have already encountered Darwin's (1871) position that thought is one of the functions of language. Andrew Carstairs-McCarthy observes that 'language could not exist without some medium of expression ... [which] must surely be subordinate to what is expressed (it is generally thought), so that what was really essen-tial for the evolution of human language must have been the cognitive developments which gave humans something to say ... But where did the drive for language come from?' (1998, 289–90).

Carstairs-McCarthy rejects the simple answer that it was due to the increased brain size, because he does not see how this would have 'led to the development of a system for communication or mental representation with precisely the characteristics that human language has' (ibid.).

My approach to this problem is to suggest that, before there was speech or verbal language, hominid mental processes were percept-based and that with the emergence of verbal language mental activity became abstract and concept-based. Out first words were our first concepts, and therefore, I propose that communication and the representation of abstract thought occurred co-terminously. As our vocabulary increased so did the complexity of our thought processes and, vice versa, as our thought processes became more complex we invented new words and more sophisticated grammatical structures. The only evidence that I can offer to support my argument here is to ask the reader to consider the contemporary and historical processes whereby new words are created as new discoveries are made and how the mastery of a technical language and the concepts that are embedded within them have led to new discoveries.

The invention of the concept of zero by Hindu mathematicians some two thousand years ago led to the term *sunya*. Sunya, which means leave a space in Sanskrit, arose from notating the results of abacus calculations when there was, for example, a result like 5 hundreds, no tens, and 3 ones. This was notated as 5 sunya (leave a space) 3 or 503. Sunya was translated by the Arab mathematicians into *sifr* – literally leave a space in Arabic – and passed on to the Italians who wrote sifr as cipher and then as zero. The term *cipher* came to have two meanings, namely, zero and a secret code. The latter meaning arose because the Church forbade the use of the Arabic number system and zero (or cipher). As a consequence Italian merchants used Arabic numerals as a secret code. Once the concept of zero in the form of the word sunya was formulated, it was not long before negative numbers and algebra followed. Negative numbers were represented by placing the sunya sign over the symbol for positive number. The sunya sign was also used to represent the unknown in an algebraic equation.

The intimate relationship of thought and language is contained in the Sapir-Whorf hypothesis, which does not speak to the origin of language but rather the way in which language influences thought. According to this hypothesis language sets up a set of categories or a mental coordinate system through which the world of senses is perceived and which constrains the way in which phenomenon are conceptualized. If words were our first and primary concepts, as we have suggested, then the Sapir-Whorf hypothesis would be a natural consequence of the emergence of language. But the relationship between words, concepts, and percepts is bi-directional. What is perceived influences what terms or words are invented and what concepts are conceived. At the same time, the words available in a lexicon influence what is perceived. Tropical people have no words for ice and snow, temperate zone people have a few, and the Inuit have many.

On the basis of these observations I would like to argue that the cognitive and communicative functionality of language co-evolved and bootstrapped each other into existence. Let us assume that the social-communication function was the initial impetus for the emergence of the first protolanguage. This development would have resulted in an improvement in the cognitive capacity of the first language users whether it was an increase in the power of conceptualization (as I claim), an increase in the ability of symbolic representation (as Deacon claims 1997), or an improvement in the power of sequential learning and processing (as Christiansen claims 1994). The increased cognitive competency would have improved the social-communicative skills of the first speakers and conferred upon them a reproductive advantage. One could reverse the argument and claim that those hominids who first improved their cognitive skills, perhaps through tool-making, non-linguistic social interactions and/or social intelligence, or mimetic communication improved their power of conceptualization, symbolic representation, or sequential learning and processing which made it possible for them to invent language and improve their social-communicative skills.

It is impossible for us to determine because of the remoteness of the events which came first, the language skills, the social-communicative skills, or the cognitive skills, but one can argue that language, social-communicative skills, and cognitive skills do form an autocatalytic set of skills that reinforce each other (or bootstrap each other into existence) and which confer upon those hominids that possess them a reproductive advantage. Both language and social-communicative skills are part of culture. Language is a cultural phenomenon and culture is grounded in language. It, therefore, should be no surprise to the reader to learn that language and culture have co-evolved. We will revisit the autocatalysis of language, social skills, and cognition when we address the role of culture in the evolution of language in chapter 12.

## Question 3:
## Was the evolution of language strictly a genetic phenomenon or did it include cultural evolution or memetics as well?

Jean Aitchison frames the question before us in the following manner: 'Perhaps the best known linguistic dichotomy is the "nature-nurture" controversy, a long standing debate on whether language is "natural' or "nurtured" … It is sometimes characterized as a distinction between "hard-wired" and "soft-wired" abilities or between "instinct" and "learning"' (1998, 18). Citing Lenneberg, Aitchison makes the point that 'language is neither "natural" or "nurtured" behaviour. Instead, children acquire it "naturally" at a particular stage in their development, provided they are properly "nurtured," that is exposed to sufficient linguistic data at the relevant time: Lenneberg (1967) labeled the phenomenon "maturationally controlled behaviour"' (ibid.).

Pinker and Bloom, however, come down on the nature-anatomical rather than nurture-cultural side of this question: 'It would be natural, then, to expect everyone to agree that human language is the product of Darwinian natural selection. The only successful account of the origin of complex biological structure is the theory of natural selection, the view that the differential reproductive success associated with heritable variation is the primary organizing force in the evolution of organisms' (1990, 50–1).

The position of Pinker and Bloom is extreme as it ignores the possible effects of culture and assumes that natural selection operates only at the genetic level and not on the language itself or the culture in which the language is embedded. Many linguists now acknowledge that the evolution of language has both a genetic and cultural component to it. In Question 2 (above), in dealing with co-evolution we encountered the ideas of Christiansen (1994) and Deacon (1997) who posit that language, an integral part of human culture, can also be considered an organism subject to natural selection. This same thought is echoed by James Hurford, who reminds us that 'languages evolve, and the human language capacity evolved, and that the two kinds of evolutionary processes are distinct in their mechanisms, but intertwined in their effects' (1998, 302). Hurford suggests that linguists are more and more adopting this position and identifies 'a movement in the late 1990s away from a focus on the genetic evolution of the innate Language Acquisition Device towards accounts invoking cultural and linguistic evolution as well' (2000, 219). Carstairs-McCarthy makes a similar point, when he writes: 'The evolution of language has involved two kinds of change, which distinguish humans from other animals. On the one hand are the technological, social and cultural advances which have accompanied it, whether as causes or effects. On the other hand are the anatomical changes which make speech possible, especially the descent of the larynx ... Which of these came first? That question oversimplifies the issue; behavioural and anatomical changes must have taken place in parallel over a long period of time' (1998, 289).

Donald's thesis that speech arose from mimetic communication contains within it the hypothesis that the evolution of language was both genetic and cultural. 'Simpler and slower than speech, "mimesis" prefigured language in being an adaptation both cognitive and cultural' (Knight 1998a, 14). The mechanism of mimesis or imitation is a purely cultural phenomenon. As reported in chapter 8, Donald reminds us that language is not preprogrammed and does not 'self-install or self-trigger' but requires 'cultural programming.'

The tradition that language is a cultural phenomena can be traced back to the time before linguists worried about evolution per se – to scholars like de Saussure who made a distinction between *langue*, as a system and a cultural institution, and *parole*, the practice of a language by an individual. De Saussure considered that 'languages were inherently collective and consensual communication systems' (cited by Donald 1998, 50). This distinction of language being a shared property of a community as well as the property of the individual who belongs to the community has been an enduring paradigm of the linguistic community. Studdert-Kennedy finds 'human speech introduced a new code, a new physical medium of transmission, and a shift from a largely

genetic to a largely cultural inheritance' (1998, 202). If speech introduced a shift in inheritance largely from genetics to culture, then one
should largely look to culture as the locus of evolutionary change and
not genetics. The emergence of verbal language itself was in all
likelihood a biological genetic phenomenon but language, once it
emerged, became subject to natural selection, as has been argued by
Christiansen (1994) and Deacon (1997), and its evolution was affected
by cultural phenomenon.

Tomasello suggests that biological genetic evolution allowed a species-
unique cognitive skill of joint attention to emerge and that with this one
cognitive advance, culture was able to take over to create the specific
cognitive skills that are verbal language. He describes a mechanism
whereby culture and language change by variation, modification, and
accumulation through sociogenesis:

> There simply has not been enough time for normal processes of biological
> evolution involving genetic variation and natural selection to have created,
> one by one, each of the cognitive skills necessary for modern humans to
> invent and maintain complex tool-use industries and technologies, complex
> forms of symbolic communication and representation, and complex social
> organizations and institutions. And the puzzle is only magnified if we take
> seriously current research in paleoanthropology suggesting that (a) for all
> but the last two million years the human lineage showed no signs of any-
> thing other than typical great ape cognitive skills, and (b) the first dramatic
> signs of species-unique cognitive skills emerged only in the last quarter of a
> million years with modern Homo sapiens.
>
> There is only one possible solution to this puzzle. That is, there is only one
> known biological mechanism that could bring about these kinds of changes
> in behavior and cognition in so short a time ... This biological mechanism is
> social or cultural transmission, which works on time scales many orders of
> magnitude faster than those of organic evolution. Broadly speaking, cultural
> transmission is a moderately common evolutionary process that enables
> individual organisms to save much time and effort, not to mention risk, by
> exploiting the already existing knowledge and skills of conspecifics ... One
> reasonable hypothesis, then, is that the amazing suite of cognitive skills and
> products displayed by modern humans is the result of some sort of species-
> unique mode or modes of cultural transmission. (1999, 2–4)

According to Tomasello, cultural traditions and artifacts accumulate modifications over time as lessons learned are passed on and used by others to make improvements in what he calls 'the ratchet effect': 'The process of cumulative cultural evolution requires not only creative invention but also, just as importantly, faithful social transmission that can work as a ratchet to prevent slippage backwards – so that the newly invented artifact or practice preserves its new and improved form at least somewhat faithfully until a further modification or improvement comes along' (1999, 5).

**Question 4:**
**In what order did the mechanisms of speech – phonology, phonemics, auditory analysis, lexicography, and syntax – appear?**

One of the interesting questions that remains unanswered, and is perhaps unanswerable, is in what order did the mechanisms of speech appear? In what order did vocalizing, phonemic articulation, phonemic generativity, auditory processing, lexicography, syntax, gesture, and prosody arise? Logic dictates that vocalization, phonemic articulation, and phonemic generativity must occur in the order listed since one has to first be able to vocalize to be able to create a large range of phonemes and one must be able to create individual phonemes before one can combine them into multi-phonemic sounds, which we have termed *phonemic generativity*. It is still an open question as to whether the first words were even vocalized or, as some believe, signed by hand gestures and only later vocalized. Putting this question aside one still is left with the question of whether syntax arose with a lexicon or whether speech at first consisted of a simple lexicon without syntax, as has been suggested by Bickerton.

The ordering suggested by John Locke is as follows: 'While it seems that vocalizing leads to talking, it also appears that talking leads to grammar ... In light of the fact that all normal human languages are spoken, it makes sense to consider the possibility that social sound-making and talking preceded the development of grammar, and that linguistic grammars represent a functional adaptation that enhanced the efficiency, utility or flexibility of vocal communication ... I submit that our evolutionary ancestors evolved a capability for utterance analysis – a critical component of grammar – in response to a rapidly increasing need to store and manipulate vocal forms that, until that point, had been poorly analyzed at the level of phonological segment' (1998, 193–4 and 198). Locke's position vis-à-vis vocalization and speech is similar to that of Donald, who also suggests that mimetic vocalization led to speech, and on the relation of lexicography and syntax it is also similar to that of Bickerton: 'Syntax could not have come into existence until there was a sizable vocabulary whose units could be organized into complex structures' (1996, 51). Studdert-Kennedy concurs: 'The necessity for hierarchical organisation discourages the notion that syntax might have emerged before the combinatorial mechanisms of phonology were well established' (2000b, 161).

In the transition from mimetic communication to spoken language there had to be a time in which phonology had an opportunity to evolve. This could not happen suddenly because of the need for phonemic generativity to develop – the syntax of combining phonemes to form words as opposed to syntax (or lexical generativity) of combining words to form sentences or propositions. When a bifurcation occurs the earlier form remains. The first spoken words to appear, therefore, were combined with the elements of mimetic communication. This explains why when we speak today we use gesture, tonality, hand signals, and body language as part of the speech act. The ratio of verbal to mimetic communication slowly increased with time. But once the idea of conceptualization emerged, humans then had a mental tool for creating more words and concepts and, hence, a selection pressure to create more types or variations of sounds arose which led to the evolution of phonological articulation or generativity. Until the first word and concepts were created, there would have been no motivation for creating the possibility of phonemic generativity. Once humans possessed the capability of phonemic generativity, new words could be created so that verbalization (lexical generation) and phonemic generativity must have co-evolved. And once the number of words that were generated reached a certain critical mass, then lexical syntax must have emerged and co-evolved with lexicography and phonemic generativity.

An interesting model for ordering has been developed by Carstairs-McCarthy, for whom 'two aspects of human language remain mysterious: its lexical elaboration and the nature of its syntactical structure' (1998,

290). For lexical elaboration he posits the existence of a synonym avoidance strategy of hominids, the Principle of Contrast, by which every call or signal has one unique meaning. He then suggests that first came the anatomical changes that allowed hominids to increase the number of calls or signals they could create in which each new call by the Principle of Contrast could represent a new meaning. The larger the usable vocabulary the hominid or human could deploy, the greater survival advantage he would enjoy over his rivals with a smaller vocabulary.

One can justify this assumption of Carstairs-McCarthy's with Ashby's Law of Requisite Variety. If one wishes to model a system accurately the model must contain the requisite variety of the system being modelled. Survival depends on carrying a mental model of one's environment; the richer one's vocabulary the richer is one's model and the more accurately it models the environment. As the number of signals with unique meanings increases inevitably, Carstairs-McCarthy claims, 'the expansion process would run up against memory limitations ... [if one] presupposes that our ancestors had to store in their memory whole calls ... There was an alternative, however: to store just short calls ... and analyse longer calls as composites of these' (1998, 292). And this, Carstairs-McCarthy claims, was the motivation for the emergence of syntax. He further proposes that the structure of human syntax was modelled on that of syllabic formation: 'The neural control mechanisms which govern syllabic structure, having been co-opted for syntax, evolved independently in that role, but left its traces of their origin in certain otherwise mysterious characteristics of human language syntax' (ibid., 294). He concludes by observing that one of the most exciting aspects of this scenario 'is the hint that certain fundamental aspects of language, not only syntactic but semantic, may be mere byproducts of a change in vocal tract anatomy' (ibid., 295).

One criticism that can be levelled at Carstairs-McCarthy's model comes from Deacon's work. Deacon is position is that the transition from autonomous animal communication to that of intentional, symbolic hominid communication was discontinuous at the cognitive level and that the emergence of changes of the vocal tract were a consequence not a cause of language evolution: 'Treating animal calls and gestures as subsets of language not only reverses the sequence of evolutionary precedence, it also inverts their functional dependence as well.

Animal calls or human nonlinguistic communication do not require words but words seem to require nonlinguistic communication, at least they did until the emergence of writing' (1997, 53). Deacon does not deny the role of primate vocalization as a pre-adaptation of Homo vocalization but sees the emergence of symbolic communication as the first step followed by the expansion of vocal capabilities: 'The superimposition of intentional cortical motor behaviors over autonomous subcortical vocal behavior is, in a way, an externalized model of a neural relationship that is internalized in the production of human speech. It graphically portrays the functional bridge that links the vocal communication of primates to the speech of humans. The evolution of speech effectively occurred at this neurological interface' (ibid., 244).

Carstairs-McCarthy's model is not unlike that of Dunbar and of Bickerton, who argue that initially there was a form of protolanguage with meaningful words but no syntax and no ability to transmit or represent abstract thoughts. I am sympathetic to their position, but find that a word by itself represents a concept. It follows then that our first words represented abstract thoughts and that some sort of primitive syntax existed from the first instances of verbal language or perhaps the first utterances in the protolanguage consisted of a single word. When babies first begin to talk their first utterances are sounds and then single words. This is a case where ontogeny seems to be recapitulating phylogeny. Actually it is more likely a case where by 'language ontogeny may parallel language phylogeny not because the course is coded in the genes, as recapitulation would have it, but it is implicit in constraints of hominid neuroanatomy and learning mechanisms, and in the logic of the development sequence from simple to complex' (Studdert-Kennedy 2000a, 124). In 1922 Watter Garstang postulated that 'ontogeny does not recapitulate phylogeny: it creates it' (1922, 82). It is not that development imitates evolution but rather development creates evolution.

If language began as single word utterances then with the increase in the size of the lexicon and the complexity of thought expressed, a primitive syntax would have emerged that would have then co-evolved with the lexicon. Given that syntax is about the generativity of propositions from a lexicon of words, then a possible justification of the existence of a syntax at the same time that the first vocabulary emerged can be found in the work of Merlin Donald (1991). Hominids would have had a generative capacity, he contends, from their toolmaking, social intelligence, and mimetic communication: 'Mimesis, Donald argues, established the fundamentals of intentional expression in hominids, and laid the basis on which natural selection could act to engender the cognitive demand and neuroanatomical machinery essential to the emergence of words and of a combinatorial syntax as vehicles for symbolic thought and communication' (Knight, Studdert-Kennedy, and Hurford 2000a, 9). Christiansen's (1994) work hints at the possibility of some form of a protosyntax existing at the time of the emergence of the first lexicon. He suggests that 'hierarchical structured behavior' may have served as a pre-adaptation for syntax and language.

Dunbar (1996, 1998), Power (1998, 2000), Dessalles (1998, 2000), and Worden (1998) have maintained that hominid and primate social intelligence created the syntactical-like reasoning power that human language requires. If their arguments are correct, then as soon as *Homo sapiens* created a lexicon they would have been able to syntactilize their utterances. Once conceptual thinking co-emerges with the first words, then the ability to create a syntax can evolve culturally rather than biologically. Once a critical mass of lexicon develops and the human mind is able to think conceptually, the ideas of syntax and placing words in an order to convey an intended meaning becomes feasible without there being a necessary change in the human genome, as has been suggested by Bickerton, who 'puts the conceptual structure associated with lexical items as the basis of syntax. Syntactical organization is largely projected from information stored in individual lexical items. In Bickerton's evolutionary scenario, there was one critical neuroanatomical change which made syntax possible, the establishment of a connection between two pre-existing systems. The two pre-existing systems were a system of "one-word" signs, with a significant and a signifie, but restricted to vocabulary only, and a "theta-role" system, linking general conceptual analysis of the world with social understanding of the "who did what to whom" variety' (Hurford 1998, 302).

Deacon argues 'that syntax and semantics are deeply interdependent facets of language' (1997, 100) and that, while 'breaking up language analytically into such complementary domains as syntax and semantics, noun and verb, production and comprehension, can provide useful categories for the linguist, and breaking it up according to sensory and motor functions seems easier from a global neuronal viewpoint, we should not expect that the brain's handling of language follows the logic of either of these categorical distinctions. The patterns we observe probably reflect, in a very indirect sort of way, the processing problems produced by mapping a symbolic reference system encoded in a serially presented modality onto the processing logic of an ape brain' (ibid., 298). For Deacon the breakthrough that made language possible was symbolic representation. Once this capability was achieved the mechanisms that facilitate the use of language then developed. He sees the 'greater intelligence, facile articulatory abilities, [and] prescient grammatical predispositions of children ... [as] supports for language complexity [whose evolution] must have been consequences rather than causes or prerequisites of language evolution' (1997, 44). According to Deacon, the expansion of the brain was not the cause of symbolic language but a consequence of it (ibid., 340).

In Chomsky's view the starting point for the emergence of language is syntax. To Chomsky, language arises from the generative grammar from which semantics and phonology flow. Universal Grammar is treated as 'an undecomposable "grammar box," no part of which would be of any use to hominids without all the rest' Jackendoff is critical of this approach, observing that 'the syntactocentric perspective in particular presents serious conceptual difficulties to an evolutionary story. Syntax is useless without phonology and semantics, since it generates structures that alone can play no role in communication or thought; so syntax could not have evolved first, because (in this architecture) they are simply passive handmaidens of syntax' (2002, 233).

Not only does Jackendoff regard syntactocentric thinking as a barrier to developing an evolutionary scenario for the emergence of language, but he also believes it represents a major mistake: 'I wish to take issue with a fundamental assumption embedded deep in the core of generative theory; that the free combinatoriality of language is due to a single source, localized in syntactic structure. I have come to believe that this "syntactocentric" architecture was an important mistake – perhaps historically unavoidable, but a mistake nevertheless ... language has multiple parallel sources of combinatoriality, each of which creates its own characteristic types of structure' (2002, 107). Jackendoff substitutes for the syntactocentric formulation of Chomsky a parallel architecture consisting of three components: phonological structure, conceptual structure or semantics, and syntactic structure. Jackendoff sees semantics as determining syntax rather than it being the other way around: 'The function of lexical items is to serve as interface rules, and the lexicon as a whole is to be regarded as part of the interface rules. On this view, the formal role of lexical items is not that they are "inserted" into syntactic derivations, but rather that they establish the correspondence of certain syntactic constituents with phonological and conceptual structures' (ibid., 131). Words behave like chemicals but with a much more complex valence structure that determines what syntactic structures are possible. Jackendoff's model completely revises Chomsky's model of the role of generative grammar in the evolution of language, while at the same time retaining Chomsky's basic notions of the UG and the LAD. Jackendoff rejects Chomsky's phylogeny but 'recapitulates' his ontogeny.

## Question 5:
**Did the emergence and evolution of language occur gradually or catastrophically, and if language is an organism, what role did autocatalysis play in its emergence and origin?**

*Continuity or Gradualism?*

As Chris Knight points out, 'one issue that needs to be resolved in the evolution of language is the question of whether the emergence of speech was a continuous or discontinuous process from pre-human ancestors' (1998a, 14). The linguistic community is more or less divided into two camps on this issue. One group, the majority, believes in a gradual, continuous process and another in a catastrophic, discontinuous one. There is nevertheless a middle ground of those who suggest some aspects of the emergence of language are catastrophic and, hence, discontinuous and some are gradual and continuous. We will review these three positions by considering the continuity school, the catastrophic school, and the middle ground.

THE CONTINUITY SCHOOL
The continuity school is not a school in the usual sense because the members of the group differ on a number of other issues and each

has her or his own reason for regarding the emergence of language as a non-catastrophic event.

One of the leading advocates of the continuity school is Robin Dunbar (1992, 1996), who writes: 'The view that language evolved suddenly with no precursors seems to be based on a naïve comparison between what humans, on the one hand, and monkeys on the other, do now, as though neither had an evolutionary history' (1998, 104–5). Dunbar attributes to animals a certain capacity for language and even grammar, 'animals naturally code the events in the world in what amounts to grammatical form ... [language] must have evolved piece-meal as more and more complex layers were added onto the existing primate communication system' (cited by Knight 1998a, 13–14). Robert Worden maintains a similar position, suggesting that language derives directly from primate social intelligence and asserts that 'essentially no new cognitive faculties or links were needed for the emergence of language' (ibid.).

Deacon argues that the emergence of language required a reorgani-zation of the brain and, hence, had to occur slowly and in a continuous manner: 'Considering the incredible extent of vocal abilities in modern humans as compared to any other mammal, and the intimate relation-ship between syntax and speech, it should not surprise us that vocal speech was in continual development for a significant fraction of human prehistory. The pace of evolutionary change would hardly sug-gest that such an unprecedented, well-integrated, and highly efficient medium could have arisen without a long exposure to the influence of natural selection' (1997, 358–9). Pinker and Bloom (1991, 50) also sup-port the gradualist position for the emergence of language, using the following four arguments:

1  That natural selection, the process, they believe, by which language emerged requires a gradual and continuous development. The expla-nation of adaptive complexity is the key reason why one should reject non-gradual change as playing an important role within evolution. An important Darwinian insight, reinforced by Fisher (1930), is that 'the only way for complex design to evolve is through a sequence of muta-tions with small effects' (ibid., 10). The work of Eldredge and Gould (1972) on punctuated equilibrium suggests that natural selection can

result in sudden discontinuous changes obviating the above argument of Pinker and Bloom, who respond by claiming that 'the positions of Gould, Lewontin, and Eldredge should not be seen as radical revisions of the theory of evolution, but as a shift in emphasis within the orthodox neo-Darwinian framework. As such they do not invalidate gradual natural selection as the driving force behind the evolution of language on a priori grounds' (1990, 721).

2 There existed 'plenty of time for language to have evolved.' Millions of years if Australopithicenes were the first to acquire language and hundreds of thousands of years if archaic *Homo sapiens* (Stringer and Andrews 1988) were the first users of verbal language. Granted there is enough time for a gradual process to have occurred. This argument is sufficient but not necessary.

3 Partial, incomplete grammars are still functional so that it was possible for syntax to evolve gradually. Still another sufficient but not necessary argument: 'Pidgins, contact languages, Basic English, and the language of children, immigrants, tourists, aphasics, telegrams, and headlines provide ample proof that there is a vast continuum of viable communicative systems displaying a continuous gradation of efficiency and expressive power (see Bickerton, 1986)' (Pinker and Bloom 1990, 758). The ironic and amusing aspect of this argument is that Pinker and Bloom make use of Bickerton's work to justify their position despite the fact that Bickerton sits on the exact opposite pole from them on the continuity controversy.

4 Broca's area seems to be visible in the cranial endocasts of hominid fossils that are two million years old (Falk 1987; Tobias 1981). Broca's area could have been a pre-adaptation for speech and have existed before speech emerged. Once again this argument is sufficient but not necessary. Christiansen (1994) argues that the Broca's area existed before speech and was associated with 'hierarchical structured behavior' and, hence, served as a pre-adaptation for language. One must also ask the question, if language evolved for two million years, as claimed by Pinker and Bloom and others, then why did the descent of the larynx in the throat only occur relatively recently?

Robbins Burling supports the Pinker-Bloom position by citing the gradual way in which children acquire language as evidence for the evolutionary slow growth of human language. He argues that since children acquire language slowly, and make use of a partial syntax as they learn to speak, there is no reason to believe that syntax came 'suddenly in evolution' (2002, 298).

## THE CATASTROPHIC OR DISCONTINUOUS SCHOOL

One of the arguments made for the sudden appearance of language is that structures already existed in the brain that had been used for other purposes and that they were exapted to provide the function of language. Gould and Lewontin proposed this in their famous spandrel model for the emergence of language (which we reviewed in chapter 6). Noam Chomsky's (1972a, 1972b, 1975) model for the sudden emergence of language could also be classified as a catastrophic model. We will go into his model in greater detail when we deal with Question 6 below and consider non-Darwinian approaches to the origin of language. Lieberman shares a similar view: 'The only model of human evolution that would be consistent with the current standard linguistic theory is a sudden saltation that furnished human beings with the neural bases for language' (1989, 200). Bates, Thal, and Marchman also seem to favour a sudden emergence of language, 'If the basic structural principles of language cannot be learned (bottom up) or derived (top down), there are only two possible explanations for their existence: either Universal Grammar was endowed to us directly by the Creator, or else our species has undergone a mutation of unprecedented magnitude, a cognitive equivalent of the Big Bang' (1989, 2–3).

Of all the models for the catastrophic emergence of language the most elaborated is that of Derek Bickerton (1990, 1995, 1998, 2000). His theory claims that there was a sudden bifurcation of speech in the form of what he terms *protolanguage*, which is a vocal system with a substantial lexicon but no syntax. Utterances consisted of spoken words without any particular order in the way they were strung together: 'Protolanguage utterances of a few (say, a maximum of three to five) words in length could have been uttered and interpreted largely without computational problems, since pragmatic and semantic factors could have been used to resolve problems of interpretation without excessive loss of time – especially if, as seems likely, the speed of protolanguage speech was noticeably slower than that of modern speech' (1998, 347).

Although Bickerton argues for the catastrophic appearance of language, he believes that there existed pre-adaptations for its emergence and assumes 'that there were, in the brains of alingual hominid predecessors (australopithecines, habilis), a number of areas adapted for purposes having nothing to do with language that were, however, potential preadaptations for language ... The origins of syntax. The answer is: the mechanism was there all the time, but it was not being used for language' (1998, 345 and 350).

Bickerton argued that long before the emergence of speech or even the hominid-pongid split primates were capable of thematic analysis, which he called 'theta-analysis.' Independent of this ability hominids also developed the capacity to make phonetic representations. Language emerged when these two areas of the brain, one 'which would represent the phonetic shapes of words' and the other 'involved in conceptual structure' linked up in what Bickerton (1998, 346 and 351) refers to as 'Monodian chance' or an 'opportunistic connection': 'Such a development needs no mutation or indeed anything beyond the natural and inevitable recombination of genetic material that occurs in all species that reproduce sexually' (ibid., 352). Those hominids able to take advantage of the new link between phonemic and cognitive representation would be capable of more complex communication and information exchange which would give them a survival advantage and begin a selection for the improvement of the vocal tract, the speed of speech, the use of syntax (Gopnik and Crago 1991), and the emergence of true language. The linkage of theta-analysis with other elements of protolanguage would not merely have put in place the basic structure of syntax, but would also have led directly to a cascade of consequences that would, in one rapid and continuous sequence, have transformed protolanguage into language substantially as we know it today (Bickerton 1995, 353).

Bickerton cites five independent lines of argument to empirically support his model of the catastrophic emergence of language (1998, 354–5):

1 The explosion of technological innovation in toolmaking circa 120,000 BC coincident with the first appearance of modern man comprise evidence of the rapid increase in cognitive abilities that speech made possible. This evidence cited by Bickerton also supports the

Extended Mind Model in which the emergence of language represents a transition from perceptual thinking to conceptual thinking.

2 There was no stage, no 'linguistic fossil,' between a pidgin language without syntax and a creole language with syntax.

3 There was no 'stable level between language and protolanguage. Either syntax is fully present, or fully absent or else it is fairly evenly degraded across its entire structure.' This contradicts the claim of Pinker and Bloom, already discussed, that partial incomplete grammars are still functional.

4 No one has been able to successfully recreate or model a possible state between full language and protolanguage.

5 There is an apparent indissociability of those properties that distinguish language from protolanguage.'

THE MIDDLE GROUND

Donald, who is in the 'continuity' camp, has suggested a slight compromise: 'There might have been a dramatic discontinuity of function in the evolution of language, but there could not have been any discontinuities of mechanism' (1998, 44). Another supporter of the middle ground is Jean Aitchison, who submits that 'we should discontinue the continuity-discontinuity debate on language origin, since enough is now known about the matter to show that it can never be resolved ... Language, like many other aspects of human behaviour, is a case of "mosaic evolution" (Gregory 1951), in which some aspects of language have strong continuity, others moderate, others little' (1998, 27 and 19).

Aitchison and Gregory have it right when they speak of a 'mosaic' evolution of language. Pinker and Bloom are correct when they suggest that Darwinian evolution (which for me includes both the human genome and language itself) is the only mechanism that can account for the construction in nature something as complex as the human language facility. I do not see, however, how this precludes discontinuities. Bickerton sees a continuous, in the sense of unbroken, chain of development of speech, as his model includes the notion that there were prehuman pre-adaptations for speech. A continuous development in the sense of unbroken does not mean that the development has to be gradual.

Perhaps the continuity-discontinuity debate is purely semantic or linguistic (pardon the pun). It should really be the gradual-catastrophic debate, as both sides of the issue believe in pre-adaptations and, hence, continuity. If the debate is framed in this manner, then I must come down on the side of catastrophic or sudden developments. The biological systems that we are dealing with, namely, the evolution of the hominid line of primates is a highly non-linear system coupled to a highly non-linear system, namely, the environment in which hominids developed and evolved. We know from the work of Prigogine, Lorenz, Feigenbaum, Mandelbrot, and other emergence theorists that non-linear dynamic systems can exhibit sudden, catastrophic transformations from one state to another. There is absolutely no reason to believe that biological systems should behave any differently than physical or chemical systems in this respect.

If we look at the evolution of notated language we find many examples of sudden changes. Each emergence of a new language represented a discontinuity of sorts, although each language borrowed heavily from the semantics and syntax of the languages that preceded it. One can say that the vocabulary of spoken language was a pre-adaptation for written language and that the number and quantitative words of speech, *one, two, three, many, more, less*, etc. were the pre-adaptation for mathematical language.

Other examples of discontinuity associated with the emergence of new forms of notated language were the emergence of the first formal schools which were organized in Sumer to teach young people the new skills associated with the notated languages of writing and mathematics. Schools to this day focus on the 3Rs of reading, 'riting, and 'rithematic (Logan 2004a). The printing press is another example of a sudden discontinuity in the evolution of notated language. It contributed to a number of cultural and political developments shortly after its advent which included the emergence of modern science, the use of vernacular languages in literature, universal education, the Protestant Reformation, and the rise of nationalism in Europe (ibid.).

Thomas Kuhn, in *The Structure of Scientific Revolutions* (1972), describes a 'mosaic' evolution of science with his distinction between 'normal' science and 'revolutionary' science. Normal science entails the articulation of a successful paradigm and represents the gradual evolution of science. Revolutionary science entails the development of a new paradigm to describe a phenomenon that cannot be explained by the older paradigms and represents a sudden discontinuity in the evolution of science.

If we look at different levels of recursion organizationally, some more complex than language and some less, by considering the evolution of notated language (more complex) and the evolution of physical and chemical systems (less complex) we find catastrophic transitions from one state to another. Is there any reason not to expect the same for the emergence and evolution of speech? I can think of none and therefore conclude that the origin and evolution of speech have been both continuous and catastrophic: Continuous in the sense that there is a continuous line of development that can be traced all the way back to the hominid-pongid split and catastrophic in the sense that some of the developments of speech have been sudden and catastrophic. This position is consistent with the notion of punctuated equilibrium of Eldredge and Gould (1972; Gould and Eldredge 1977), 'according to which most evolutionary change does not occur continuously within a lineage, but is confined to bursts of change that are relatively brief on the geological time scale, generally corresponding to speciation events, followed by long periods of stasis' (Pinker and Bloom, 1990, 719).

*The Emergence of Language as an Autocatalytic Set of the Elements or Mechanisms that Make Speech Possible*

In chapter 7 we reviewed the mechanisms that made language in the form of speech possible. In this section we will explore the hypothesis that these mechanisms form an autocatalytic set. We also explore the notion that language represents an emergent phenomenon in that its properties cannot be predicted from, derived from, or reduced to those of the components of which it is composed. We will make use of a more generalized form of autocatalysis than the one Kauffman used to describe the origin of life from complex organic chemicals. We propose that any set of mechanisms or ideas that catalyze each other's existence is an autocatalytic set – an autocatalytic set of mechanisms or ideas. In the case of language, we therefore, posit that language is the result of an autocatalytic process among the various components of which it is composed and like a living organism has the 'capacity to catalyze its own reproduction.' Language is collectively an autocatalytic whole. We further posit that as such language is an emergent phenomenon, as its properties cannot be reduced to those of the components of which it is composed. If we were to describe all of the mechanisms of language, we would still not be able to explain the origin of language because language is more than the sum of its mechanisms.

Tecumseh Fitch makes the point that to understand language, and in particular its origin and evolution, one must consider all of the components that make up language or make language possible: 'As recently stressed [in] Hauser et al. (2002a), it is unproductive to discuss "language as an unanalyzed whole." Thus a critical first step in analyzing language evolution is to distinguish among its various component abilities. Most generally, any mechanism involved in language is part of the faculty of language in a broad sense (FLB). Mechanisms that are both specific to language and uniquely human can be termed the faculty of language in a narrow sense (FLN), which is a subset of the FLB. The contents of the FLN must be determined empirically rather than a priori' (2005, 194).

The components of language, without which language could not exist, include the following: vocal articulation, vocal imitation, phonemic generativity, lexical creation, morphology, conceptual representation, comprehension, a theory of mind, joint attention, altruistic behaviour, syntax especially recursion, grammaticalization, and generativity of propositions. As has already been noted, speech serves two functions: (1) social communication and (2) conceptualization, or as a medium for abstract thought. Of the above components almost all of them belong to FLN, only vocal articulation and vocal imitation are part of FLB. Many animals are capable of vocal articulation but have a limited range of signals that they can produce which is not more than twenty or thirty distinct sounds, and they cannot use these signals generatively, that is, make a combination of two signals to produce a new third signal. Some animals such as parrots, myna birds, harbour seals, bats, whales, and dolphins are capable of vocal imitation (Fitch 2005, 197). It is important to note, however, that our closest relatives in the animal world, the great apes, do not possess this capability. Human vocal imitation was not, therefore, inherited genetically but developed sometime during the evolution of genus Homo.

Rather than defining FLN as a subset of FLB as do Hauser et al. (2002) we shall define two new sets $L_1$ and $L_2$, where $L_2$ is the same as FLN but the set $L_1$ consists of those components of FLB that are not also members of FLN. Thus,

$$L_1 = FLB - FLN, \text{ and}$$
$$L_2 = FLN.$$

The set $L_2$ consists of all those components that make human language possible and is uniquely human. The set $L_1$ also contains components that make human language possible but consists exclusively of those components of FLB that are prehuman and as such includes all the pre-adaptations for members of the set FLN or $L_2$. With this definition of $L_1$ and $L_2$, we suggest that the set $L_2$ emerges from the set $L_1$ – in the classical sense of emergence – since the properties of $L_2$ cannot be predicted from, derived from, or reduced to those of $L_1$. This emergence parallels the emergence of life from organic chemistry, for example.

Using Philip Clayton's (2004) description of the emergence of a level $L_2$ from a less complex level $L_1$, it becomes clear that human language is an emergent phenomenon and $L_2$ or FLN emerges from $L_1$ or FLB – FLN. Clayton describes the relationship between two levels $L_1$ and $L_2$, where $L_2$ emerges from $L_1$ as follows:

For any two levels, $L_1$ and $L_2$ where $L_2$ emerges from $L_1$,

(a)   $L_1$ is prior in natural history.
(b)   $L_2$ depends on $L_1$, such that if the states in $L_1$ did not exist, the qualities in $L_2$ would not exist.
(c)   $L_2$ is the result of a sufficient complexity in $L_1$. In many cases one can even identify a particular level of criticality which, when reached, will cause the system to begin manifesting new emergent properties.
(d)   One can sometimes predict the emergence of some new or emergent qualities on the basis of what one knows about $L_1$. But using $L_1$ alone, one will not be able to predict (i) the precise nature of these qualities, (ii) the rules that govern their interactions (or their phenomenological patterns), or (iii) the sorts of emergent levels to which they may give rise in due course.
(e)   $L_2$ is not reducible to $L_1$ in any of the standard senses of 'reduction' in the philosophy of science literature: causal, explanatory, metaphysical, or ontological reduction. (2004, 61)

Taking $L_2$ to be FLN and $L_1$ to be FLB – FLN then each of the five conditions that Clayton articulates are satisfied:

(a)  $L_1$ certainly took place before $L_2$.

(b)  $L_2$ would not be possible without $L_1$, as $L_1$ contains the pre-adaptations of $L_2$.

(c)  $L_2$ is certainly more complex that $L_1$.

(d)  One cannot predict on the basis of animal signalling the emergence of the various manifestations of human language such as generative grammar, writing, narrative, mathematics, science, computing, and the Internet (Logan 2004b).

(e)  Human language cannot be reduced to animal signalling in any of the senses of reduction identified by Clayton in (e) above.

### Autocatalysis and the Emergence of Language

To complete the argument that the emergence of language is due to the autocatalysis of its components, we have to demonstrate that the components or subsystems that make up language that we identified above catalyze each other. If human language is an emergent phenomenon, as I believe we have just demonstrated using Clayton's definitions, it explains why theories of the origin of language that do not take into account all of the components or subsystems that make up language have proven to be less than satisfactory.

As has been suggested by Fitch, in 'analyzing language evolution,' it is necessary 'to distinguish among its various component abilities' (2005, 194). 'It is unproductive to discuss language as an unanalyzed whole' (ibid.), but looking at language as an analyzed whole, as a non-linear dynamic system, has great merit. The most productive course would be to look at each of the components or subsystems of language and the system of language that emerges from the autocatalytic interactions of these components. I will attempt to show how some of the components of language catalyze the emergence of other components. I do not claim to be able to execute a complete analysis of the dynamic system of language and its components, but hope I that by providing a few examples I may be able to point the reader in a direction that might prove fruitful with time.

The term *catalysis* arises most naturally in chemistry and was used to great effect by Kauffman in his model to explain the emergence of life as the autocatalysis of organic chemicals. We would like to suggest that the analogue to autocatalysis that might be most appropriate when considering the evolution of *Homo sapiens*, the most advanced species in the biosphere, is co-evolution. By autocatalysis we mean that as one function or mechanism required for language develops it creates an environment that facilitates the development of other mechanisms equally essential for language. This is the sense in which we can use the term *autocatalysis* to describe how the various mechanisms necessary for the emergence of language might have bootstrapped each other into existence, that is, this is how the various mechanisms might have co-evolved.

We have already begun to address the co-evolution of the mechanisms and functions of language. In chapter 9, on the phylogeny of language, we addressed Question 2: How have co-evolutionary processes affected the emergence and evolution of language? We looked at the co-evolution of (1) the human capacity for language and language per se, (2) the functions and mechanisms of language, (3) the mechanisms of language, and (4) the communicative and cognitive functionality of language. To support our argument that language emerged as the autocatalysis of its components, we review some of these instances of co-evolution.

## THE CO-EVOLUTION OF MECHANISMS

*Vocal articulation* is, a mechanism that we share with many non-human animals. It is obviously ground zero for speech, but there is controversy among linguists as to whether language began as a vocalized system (as is true of all of today's languages) or as a system of hand signals (as is the case with the signed language of the deaf, e.g., like American Sign Language, which is derived from spoken language. There are compelling arguments on both sides of this dispute. We will pursue a Solomon-like neutrality and remain agnostic as to whether human language was first signed or vocalized. I personally favour the position of Merlin Donald (1991), in *The Origin of the Modern Mind*, in which he claims that language arose from mimetic communication consisting of hand signals, mime, gestures, and non-verbal prosodic vocalization. It is therefore not a question of either hand signals or vocalization but probably a combination of both. That it is almost impossible to speak without simultaneously using mimetic signals argues for the emergence of speech from both hand signalling and vocalization. The elements of mimetic communication identified by Donald (ibid.) belong to $L_1$ as we have defined it above, that is, they are part of FLB but not FLN.

*Vocal imitation* is absolutely necessary for the acquisition of language by infants and hence the reproduction of the organism of language, that is, the transmission of language from parents and caregivers to their children and wards. Vocal imitation obviously co-evolved with phonemic articulation, as imitation could not take place until phonemic articulation emerged. But is it possible that vocal imitation contributed to phonemic articulation?

*Phonemic generativity, lexical creation,* and *conceptualization* must have co-evolved because without phonemic generativity it would not be possible to create or produce the rather extensive vocabulary characteristics of all the world's languages. The mechanism of morphology would have also contributed to the generation of lexical items. But it was the pressure for a larger vocabulary that conceptualization generated that gave rise to phonemic and morphemic generativity, and it was lexical creation that co-evolved with conceptualization as our first concepts were our first words. Phonemic generativity catalyzed lexical creation and conceptualization catalyzed lexical creation which in turn catalyzed phonemic generativity. All three bootstrapped each other into existence.

*Conceptual representation* and *comprehension* are linked to the symbolic and conceptual nature of language, as described by Deacon (1997) and Logan (2000, 2006a) respectively, and must, therefore, have co-evolved. The desire to communicate verbally has been attributed to three closely related attributes of human cognition, namely, a *theory of mind*, the sharing of *joint attention*, and the advent of *altruistic behaviour.* In order to want to engage in the *joint attention* that Tomasello (1998, 208–9) suggests was essential for the emergence of language, it is necessary to have a *theory of mind* (Dunbar 1998, 102), namely, the realization that other humans have a mind, desires, and needs similar to one's own mind, desires, and needs. At the same time there must have developed a spirit of *altruism* (Ulbaek 1998, 41) once a theory of mind emerged so that human conspecifics would want to enter into the cooperative behaviour that is entailed in the sharing of information. Theory of mind and joint attention catalyzes the social function of communication and cooperative behaviour and vice versa. The mechanisms of social communication and cognition through language also form an autocatalytic subset.

A number of scholars have suggested that a primitive *syntax* emerged at the same time as the first lexicon. Donald (1991, 250), Levelt (1989), and Hudson (1984) support the *lexical hypothesis*, which holds that lexical items are the central focus of language and that they carry with them their pronunciation, meaning, and grammatical and morphological possibilities all at once. For Christiansen and his co-workers, syntax existed at the very beginning of language because it arose from the adaptation of the capabilities of the learning and processing of sequential information that existed before the advent of language. *Grammaticalization* is a mechanism in which semantics gives rise to *syntactical* possibilities: Semantics catalyzes syntax and syntax catalyzes semantics. They bootstrap each other. *Syntax or grammar* and the *generativity of propositions* share a similar dynamics.

**Question 6:**
**What role, if any, did emergence theory or complexity play
in the origin of language?**

The only credible alternative to the Darwinian natural selection model for the origin of language is offered by emergence theory or complexity. This is a position taken by Noam Chomsky, who has suggested 'that our biological endowment embodies innately determined universal grammar that accounts for the major structural properties of the world's languages and helps to shape the acquisition by children of particular grammars' (Newmeyer 1998, 305). Chomsky explains the phylogenesis of the Universal Grammar in terms of physical principles related to the large number of neurons and their cross-links that emerged with the encephalization of hominids. He asserts that language is not 'simply a more complex instance of something to be found elsewhere in the animal world, [but rather] is an example of true "emergence" – the appearance of a qualitatively different phenomenon at a specific stage of complexity of organization' (1972b, 70). Furthermore, writes Chomsky, 'we know very little about what happens when $10^{10}$ neurons are crammed into something the size of a basketball, with further conditions imposed by the specific manner in which this system developed over time. It would be a serious error to suppose that all the properties, or the interesting properties of the structure that evolved, can be "explained" in terms of natural selection' (1975, 59).

Bickerton takes the opposite point of view of Chomsky and argues that it was not the large brain size that led to language but the other way around – the brain increased in size to accommodate language: 'Our unprecedented brain growth must surely have involved the creation of some specific and equally unprecedented capacity. Language fits the description of such a capacity, and indeed may be the only thing that does. The view that language was the main driving force in the increase of brain size is shared by at least some paleoneurologists, such as Bradshaw (1988) and Falk (1987)' (1995, 44). Bickerton also points out that during the two-million-year time span of the evolution of Homo erectus brain size increased but there was no major breakthroughs in the cultural development of Homo erectus. It was only after the brain size of the Homo line stabilized to its current level that the break-throughs in culture started, beginning with Cro-Magnons (ibid., 49).

While Chomsky's argument for emergence based on the size of the brain has been neutralized by Bickerton's arguments, the idea of using emergence to explain the origin of language has been taken up by a new generation of scholars who look to complexity and emergence theory as a possible explanation of the mystery of the origin of human language. They have developed computational models which suggest that linguistic structures 'arise by self-organization from the process of interaction itself without the benefit of standard selection pressures' (Knight, Studdert-Kennedy, and Hurford 2000a, 11). These researchers simulate the genesis of semantics and syntax among agents through the exchange of information 'using basic learning algorithms and without selection pressure for successful communication' (Ragir 2002, 284). Luc Steels (1998) has presented 'an alternative explanatory paradigm to the Darwinian phylogenetic one. Steels' research programme is an effort to minimize the amount of domain-specific genetic information one needs to postulate in order to account for the structure of language ... It shows that some aspects of the co-ordinated communication behaviour of individuals interacting in a group can be accounted for simply as emerging from the very fact of interaction' (Hurford, 1998, 302). By explaining some features of language that might have emerged from self-organization the number of features that need to be innate and a product of biological evolution is reduced and the time frame in which language emerged does not have to be so long (de Boer 2000, 196).

From studies of the emergence of indigenous sign languages, Sonia Ragir offers evidence to argue that human language is the result of self-organization rather than an innate cognitive facility:

There are six communities with indigenous sign systems that have been studied in detail ... In three instances – Martha's Vineyard, Nicaragua, and

Enga (New Guinea) – conditions encouraged the growth of well-developed context-independent lexicons and grammars. In three others – Noyha (Guatemala), Grand Cayman Island, and Providence Island – social marginalization inhibited language formation, and, as a result, the indigenous sign systems remained static and context-dependent for many generations. When studied together, these field studies make a convincing case for language formation processes that are epigenetic and self-organizing rather than innate. (2002, 275)

The lack of language development in communities in which signed pidgins are passed from deaf parent to deaf child for five or six generations ought to create serious doubts about the existence of universal, innate language-specific parameters. Semantics and syntactic parameters that are sensitive to social marginalization, despite early access to sign, suggest that language formation is dynamic, self-organizing, and epigenetic. (ibid., 275 and 282)

Another dimension of the question we are considering is whether or not emergence theory is in actuality an alternative to Darwinian evolution. If Darwinian evolution and natural selection are indeed a consequence of emergence within non-linear dynamic biological systems interacting with each other, perhaps what we have is two different languages for describing the same phenomena. Perhaps we are on the threshold of a development that will show the equivalence of these two approaches in a way similar to the way in which thermodynamics and statistical mechanics were found to be equivalent or the way in which Schroedinger's wave mechanics and Heisenberg's matrix mechanics were found to be equivalent expressions of non-relativistic quantum mechanics. Stuart Kauffman's explanation of the origin of life in terms of the autocatalysis of certain organic chemical reactions is an example of a model that incorporates emergence and phylogenetics:

We must encompass the roles of both self-organization and Darwinian selection in evolution. But these sources of order may meld in complex ways that we hardly begin to understand. No theory in physics, chemistry, biology or elsewhere has yet brokered their marriage. We must think anew. Among the progeny of this mating of self-organization and selection may be new universal laws ... For what can the teeming molecules that hustled themselves into self-reproducing metabolisms, the cell coordinating their behaviors to form multicelled organisms, the ecosystems, and even economic and political systems have in common? The wonderful possibility, to be held as a working hypothesis, bold but fragile, is that on many fronts, life evolves toward a regime that is poised between order and chaos. The evocative phrase that points to this hypothesis is this: life exists at the edge of chaos. (1995, 26)

These excerpts from Kauffman's work lend support to the position that I am trying to develop in this monograph on two fronts. The first is the notion, central to my model for the origin of language, that 'life exists at the edge of chaos.' If language is an organism, as I and others contend that it is, then it must be treated as a form of life. Kauffman's suggestion that 'life exists at the edge of chaos' supports my notion that chaos and complexity motivated the emergence of language first in the form of speech, then as writing, mathematics, science, computing, and the Internet. A second area of support is that Kauffman submits that both self-organization and selection contributed to the origin of life. This idea, together with the position that language is an organism, supports my assertion that both emergence and natural selection played a role in the origin of language. The emergence of new biological structures through self-organization occurs at what Prigogine calls far from equilibrium and what Kauffman identifies as 'the edge of chaos.' This is the basis of my hypothesis that the emergence of language and its evolution into five different notated forms occurred as a result of an information overload that each time required a new form of information processing.

Kauffman challenges the notion that Darwinian natural selection alone can account for evolution, stating: 'I will show that the genome itself can be thought of as a network in the ordered regime. Thus some of the orderliness of the cell, long attributed to the honing of Darwinian evolution, seems likely instead to arise from the dynamics of the genomic network – another example of order for free ... Selection is not the sole source of order in the living world. The powerful spontaneous order we are discussing now is likely to have played a role not only in the emergence of stable autocatalytic sets, but in the later evolution of life' (1995, 85–6). To this I would add: also in the later evolution of language.

Carina Buckley and James Steele suggest that perhaps it was a combination of genetic evolution and self-organization that led to the emergence and full development of verbal language: 'A synthesis of the genetic and self-organizing perspectives is, however, provided by the hypothesis of a "Baldwin effect." In which – as language emerges through self-organization and becomes perpetuated by cultural transmission – individual variability in features advantageous to language production and comprehension becomes subject to natural selection, leading to "genetic assimilation" of linguistic structures' (2002, 28). Not only does this suggest that both genes and memes played a role in the emergence of verbal language, but it also bears on the previous question regarding the order in which the mechanisms necessary for speech emerged. By this account it becomes clear that the development of semantics, syntax, phonology, and comprehension all overlapped and bootstrapped each other into existence.

### Question 7:
### Are the questions related to the origin of language subject to scientific inquiry as defined by Popper in that one can formulate propositions that can be falsified?

Pinker and Bloom make an important point about the kinds of speculations that underpin the models of the origin of language with which we are dealing: 'The entire theory of natural selection may be literally unfalsifiable in the uninteresting sense that elaborations can always rescue its empirical failings, but this is true of all large-scale scientific theories. Any such theory is supported to the extent that individual elaborations are mutually consistent, motivated by independent data, and few in number compared to the phenomena to be explained' (1990, 717).

Karl Popper's criteria for what makes a scientific theory might rule out all of models for the origin of language, but I personally fall back on Thomas Kuhn's (1972) work and suggest that the criteria for selecting any particular paradigm are not necessarily objective and are not always completely determined by empirical considerations. Within a certain fixed data set there are a number of possible different explanations, the choice of which is often a question of personal taste. For example, there has never been a resolution to the difference in views on the nature of quantum mechanics as expressed by Einstein and Bohm, on the one hand, and Bohr and the Copenhagen school, on the other. This debate has raged for over seventy years and shows no signs of ever being resolved despite the fact that so much data have been collected and that quantum mechanics has had such unprecedented success in describing empirical data or, more pertinently, explaining data in terms of its basic assumptions. The last point made by Pinker and Bloom in the above excerpt – that elaborations be few in number – is similar to a caveat used in physics which states that one should use as small a set of parameters as possible for, given enough parameters, a model will be able to describe any data set presented to it.

# PART 4

## The Synthesis of the Extended Mind Model with Other Approaches

In addressing the issues surrounding the origin and evolution of language in chapters 6 through 9, I have made use of many sources but I have been particularly drawn to the work of Donald (1991, 1998) and his use of mimesis; Christiansen (1994, 1995), Christiansen and Delvin (1997), Christiansen, Dale, Ellefson, and Conway (2002), Christiansen and Ellefson (2002), and their notion of the adaptation from sequential learning and the idea of language as an organism; Deacon (1997) and his notion of symbolic representation; and Tomasello (2003b) and his model of joint attentional interactions and sociogenesis.

In chapter 10, I will demonstrate an attempt to link up these four approaches with the Extended Mind Model, which I developed in chapter 3, which in turn emerged from my work on the evolution of notated language, as described in chapter 2. I propose that a synthesis of the four approaches with my work is possible and that, taken together, the five models represent a reasonable scenario for the emergence of language that is consistent with existing data. I also find overlap with and support of my ideas in the Extended Mind Model with Clark's (1997) notion of embedded cognition, Jackendoff's (2002) work on the role of the lexicon in language, and Schumann's notion of the symbolosphere, which I will address in chapter 11.

# 10 The Synthesis of Five Approaches to the Origin of Language

I enter into this exercise of synthesis with some trepidation because I am appropriating the work of others into my Extended Mind Model, perhaps making use of Clark's (1997, 45) sense of scaffolding is a better way of putting it. This is the nature of the scientific enterprise, however, and I believe it is intellectually honest to make my appropriation of the ideas of others explicit. I offer my apologies in advance for any inaccuracies that I might make and hope the authors will set me straight if I misrepresent them in this work in progress. I will begin by summarizing what I see as the main points of overlap of the five approaches (mimetics, sequential learning, symbolic representation, sociogenesis, and the bifurcation from percepts to concepts) and then delineate the differences in them but show that these differences are not so much substantive as merely differences in emphasis.

The first thing that drew me to each of four thinkers – Donald, Christiansen, Deacon, and Tomasello – cited above is that co-evolution plays a central role in their respective approaches, as I have pointed out in Question 2 of chapter 9. Many of the controversies in the literature simply disappear when the notion of co-evolution is introduced. As I have mentioned earlier a both/and position is more productive than an either/or one, a sentiment I share with Jean Aitchison who wrote, 'I support the notion that progress can be made by discussing dichotomies, but suggest that the continuity-discontinuity dichotomy should be abandoned, and that we should go beyond this to further controversies, which are in turn dissolving as research proceeds' (1998, 18). Given that the evolutionary processes of biology and those of culture are both emergent and non-linear, it is no wonder that the mechanism of co-evolution is the norm. A biological system cannot evolve in isolation from its environment.

A perfect example of the kind of controversy one finds in the literature is the debate as to whether the evolution of language is gradual or discontinuous. Each of the five approaches I am attempting to synthesize assumes a gradual evolution of language that can be traced back to Homo habilis and even possibly Australopithecus, but each assumes that there have been discontinuities as new cognitive and/or linguistic skills emerged, especially the burst of linguistic activity that characterized the transition to *Homo sapiens*: 'Up until about 35,000 years before the present, I hypothesize that the evolution of language was quite slow, perhaps only involving the addition of relatively few vocabulary items, but following the explosion of cultural artifacts from this point in evolutionary history, we would have seen a dramatic growth in the number of words (referring to the new artifacts and other aspects of the rapidly evolving culture), and perhaps, a more complex syntax allowing for the expression of more complex situations and events' (Christiansen 1995, 21). The other three authors concur. Donald (1991, 44) points out, as we mentioned earlier, that perhaps the functions of language are discontinuous but not the mechanisms. He also claims that 'the modern vocal apparatus ... appears to have evolved much later than erectus' (ibid., 181). Deacon suggests that 'it should not surprise us that vocal speech was in continual development for a significant fraction of human prehistory' (1997, 359). Tomasello, on the other hand, believes 'the first dramatic signs of species-unique cognitive skills emerged only in the last quarter of a million years with modern Homo sapiens' (1999, 4).

The presence of continuities and discontinuities are typical of non-linear dynamic systems. The equations describing such a system are continuous, but the solutions to these equations suffer bifurcations or discontinuities. It should be no surprise that something akin to the butterfly effect operates in the evolution of the human mind, where a small change in the initial variable can make a large change in the behaviour of the system. I find that this corresponds to something akin to punctuated equilibrium (Eldredge and Gould 1972), according to which 'species, once they originate, tend to remain stable, while change occurs by rapid events of branching by small populations splitting off from ancestral species' (Brockman 1996, 36).

Another point of concurrence among four of the five models is that each sees a direct connection between speech and manual articulation or hand signaling. Donald, who posits that mimetic skills and communication laid the foundation for human language, also sees a strong connection between toolmaking and mimetics: 'Toolmaking was probably the first instance of behavior that depended entirely upon the existence of self-cued mimetic skill' (1991, 179). Deacon, submits that 'signing might be the missing link in the language origins story ... Gesture likely comprised a significant part of early symbolic communication [which] existed side by side with vocal communication' (1997, 355–6). Christiansen suggests a similar origin of language: 'Language might therefore have originated with (Homo habilis) as a kind of systematic set of manual gestures (hence the importance of bipedalism freeing of the hands from participation in locomotion, cf. Corballis, 1992)' (1995, 16). In the Extended Mind Model, the freeing of the hands led to toolmaking and signalling, which increased the complexity of hominid, life creating the conditions for the bifurcation from perception to conceptualization. Tomasello, however, seems to be agnostic on this point.

A fourth point of overlap is that each of the authors holds that a primitive syntax emerged at the same time as the first lexicon. Donald argues that 'the linkage to reference invests the utterances of the phonological system with meaning and syntactical structure. The primary symbolic device in this reference system is the "word" ... The idea that the lexicon is at the center of the language system is sometimes called the lexical hypothesis. The lexical hypothesis holds that lexical entries are unifying devices that tie together grammar, meaning, phonology, and specific morphological rules' (1991, 250). Support for the lexical hypothesis is also found in the work of Levelt (1989) and Hudson (1984).

For Christiansen and his co-workers, syntax existed at the very beginning of language because it arose from the adaptation of the capabilities of the learning and processing of sequential information that existed before the advent of language: 'We show how language and sequential learning are intertwined, and how universal constraints on basic word order and complex question formation can be explained in terms of non-linguistic constraints on the learning of complex sequential structure'

(Christiansen and Ellefson 2002, 340). Deacon arrives at the same conclusion, if from a slightly different perspective: 'Symbol learning in general has many features that are similar to the problem of learning the complex and indirect architecture of syntax. This parallel is hardly a coincidence, because grammar and syntax inherit the constraints implicit in the logic of symbol-symbol relationships. These are not, in fact, separate learning problems, because systematic syntactic regularities are essential to ease the discovery of the details' (1997, 136).

My argument within the context of the Extended Mind Model is similar to Deacon's: Once conceptualization has taken place with the creation of the first words, this cognitive skill allows for the conceptualization of propositions consisting of different elements of the lexicon and, hence, the simultaneous appearance of grammar.

Tomasello, with the cognitive-functional grammar that he adopts, makes no strong distinction between syntax and semantics, as Deacon does. For Tomasello, 'all language structures are symbolic instruments that serve to convey meaning, from the smallest morpheme to the most complex constructions' (1998, xi).

All of the models under consideration are critical of the notion that the Universal Grammar (UG) and the Language Acquisition Device (LAD) were hard-wired into the human brain. Donald has indicated, as mentioned previously, that the 'language brain' is not 'preprogrammed' nor does it 'self-install or self-trigger' (1998, 49). In referring to the UG approach, Christiansen and Ellefson write: 'More recently an alternative perspective is gaining ground, advocating a refocus in thinking about language evolution. Rather than concentrating on biological changes to accommodate language, this approach stresses the adaptation of linguistic structures to the biological substrate of the human brain' (2002, 336).

Deacon strikes a similar chord: 'Children's minds need not innately embody language structures, if languages embody the predispositions of children's minds ... We don't design language at all. It "designs" itself ... Every effort to design a language has flopped' (1997, 109). Deacon also argues against the hard-wiring of the brain by pointing out how the different cognitive skills associated with language are distributed in different parts of the brain: 'So if there is a grammar module, then the parts of this module map in very different ways to different grammatical operations, depending on the relative importance of positional or inflectional tricks for cueing grammatical decisions in different languages. This sort of module is a will-o'-the-wisp' (ibid., 307).

Tomasello, who we discussed earlier is chapter 8, makes the point that children acquire a language complete with its grammar 'on the basis of their own categorization skills working on the language they hear' (1998) rather than arriving at it innately.

While rejecting the notion of the hard-wiring of the UG, each author with the exception of Tomasello, accepts its validity and each provides a mechanism of how the UG might have arisen as an adaptation and/or an exaptation of prelingual cognitive capabilities. For Donald the mechanism that gave rise to grammar is mimetic representation, which includes toolmaking, social intelligence, and mimetic communication: 'Mimetic representation involves the ability to "parse" one's own motor actions into components and then recombine these components in various ways, to reproduce the essential features of an event' (1991, 171).

Deacon sees iconic and indexical representation leading to symbolic representation and from there to UG: 'The earliest symbolic systems would necessarily have been combinatorial and would have exhibited something like this operator-operand structure (and probably subject-predicate structure) right from the start. This is the minimum requirement to make the transition from indexical to symbolic reference. In other words, some form of grammar and syntax has been around since the dawn of symbolic communication. There was never a protolanguage that lacked these and yet possessed words or their equivalents. This satisfies the first requirement, consistency across all languages throughout time' (1997, 334). Deacon's explanation of the universality of grammars is that 'they have emerged spontaneously and independently in each evolving language, in response to universal biases in the selection processes affecting language transmission. They are convergent features of language evolution in the same way that the dorsal fin of sharks, ichthyosaurs, and dolphins are independent convergent adaptations of aquatic species' (1997, 116).

For Christiansen, Dale, Ellefson, and Conway the mechanism that gave rise to UG is sequential learning and processing plus the fact that each language acting as an organism evolved to match universal human extra-lingual sequential learning processes and, hence, universal rules of organization emerged for all the languages of the world (2002, 149).

Although Tomasello does not accept the validity of the UG, he does have an explanation of how grammar is generated. In his model for the emergence of language, Tomasello invokes the idea that there were cognitive skills of categorizing that served as a pre-adaptation for verbal language, which is similar to Christiansen's notion that linear processing and learning functioned as a preadaptation for verbal language: 'The point is not that language creates ex nihilo the ability to categorize, to perspectivize, or to make analogies or metaphors. That is impossible because language depends on these skills, and they may be present in basic form in either nonhuman primates or prelinguistic infants. But what has happened is that in collaboration over historical time human beings have created an incredible array of categorical perspectives and construals on all kinds of objects, events, and relations, and then they have embodied them in their systems of symbolic communication called languages' (1999, 169).

Whereas Christiansen starts with the biological genetically derived cognitive skills of linear processing and learning and then suggests that languages evolved to be easily acquired, Tomasello takes a slightly different tack. He starts with a different set of biological genetically derived cognitive skills, namely, categorization and perspectivization, and explicitly attributes the evolution of the language to the cultural mechanism he calls 'the ratchet effect,' whereby the culture accumulates modifications over time through creative invention and retention of these modifications through faithful social transmission (1999, 5).

In the Extended Mind Model I have proposed the bifurcation from perceptual thought to conceptualization as the mechanism that gave rise to grammar, but I defer to Deacon and Christiansen as providing the most cogent explanation for the universality of that grammar across the many forms of human language.

## The Synthesis of the Five Models and the Four Why's

I believe I have established the consistency of the five models under consideration. I would now like to pursue their synthesis by evoking Tinbergen's 'Four Why's' once again, but applying them not just to the biological phenomenon of human language but, more specifically, to the emergence of language. I will attempt to show that among the five approaches we have reviewed in this chapter that some combination of the five is able to address each of the 'Four Why's' as applied to the emergence of language, namely, (1) the function or purpose, (2) the mechanisms or machinery, (3) ontogeny or development, and (4) phylogeny or evolutionary history.

*Function or Purpose*

Language would not have emerged unless it served some function or purpose: 'Individuals can perform a variety of difficult functions without language, without even the possibility of internal speech. The range of their cognitive competence is impressive: it includes intentional communication, mimetic and gestural representation, categorical perception, various generative patterns of action, and above all the comprehension of social relationships, which implies a capacity for social attribution and considerable communicative ability' (Donald 1991, 166).

If mimetics which predated speech provided an adequate system of communication, then it would seem that the principal function for the emergence of language is conceptualization (Logan 2000) or symbolic representation Deacon (1997). This is consistent with the following point made by Donald: 'Although language was first and foremost a social device, its initial utility was not so much in enabling a new level of collective technology or social organization, which it eventually did, or in transmitting skill, or in achieving larger political organizations, which it eventually did. Initially, it was used to construct conceptual models of the human universe' (1991, 215).

The Extended Mind Model parallels Donald's model in that the transition from mimetic culture to semiotic culture is the transition from percept-based mental processes to concept-based ones, as Donald regards the mental processes of mimetic culture as percept-based: 'Mimes must generate the representation directly from a perceptual model. They cannot proceed in any other way; there are no other data to go on. For example, a fight might be mimed by retrieving an episodic memory of a fight and re-enacting it fairly literally; or by means of a more abstract, prototypical mime. Either way, the mimetic act is guided by perceptual metaphor. It is understood by the perceiver by means of perceptual metaphor ... The primary human adaptation was not language qua language but rather integrative, initially mythical thought. Modern humans developed language in response to pressure to improve their conceptual apparatus, not vice versa' (1991, 226 and 215).

For Tomasello, the initial purpose of language was joint attention, but this led to sociogenesis and the conversion of simple cognitive skills into complex ones so that the function of language became conceptual. Tomasello claims that 'the process of acquiring and using linguistic symbols fundamentally transforms the nature of human cognitive representation,' in contrast to other researchers who 'do not believe that acquiring a language has any great effect on the nature of cognitive representation because they view linguistic symbols as simply handy tags for already formulated concepts (e.g., Piaget 1970)' (1999, 123–4). Tomasello supports the hypothesis in the Extended Mind Model that concepts and words emerged together at the same time. He also points out, as I have, that words entail concepts and go beyond mere perceptual representation: 'As the child internalizes a linguistic symbol – as she learns the human perspectives embodied in a linguistic symbol – she cognitively represents not just the perceptual or motoric aspects of a situation ... The way that human beings use linguistic symbols thus creates a clear break with straightforward perceptual or sensory-motor representations, and it is due entirely to the social nature of linguistic symbols' (ibid.). My only quarrel with Tomasello, and it is a minor one, is his use of the word 'entirely' in the last phrase of the last sentence. I believe the break with perceptual representations while due in part to social considerations, as suggested by Tomasello, is, in fact, primarily due to the conceptual nature of linguistic symbols.

Tomasello does make the point that the social nature of shared linguistic symbols provides an extra richness to them above and beyond the fact that they are used to represent concepts: 'The intersubjectivity of human linguistic symbols – and their perspectival nature as one offshoot of this intersubjectivity – means that linguistic symbols do not represent the world more or less directly, in the manner of perceptual or sensory-motor representations, but rather are used by people to induce others to construe certain perceptual/conceptual situations – to attend to them – in one way rather than another' (1999, 128).

*Mechanisms*

The cognitive mechanism or machinery by which semiotics – based communication emerged is some combination of sequential learning, as suggested by Christiansen, and mimetic culture with its generativity and intentional expression, as suggested by Donald. The overlap of the two mechanisms is considerable, and it might be that they represent different ways of describing the same phenomena: 'Generativity involves a process of combinatorial sequential analysis that is not unlike the concept of analytic thought except that it is not language bound' (Donald 1991, 73). Manual articulation is a key element of mimetic culture, and, at the same time, a prototypical example of sequential learning and processing. Other aspects of mimetic culture such as dyadic social interactions and mimetic communication are additional examples of cognitive skills, which require sequential learning and processing.

Imitation is an important mechanism for Tomasello's social-cognitive model of language acquisition by which children first comprehend and then use verbal language employing the following steps: (a) joint attentional scenes as the social-cognitive grounding of early language acquisition; (b) understanding communicative intentions as the main social-cognitive process by means of which children comprehend adult use of linguistic symbols; and (c) role-reversal imitation as the main cultural learning process by means of which children acquire the active use of linguistic symbols (1999, 96).

Deacon sees toolmaking or manual articulation as playing a leading role in the emergence of language: 'Stone and symbolic tools, which were initially acquired with the aid of flexible ape-learning abilities, ultimately turned the tables on their users and forced them to adapt to a new niche opened by these technologies. Rather than being just useful tricks, these behavioral prostheses for obtaining food and organizing social behaviors became indispensable elements in a new adaptive complex. The origin of "humanness" can be defined as that point in our evolution where these tools became the principal source of selection on our bodies and brains. It is the diagnostic trait of Homo symbolicus' (1997, 345). Deacon's hypothesis incorporates McLuhan's notion that we shape our tools and thereafter our tools shape us.

*Ontogeny*

Of the five models under consideration the strongest for explaining the ability of young children to acquire language are those of Tomasello, Deacon, and Christiansen. Christiansen developed the notion of 'language as an organism,' which evolved in such a way as to make itself compatible with the cognitive skills of the young child and, hence, easily learned. Deacon (1997) incorporated this notion into his model of language acquisition. Christiansen's expression of this idea is best represented by the following quote: 'The fact that children are so successful at language learning is therefore best explained as a product of natural selection of linguistic structures, and not as the adaptation of biological structures, such as an innately specified linguistic endowment in the form of universal grammar (UG)' (Christiansen, Dale, Ellefson, and Conway 2002, 167).

Tomasello's model of language growing through cultural transmission parallels Christiansen's notion of the evolution of language taken metaphorically as an organism:

> The evidence that human beings do indeed have species-unique modes of cultural transmission is overwhelming. Most importantly, the cultural traditions and artifacts of human beings accumulate modification over time in a way that those of other animal species do not – so-called cumulative cultural evolution. Basically none of the most complex human artifacts or social practices – including tool industries, symbolic communication (i.e. language), and social institutions – were invented once and for all at a single moment by a single individual or group of individuals. Rather what happened was that some individual or group of individuals first invented a primitive version or the artifact or practice, and then some later user or users made a modification (which others improved upon) ... and so on over historical time in what has sometimes been dubbed 'the ratchet effect.' (Tomasello 1999, 5)

In addition to languages having evolved to be easily learned, the skills that developed in mimetic culture of imitation would also facilitate language learning of the young. If mimetic culture is two million years old, as is suggested by Donald, then the ability to imitate would have been selected for. Imitation is an automatic percept-based skill that the user would not have to be conscious of. It could be the mechanism that allows children to acquire language without any effort. Children do not think about learning language, they just do it. This is consistent with Elissa Newport's (1990, 24; cited by Christiansen 1995) 'less is more' hypothesis that proposes 'paradoxically, that the more limited abilities of children may provide an advantage for tasks (like language learning) which involve componential analysis.'

*Phylogeny*

Each of the five models suggests a different stepping stone from which speech emerged: mimesis for Donald; sequential learning and processing for Christiansen; symbolic representation for Deacon; joint attentional interactions and sociogenesis for Tomasello; and the bifurcation from percept to concept in the Extended Mind Model: 'There could not have been selection pressure to evolve such a sophisticated, high-speed communication system as modern language unless there was already a simpler slower one in place. Mimesis fulfills that condition: it provides the preconditions out of which language, improbable an adaptation though it may seem, might have evolved simply as the need for disambiguation grew ... Mimetic skill is a powerful device for communication: it can convey requests and commands, capture and hold the attention of others, show or declare, establish and maintain contact, refer explicitly to actions or events, demonstrate, oversee the actions of others and convey emotion' (Donald 1998, 60–2).

Christiansen, Dale, Ellefson, and Conway (2002, 171), however, proposed that 'language to a large extent "piggy-backed" on pre-existing sequential learning and processing mechanisms, and that limitations on these mechanisms in turn gave rise to many linguistic constraints observed across the languages of the world.' Deacon suggests still another mechanism, namely, that 'selection for the core symbolic function distributed selection to a wide variety of supportive adaptations that became significant only once this core function was established. These in turn distributed selection pressure back on the core functions as they became entrenched in later epochs of the process. As a result, the prefrontal cortex became additionally recruited for other supportive functions as well, as did the other systems. Numerous serendipitous "spin-offs" would thus become co-opted, or exapted, by the growing cluster of language adaptations' (1997, 353).

Tomasello, suggests that we biologically inherited the ability to identify with conspecifics and enter into joint attentional interactions, which in turn gave rise to the 'skills of metacognition, representational redescription and dialogic thinking' (1999, 10). But the Extended Mind Model (chapter 3, and Logan 2000b) posits that language emerged as the bifurcation from percept-based to concept-based thought, where the first concepts were words. The bifurcation arose because of the increased complexity of hominid existence.

Although the five models seem to nominate five different mechanisms for the emergence of speech, namely, mimesis, sequential learning and processing, symbolic representation, joint attentional interactions, and the bifurcation from percept-based to concept-based thought, I see an overlap of the five mechanisms. In terms of the mechanics of the emergence and evolution of language, sequential learning and processing and mimetic representation began at the perceptual level and entailed manual articulation and toolmaking: 'Toolmaking is primarily a visual-manual skill, but it also involved obtaining the necessary materials, fashioning the appropriate tools at the right time, apportioning responsibility and so on ... Toolmaking was probably the first instance of behavior that depended entirely upon the existence of self-cued mimetic skill' (Donald 1991, 171 and 179). In other words mimetic representation entails sequential processing. The features of mimetic culture, thus, entail toolmaking, social organization, large-scale co-ordinated hunting, and mimetic communication – all of which would have reinforced and expanded sequential learning and processing. Although Donald and Christiansen start from different points their approaches converge. One may regard Donald's (1991) mimetic communication as a preadaptation for Tomasello's joint attentional interactions. Mimetic communication would have been just as effective for creating joint attentional scenes as verbal language. And in both Donald's and Tomasello's approaches mimetic communication and joint attentional interactions respectively evolved into more sophisticated cognitive skills involving conceptualization.

In Deacon's model, symbolic representation emerges from iconic and indexical representation. While Deacon does not explicitly indicate that these forms of representation are perceptual, he does refer to them as conditioned responses. He also attributes them to non-human primates and indicates that they are non-symbolic, which in my language makes them percept-based mental processes. Therefore, Deacon's model entails the transition from percept-based to concept-based mental activity. Sequential learning and processing provide the mechanism for the process of symbolic representation, which as described by Deacon, requires a mapping of the symbolic tokens into a net of relationships. The sequential ordering capability is the mechanism for this process. Mimetic culture and sequential learning and processing provided the complexity of hominid mental life which fueled the complexity that led to the bifurcation from percepts to concepts in the form of words (or symbolic tokens to use the language of Deacon).

A concept provides a mapping from multiple perceptual experiences associated with that concept to a single word, which represents the concept symbolically. I suggest that there exists a parallel between Deacon's connection of symbol tokens to indices and icons with my connection of a single concept to multiple perception events. Symbols represent a mapping between a signal and a concept. The emergence of language involved the emergence of concepts in the form of words, and those words immediately became symbols of those concepts. Words, concepts, and symbols bootstrapped themselves into existence.

It is possible that an experience or perceptual event consists of a number of individual percepts, which in turn connect to a number of different concepts and, hence, creates a web of relationships among the concepts or the symbol tokens as described by Deacon. This network of concepts and percepts, which I will call a percept-concept net, connects different concepts or symbols creating what Deacon has identified as symbol-symbol relationships, which, as Deacon claims, are essential for grammar and syntax.

Tomasello also suggests that a web of relationships exists between words. He points out that choosing one word as opposed to another to describe an event or an object provides a particular perspective on that event or object and that by using different words language users can give whatever twist they like to their utterances: 'What makes linguistic symbols truly unique from a cognitive point of view is the fact that each symbol embodies a particular perspective on some entity or event; this object is simultaneously a rose, a flower, and a gift' (1999, 107).

I would suggest that in addition to this that whatever word is chosen it provides a multiple of perspectives on that event or object because the word chosen has multiple meanings that have accrued to it on two levels: (a) its previous use in different contexts has given it different shades of meaning and (b) the word itself is a strange attractor for all of the experiences associated with the concept that the word represents. It is the richness of this multi-perspectival aspect of words that poets take advantage of to weave a rich picture of ideas and imagery. Thus, the word *rose* given as a gift denotes a flower, but it denotes a flower with thorns so even if the speaker chooses the word rose instead of flower there is the association with the thorns, so it is a gift with the possibility of pricking the receiver. If the word *flower* was used instead, it could connote the concept of florescence or growth, so that the gift strengthens a growing bond. I would, therefore, suggest two levels of multiple perspective: one, depending on which word is chosen to represent an event or object and, two, the multiple meanings of that word.

In the Extended Mind Model, as developed in chapters 3 and 4, I suggested that language or words extended the brain, which before language served as a percept processor, into the human mind capable of abstract conceptual thought. In the same year, 1997, that I first communicated this model, unbeknownst to me Terry Deacon came up with a very similar idea: 'The evolutionary miracle is the human brain. And what makes this extraordinary is not just that a flesh and blood computer is capable of producing a phenomenon as remarkable as the human mind, but that the changes in this organ responsible for this miracle were a direct consequence of the use of words. And I don't mean in a figurative sense. I mean that the major structural and functional innovations that make the human brains capable of unprecedented mental feats evolved in response to the use of something as abstract and virtual as the power of words. Or, to put this miracle in simple terms, I suggest that an idea changed the brain' (1997, 321–2).

## Summary and Conclusion

To summarize this synthesis of the five models for the origin of language, I suggest that the syntactical interconnection of the symbols tokens or concepts through the percept-concept net or symbol-symbol network are made possible by sequential learning and processing as identified by Christiansen. Mimesis including phonological imitation and cultural transmission through joint attentional interactions and sociogenesis provides a mechanism for the transmission of language from one generation to another as the sequential acquisition and processing of symbol tokens acting as concepts (or of concepts acting as symbol tokens). Conceptualization and symbolic representation provide the lexicon of language, sequential learning and processing its syntax, and mimesis and joint attentional interactions the medium for its transmission. The cognitive processes of sequential ordering, symbolic representation, and conceptualization emerged as a combination of the adaptation and exaptation of the communication function that developed in mimetic culture. Mimesis bifurcated into the figure of verbal language with mimesis now acting as the ground that surrounds speech rather than serving as the main communication channel as it did in mimetic culture. Joint attentional interactions provided the multi-perspectival and construal nature of language. I therefore conclude that mimetics, joint attentional interactions, sequential learning and processing, symbolic representation, the bifurcation from concept-based thought to percept-based thought, and language as an organism form an autocatalytic set of ideas that are mutually self-supporting. And furthermore, these mechanisms, which incorporate both Darwinian selection and self-organization, contributed to the origin of language.

In none of the five models is the emergence of language seen as a purely biological phenomenon. The evolution of culture and/or language is seen as playing a fundamental role in the origin of language. Both Christiansen and Deacon treat language as an organism that evolved in such a way to facilitate its acquisition, whereas language evolves in Tomasello's approach through cultural transmission and accumulation. In Deacon's model cultural elements, such as marriage and ritual, play an important role in the emergence of symbolic representation, which is similar to Tomasello's approach. In Donald's approach language is seen to emerge against the background of the evolution of culture from the episodic culture of apes to the mimetic culture of hominids to the mythic (semiotic) culture of modern *Homo sapiens*. I embrace the approach of all four of these seminal thinkers whose ideas, I believe, are compatible with the Extended Mind Model.

# 11 Overlaps of the Extended Mind Model with the Work of Clark, Jackendoff, and Schumann

In chapter 10, we developed a synthesis of the Extended Mind Model with the work of Christiansen (1994), Deacon (1997), Donald (1991), and Tomasello (1999) because of my perception of an overlap of our approaches. In this chapter, I wish to consider in greater detail the ideas of Andy Clark (1997), Ray Jackendoff (2002), and John Schumann (2003), whose ideas have helped me extend my hypothesis.

## Embodied Cognition and the Extended Mind

I did not encounter Andy Clark's marvelous book *Being There* (1997) or his (co-authored) article 'The Extended Mind' (Clark and Chalmers 1998) until 2004, long after I developed almost all of the ideas in this book. Our work obviously has a common link if we both used the phrase 'the extended mind' in the title of our work. I am in complete agreement with Clark's (1997, 179) suggestion that what makes humans so much more cognitively capable is not merely the improved structure of their brains but their 'amazing capacities to create and maintain a variety of special external structures (symbolic and social-institutional),' by which Clark means language and culture. Clark even muses: 'Are brains somehow the improper object of study?' (ibid., 82). And he concludes: 'It is the human brain plus these chunks of scaffolding that finally constitutes the smart, rational inference engine we call mind' (ibid., 180). The chunks of scaffolding Clark is referring to is language and culture and, hence, this proposition parallels my notion that the mind = brain + language, and he emboldens me to enlarge on this equation, so that in chapter 12 I will suggest that mind = brain + language + culture.

Clark (1997, 198) proposes that the discontinuity in the cognitive skills between humans and non-human primates, while affected by some subtle changes in the structure of the brain, are in fact due primarily of the human ability to exploit language and culture as an external resource or a *scaffold*, a term he makes liberal use of and to great effect and which he defines as follows: 'We have called an action "scaffolded" to the extent that it relies on some kind of external support. Such support could come from the use of tools or from the exploitation of the knowledge and skill of others; that is to say, scaffolding denotes a broad class of physical, cognitive, and social augmentations – augmentations that allow us to achieve some goals that would otherwise be beyond us' (ibid., 194). The subtle change in the structure of the brain that he refers to could well be the mutation, suggested by Tomasello, to be responsible for joint attentional interactions (see the section, 'Language Acquisition, Ontogeny, and a Theory of Mind' in chapter 8). ·

Clark does not see language as just the medium for the communication of thought but rather the engine of thought: 'Language is not the imperfect mirror of our intuitive knowledge. Rather it is part and parcel of the mechanism of reason itself' (1997, 207). Clark created an interesting metaphor, 'the mangrove effect,' to describe the relationship of language and thought. The mangrove effect is based on the fact that mangrove seeds root in the shallow sea water adjacent to the coast of a tropical ocean and grow into plants with stiltlike roots which trap floating soil, weeds, and debris – creating land. So it is not that the land creates a place for the plant but rather the plant creates the condition for new land. So it is with words and thoughts, according to Clark: 'Something like the "mangrove effect," I suspect is operative in some species of human thought. It is natural to suppose that words are always rooted in the fertile soil of preexisting thoughts. But sometimes, at least, the influence seems to run in the other direction ... Perhaps it is public language that is responsible for a complex of rather distinctive features of human thought – viz., the ability to display second order cognitive dynamics' (1997, 208).

These thoughts of Clark parallel my notion that our first concepts were our first words, and they collected the debris of our percepts to create the soil out of which our thoughts grew. Clark identifies one class of thoughts for which the fact that they emerged because of language cannot be doubted: 'Thinking about thinking is a good candidate for a distinctly human capacity – one not evidently shared by the non-language using animals that share our planet. Thus, it is natural to wonder whether this might be an entire species of thought in which language plays the generative role – a species of thought that is not just reflected in (or extended by) our use of words but is directly dependent on language for its very existence' (1997, 209).

One of the aspects of Clark's work that I find so enjoyable is that, without making explicit reference to McLuhan, he recapitulates some of McLuhan's ideas, particularly McLuhan's notion that tools are extensions of the body and media are extensions of the psyche. But there is a flip, as we through the use of our tools become their extensions: 'To behold, use or perceive any extension of ourselves in technological forms is necessarily to embrace it. By continuously embracing technologies, we relate ourselves to them as servo-mechanisms' (McLuhan 1964, 46). At first, technology serves as an extension of humankind, and then suddenly a flip occurs and humankind is transformed into an extension of its technology. If we consider language a tool and a technology, then Clark expresses a similar thought: 'There is, after all, a quite general difficulty in drawing a line between a user and a tool' (1997, 214).

Another parallel with McLuhan is the similarity of the following thought of Clark's from his book *Natural-Born Cyborgs* (2003) and McLuhan's (1967) oft-quoted remark: 'We shape our tools and thereafter our tools shape us': 'It is the mind-body-*scaffolding* problem. It is the problem of understanding how human thought and reason is born out of looping interactions between material brains, material bodies, and complex cultural and technological environments. We create these supportive environments, but they create us too' (Clark 2003, 11).

We can see how McLuhan foreshadows Clark's notion of a 'natural-born cyborg,' if we compare McLuhan's forty-year-old quote with Clark's definition of a 'natural-born cyborg.' McLuhan wrote: 'In this electric age we see ourselves being translated more and more into the form of information, moving toward the technological extension of consciousness ... By putting our physical bodies inside our extended nervous systems, by means of electric media, we set up a dynamic by which all previous technologies that are mere extensions of hands and feet and bodily heat-controls – all such extensions of our bodies, including cities –

will be translated into information systems' (1964, 57). Whereas Clark's definition of a 'natural-born cyborg' reads as follows:

> The biological design innovations that make all this possible include the provision (in us) in an unusual degree of cortical plasticity and the (related) presence of an unusually extended period of development and learning (childhood). These dual innovations (intensively studied by the new research program called 'neural constructivism') enable the human brain, more than that of any other creature on the planet, to factor an open-ended set of biologically external operations and resources deep into its own basic mode of operation and functioning. It is the presence of this unusual plasticity that makes humans (but not dogs, cats, or elephants) *natural-born cyborgs*: being primed by Mother Nature to annex wave upon wave of external elements and structures as part and parcel of their own extended minds. (2003, 31)

Clark regards language as one of the scaffolds of the human mind: 'Language is in many ways the ultimate artifact: so ubiquitous that it is almost invisible, so intimate it is not clear whether it is a kind of tool or a dimension of the user. Whatever the boundaries, we confront at the very least a tightly linked economy in which the biological brain is fantastically empowered by some of its strangest and most recent creations: words in the air, symbols on the printed page' (1997, 218). But for Clark language is but one tool or external scaffold that led him to surmise: 'And I am led to wonder whether the intuitive notion of mind itself should not be broadened so as to encompass a variety of external props and aids, – whether, that is, the system we often refer to as "mind" is in fact much wider than the one we call "brain." Such a more general conclusion may at first seem unpalatable. One reason, I think, is that we are prone to confuse the mental with the conscious. And I assuredly do not seek to claim that individual consciousness extends outside the head' (ibid., 215).

Clark and Chalmers justify the claim that the mind extends outside of the skull in their article entitled 'The Extended Mind' (1998, 10): 'If, as we confronted some task, a part of the world functions as a process which, were it to go into the head, we would have no hesitation in accepting as part of the cognitive process, then that part of the world is (for that time) part of the cognitive process.' According to this argument, and others made by Clark, not only does language extend the brain into the human mind, but so does culture and all the tools and aids that a culture creates. I am in great sympathy with this conjecture and in fact will examine in Chapter 12 the role of culture in cognition and discuss the co-evolution of language and culture and come to conclusions similar to Clark's.

## Jackendoff's Theory of the Emergence of the Lexicon and the Notion of Conceptualization in the Extended Mind Model

Although I do not always agree with Ray Jackendoff's positions, especially with respect to his support of Chomskyan generative grammar, I admire him for his even-handedness and his desire to find ways to reconcile conflicting opinions within the field of linguistics. Jackendoff has stimulated some interesting thoughts that I would therefore like to share with the reader, even if they are highly speculative and are offered as probes to stimulate further thought and debate.

Jackendoff suggests a mechanism for the way in which concrete nouns gave rise to abstract nouns: 'Not all nouns denote concrete objects; all words for concrete objects are nouns ... Having learned the words for concrete objects, children f-know that these words are going to be nouns. In turn, this enables them to f-look for the grammatical properties of nouns, from which they can start f-figuring out *storm, cost,* and the like' (2002, 125). I believe that this ontogeny perhaps recapitulates the phylogeny of human language development. First came concrete nouns, then abstract, conceptual nouns. A concrete noun is the beginning of conceptualization, which then becomes more abstract. From the word for a concrete object, an orange, comes the colour word 'orange.'

Jackendoff's model for lexical access in the production of speech is that 'the conceptual department of working memory contains some thought than the speaker wishes to express ... The initial event has to be a call to the lexicon: what words potentially express parts of this thought? As in perception, it is an open question whether the call to the lexicon should be thought of as an actual call from "working memory" or as the lexicon actively intruding itself on working memory' (2002, 211–12). I do not think this is a real problem. Within the framework of the Extended Mind Model, where each word is a concept, the lexicon is a collection of concepts for which there exists a phonological handle. Thus, the lexicon has intruded itself in working memory as soon as a concept arises since the concept is instantiated as a word or set of words.

Jackendoff proposes that 'since lexical items must be stored in long-term memory, so must lexical concepts' (2002, 333). But in the Extended Mind Model there is no distinction between a lexical item and a lexical concept – they are the same. Some words and, hence, concepts share the same phonological handle such as homophones like to, two, and too, or words such as bug which have multiple meanings depending on the context in which they are used.

Jackendoff recognizes the importance of symbol representation or conceptualization to the emergence of language and, like Bickerton, suggests human language began as one-word utterances: 'Deacon (1997), Donald (1991) and Aitchison (1998) are correct in seeing symbol use as the most fundamental factor in language evolution ... A single vocalization, as in a one-year-old's single-word utterance, can clearly serve symbolically. I therefore concur with most speculation on the subject in thinking that this initial stage consisted of single-symbol utterances, lacking combinatoriality. Single-symbol utterances in young children go beyond primate calls in important respects that are crucial in the evolution of language. Perhaps the most important difference is the non-situation-specificity of human words' (2002, 238).

While recognizing the importance of conceptualization to the emergence of language, Jackendoff sees language and thought as two separate activities whereas I believe abstract conceptual thought and language cannot be separated: 'An important aspect of the present view is that thought is independent of language and can take place in the absence of language. This goes against the common intuition that thought takes place "in a language," as in "Do you think in English or in French?" My position is that linguistic form provides one means for thought to be made available to awareness (another is visual imagery) ... The correct level for carrying out reasoning is conceptual structure [a part of Jackendoff's linguistic architecture], and reasoning can take place without any connection to language, in which case it is unconscious' (2002, 273–4).

The error that Jackendoff is making in my humble opinion is that he does not distinguish between perceptual thinking and conceptual thinking which is a critical distinction made in the Extended Mind Model. The visual imagery that he alludes to in the above excerpt is pure perceptual thinking, as he himself later admits: 'In the old days one might have tried to make the distinction by claiming that there is an "imaging" part of the brain separate from the "perception" part' (2002, 312). Analytic, abstract, deductive thinking, the kind that is used in planning, engineering, science, or story telling is conceptual.

If thought is independent of language, as Jackendoff proclaims, then why is it that humans are the only species with verbal language and at the same time they have thought patterns several orders of magnitude more sophisticated than their closest rivals in the animal world? Jackendoff would have us believe that this correlation is accidental, when in fact the simplest explanation of this fact is that thought and language are intertwined and speech is basically vocalized thought.

There is a possible connection between intentionality and conceptualization for in order to have an intention one must conceive of a goal or an objective. It is true that animals act with intention, but it as though they are operating on some form of automatic pilot driven by their intuitions because they can only act with intention if the object of their desire is immediately perceivable. The predator sees its prey and acts automatically. Domestic pussycats that are provided with all the food they could possibly want will still chase birds and pounce upon insects in an instinctual way without necessarily being motivated by the need for food. It is interesting that Jackendoff wishes to detach intentionality from language in the same way he detaches thought from language except as a medium to express thought: 'I am hoping that we can indeed arrive at a naturalized view of meaning without invoking intentionality' (2002, 279).

Language is a process whereby humans are able to represent their percepts in terms of words or concepts. Percepts are generalized as words or concepts. Language is the beginning of science because language pursues many of the same processes as science. It observes, describes, classifies, and generalizes. The word *dog* describes a class of four-legged creatures, which share certain features. Language, like science, is constantly testing whether it has successfully communicated, as the next two quotes from Emmon Bach and Herbert Clark illustrate: 'In general, to determine whether a sentence is true or false, two things are necessary: (1) you must know what the sentence means and (2) you must face the sentence with some situation in the real world and see whether it corresponds to the meaning of the sentence' (Bach 1989, 8). Herbert Clark emphasizes that 'linguistic communication is not a one-way street, a speaker making utterances and a hearer passively taking them in. Rather, virtually all communication involves a delicate negotiation between speaker and hearer in a joint effort for both to be assured that the intended message gets across' (1996).

Jackendoff sees conceptual structure as innate but not part of UG: 'What is part of UG, of course, is the architecture of the interface components that allow conceptual structures to be expressed in syntactic and phonological structures' (2002, 417). Clearly, for Jackendoff, cognitive structures and language are two separate things.

## The Semantic Uncertainty Principle and a Linguistic Lemma of Gödel's Theorem

Jackendoff engages in a philosophical discussion of how it is that the mind is able to grasp language which some regard as an abstract object. David Lewis suggests there are two topics of interest, one 'the description of possible languages or grammars as abstract semantic systems whereby symbols are associated with aspects of the world,' and the other, 'the description of the psychological and sociological facts whereby one of these abstract semantics systems is used by a person or population' (1972, 170). But to this Jackendoff retorts: 'This view of language is of course profoundly at odds with the outlook of generative grammar, which places language in the f-mind of the language users ... One way to eliminate the problem of how the mind grasps language [as an abstract semantic system or object] is to push language entirely into the mind' (2002, 297 and 300).

The Extended Mind Model, along a similar line, solves this problem simply by avoiding it, since words are concepts in the mind and concepts are words or combination of words. The mind is language plus the brain where the brain before language was merely a percept processor. But with language the brain bifurcates into the mind, which is both a percept processor and a conceptualizer capable of abstract thought. One does not have to push language into the mind since the brain with language becomes a mind capable of conceptualization, which the brain without language was not capable of. This argument is necessarily circular, as is the description of any non-linear dynamic system, since language-words are a product of the mind and at the same time create the mind in a bootstrap operation. There is an analogy in elementary particle physics in which the forces create the particles and the particles generate the very same forces that bring them into existence.

\* \* \* \* \*

### Bootstrap Argument

*In order to grasp the nature of the bootstrap argument from elementary particle physics, let us simplify the argument by considering a universe with only two elementary particles, the pi meson and the rho meson. The rho meson is a resonance of two pi mesons and the force, which creates the resonance of the two pi mesons arises from the exchange of the rho meson between the two pi mesons. And that rho meson, which is exchanged by the two pi mesons is nothing more than two other pi mesons exchanging a rho meson, which is two more pi mesons exchanging a rho meson ... on so on ad infinitum.*

*Extending the argument to the bootstrap of language and the mind, consider the hominid brain before hominids achieved speech or language. The brain was essentially a percept processor. As the hominid began to create concepts in the form of words as strange attractors of the percepts associated with those concepts, it was able to create more words because of its ability for abstract thought and conceptualization, which made it more capable of abstracting more precepts into words or concepts, which increased its conceptualization creating more words ... on so on ad finitum until human language and a mind capable of abstract conceptual thought emerged. This argument is similar to Andy Clark's mangrove effect which we encountered at the beginning of this chapter.*

\* \* \* \* \*

The issues that Jackendoff raises are the linguist's version of the mind-body problem. The solution(s) to this problem cannot be precise, because of the existence of a semantic uncertainty principle not unlike

Heisenberg's uncertainty principle in physics, which states that an exact measurement of both a particle's position and momentum cannot be made because the very act of measuring a particle changes its momentum and/or position. In a similar vein, the semantic uncertainty principle states that a semantic model will be imprecise because the definitions of the words needed to describe the semantic model are themselves subject to uncertainties. Also, with respect to the Extended Mind Model, the concepts required to conceive the notion of a concept are imprecise because of the way in which the semantic model in which they are embedded has been conceived.

Word meanings are personal, belonging to the individual producing them or interpreting them. My word for cat and another person's word for cat have different meanings because our experiences with cats have been different. The meaning that two communicating individuals give to the word cat is close enough for them to understand each other to a certain degree but that understanding is never perfect. Human communication is rife with miscommunication because certain nuances in meaning are not shared. There are times when a person says 'yes' when they mean 'no' and the communication of the true meaning is in the tone or the accompanying facial gesture and body language. The word cat has a smear of meanings, $\Delta$ cat, and similarly love has a smear of meanings $\Delta$ love. Subjective words such as good, happiness, truth, beauty, and hope have a greater smear of meaning and variation than words like house, ball, or the number two.

The uncertainty associated with linguistic models and the lack of consistency should not be a surprise, given that the Universal Grammar was formulated as a mathematical model. In light of Gödel's theorem, which states that a mathematical or logical system cannot be both logically consistent and complete at the same time, neither Chomsky's nor Jackendoff's version of Universal Grammar can be both complete and logically consistent at the same time. Remember that it was the failure of the Russell-Whitehead project to derive all of mathematics from a logically consistent set of axioms that motivated Gödel to derive his theorem. I believe that Chomsky, Pinker, and Jackendoff were unable to do for language precisely what Russell and Whitehead were unable to do for mathematics, namely, derive the entire system from a small set of logically consistent principles. This does not mean that formal mathematics and verbal language are not systematically organized, but only that consistency and completeness are not simultaneously possible. This thought motivated me to formulate a linguistic lemma of Gödel's Theorem.

**The Linguistic Lemma of Gödel's Theorem: No human language can be semantically complete and syntactically consistent.**

The support for this lemma is the fact that the world's linguists cannot agree whether the UG exists and if it does what exactly it is and how it came about. That there are always exceptions to the rules of UG (or other models) is another consequence of this lemma. The term *semantic completeness* is not intended to mean that a language contains all the possible words needed to describe the world but rather that a complete theory of meaning is not possible.

The formulation of the lemma is not intended as a put-down of the field of linguistics. The reader should bear in mind a similar controversy rages in physics as to whether or not quantum theory is a complete theory. There is a respected wing of the field led by the likes of Albert Einstein and David Bohm, who believed that quantum mechanics is incomplete and that there are hidden variables, which once they are discovered will restore full causality to physics. Another respected wing is led by Nils Bohr, who believed quantum theory as presently formulated is a complete theory. This only proves there are many ways to skin Schrödinger's cat or formulate a theory of language.

Another philosophical issue that Jackendoff raises is the connection of the mind to the world through the medium of language: 'If language is in the minds of language users, it is necessary to invoke some mystical connection from the mind to the world, either at the level of language or at the level of concepts the language expresses' (2002, 303). Within the framework of the Extended Mind Model this is a non-issue because the words of the language are mental objects and strange attractors of the percepts related to the concept embraced by the word and, hence, are also mental objects. To put it differently, language describes our mental perceptions of the world, as they are the filters through which the brain experiences the world. This point is conceded by Jackendoff: 'We should properly think of "the perceptual world" ... not as absolute reality but as the "reality" constructed by our perceptual systems in response to whatever is "really out there" ... Thus the perceptual world is reality for us' (ibid., 308).

The philosophical issue that Jackendoff is concerned with is not the connection of language and the 'real' world but rather the connection of our perceptions of the world and the 'real' world. This is a philosophical issue as old as philosophy itself and one that cannot be resolved by inserting language into the problem, as Jackendoff concedes at the end of his discussion of this issue: 'In short, the problem of reference for the intuitively clear cases is not at bottom a problem for linguistic theory, it is a problem for perceptual theory: how do the mechanisms of perception create for us the experience of a world "out there"?' (2002, 309). This is basically correct. The way in which linguistics enters perceptual theory from the standpoint of the Extended Mind Model is that the language incorporates our concepts of the world, which in turn mould our percepts à la the Sapir Whorf hypothesis from which we derive our concepts. In other words, we have a non-linear dynamic system in which the elements are language, concepts, and percepts. Language is the medium in which percepts and concepts bootstrap each other into existence.

### The Symbolosphere, the Extended Mind, and Neo-Dualism

John Schumann (2003a, 2003b) together with his colleague Namhee Lee (Lee and Schumann (2003) have developed the notion of the symbolosphere, in which language is seen as a cultural artifact that 'is neither of the brain nor in the brain' (Lee and Schumann 2003). It is not transmitted biologically but rather culturally and 'exists as a cultural artifact or technology between and among brains' (ibid.). It is an artifact that is invisible and non-material and, hence, is not part of the biosphere but rather forms the symbolosphere, which includes all forms of symbolic communication including such things as written language, mathematics, science, music, and the arts.

Schumann argues that humans live within the symbolosphere, which influences their lives as much as the biosphere and, hence, introduces a duality between these two spheres of influence on human existence. He suggests that a distinction should be made between the brain and the mind 'because there is an implicit recognition that aspects of mental life take place, not only in the physical brain, but also in some nonphysical medium. Could this mind actually be the symbolosphere?' asks Schumann (2003b).

The symbolosphere is embedded within the semiosphere, the set of all signs, whether they are iconic, indexical, or symbolic. The symbolo-sphere includes all of the phenomena mediated by symbols and, hence, includes all abstract human thought and communication. Embedded within the symbolosphere one can imagine a memeosphere or culturo-sphere, the set of all memes or cultural replicators. The complement to the semiosphere and the symbolosphere is the physiosphere within which is embedded the biosphere

Schumann and I, in discussing our respective approaches to under-standing the origin of language, realized that our approaches both embraced a form of dualism, which in most scientific circles would be scoffed at. We felt rather than a weakness that properly formulated as neo-dualism this idea had merit.

One can trace dualism back to Plato but the modern tradition of dualism begins with Descartes, who distinguished between two types of substances or ontological categories *res extensa* and *res cogitans*. Res cogi-tans represents for Descartes all the beings that think, which for him is the set of human minds and God. Res extensa was all the rest, the mate-rial world which has extension and, hence, physicality. Res cogitans has no extension or physicality. Descartes' formulation is known as 'sub-stance dualism' in which two types of substances, res extensa and res cogitans, are posited. Logan and Schumann (2005), however, argue that a property dualism is a more appropriate description of the mind-brain system. We therefore posited that 'the human brain can have two sets of properties, one physical made of flesh and blood and the other mental composed of thoughts and consciousness' (ibid.).

We contend that this philosophical debate between substance and prop-erty dualism is not amenable to a scientific resolution. Since we do not understand the relationship between the physical events that take place in the brain and the emergence of thought, it is folly to try to speculate as to whether they are the same substance. At our present level of under-standing, the only practical way to deal with understanding the nature of human mentality is to describe the activities of the brain, on the one hand, and of human thought and emotions which make up the human mind, on the other hand, and try where possible to find links between these two levels of phenomena, namely, the physical brain and human thought and emotion.

If we adopt a cybernetic point of view by invoking Ashby's (1957) Law of Requisite Variety, the only way to model the phenomena of cognition, language, brain, and mind, given our present understanding of neuroscience, is to make a distinction between mental properties and physical properties, that is, to adopt a property dualist position. Any attempt to speculate about the possibility of a monist position, namely, that mental and physical events are of a single property or substance enters the realm of theology and is no longer within the domain of science, since any proposition of this nature is not falsifiable.

It is our position that one way to explore the relationship between the brain and the human mind is by studying the origin and production of language as well as its many subsequent consequences. We note that language gives rise to concepts, ideas, thoughts, beliefs, values, and consciousness, which in our opinion make up the essential unique features of the human mind. Thus, we would like to introduce a new dualism, that of res extensa, one of Descartes' original substances and *res linguistica*. Res extensa is the natural physical and material world, which we will sometimes refer to as the physiosphere and res linguistica is the world of language, symbols, semantics, syntax, metaphors, concepts, thoughts, ideas, consciousness, culture, and the human mind, which Schumann (2003b) refers to as the symbolosphere. There is a certain parallel of our approach with Descartes, in that he started with what he saw as two certainties, namely, the existence of God and his own existence via the *cogito ergo sum* argument. We, however, begin with our belief that the one unique quality that differentiates humans from non-human animals is our ability to use non-material language, which in turn gives rise to another uniquely human phenomenon, namely, the human mind.

Within the framework of the neo-dualism that we have just formulated we make no distinction between substance dualism and property dualism. The notion that one describes the world in terms of substances is an outdated mode of philosophical analysis that does not particularly illuminate our understanding of human language, thought, or culture. In other words, the term *substance* when used in the context of understanding human cognition is without substance (pun intended). Therefore, to debate whether there are two types of substances in the universe or one substance with two types of properties is fruitless. It is clear to us that a description of human behaviour requires consideration of physical interactions that are understood in terms of physics, biochemistry, and biology and cognitive interactions, which we believe are language– and symbol–based. To talk of language as a property of the brain, or as some separate substance, does not add in any way to our understanding of the nature of cognition, consciousness, or the mind itself. Language is both a property of the brain and at the same time a phenomenon that can be studied independently of understanding the mechanisms of the brain. Thus, we are proposing an emergent dualism without a disconnect from the brain.

The neo-dualistic formulation that we are proposing differs from Descartes in that we do not think of res linguistica as a substance but rather as a description of human cognition. Our formulation parallels Descartes dualism. Res extensa remains unchanged. Res cogitans is replaced with res linguistica, which like res cogitans incorporates the human mind and all its thought and communication processes, but does not include God. We remain agnostic with respect to the existence of God, but treat the spiritual dimension of human cognition as a cultural artifact or value. The neo-dualistic split that we are championing makes a distinction between the description of physical phenomena and abstract, symbolic mental phenomena. We carefully make a distinction between percepts, the nervous system's response to physical stimuli, which belong to the physiosphere, and concepts, the symbol-based processes of human thought and communication, which are part of the symbolosphere. Res linguistica, the symbolosphere, and conceptualization are exclusively properties of humans and separate us from non-human animals. With respect to acculturated non-human primates (and hominids) we believe they might now possess (or might have possessed) some primitive elements of res linguistica but that the creation of the symbolosphere was basically a human creation.*

---

* This section has been excerpted from the article 'The Symbolosphere, Conceptualization, Language and Neo-Dualism,' *Semiotica* (2005) 155: 201–14, with the permission of my co-author, John Schumann.

One of the key elements of the argument just presented for a neo-dualistic position is our lack of understanding of the relationship between the physical operations of the brain and the mental operations of the mind. Andy Clark has argued that this situation might not be so easily overcome by citing the following quote of unknown authorship: 'If the brain were so simple that a single approach could unlock its secrets, we would be so simple that we couldn't do the job!' (1997, 175). In other words we will be limited by a neuroscience uncertainty principle. The Heisenberg uncertainty principle arises from the fact that the only way to measure quantum objects is with using other quantum objects and so it is with neuroscience, brains are required to measure and understand brains.

# PART 5

---

## The Co-evolution of Culture:
## Language and Altruism and the Emergence
## of Universal Culture

# 12 The Co-evolution of Culture and Language

In chapter 9 we considered the question: Was the evolution of language strictly a genetic phenomenon or did it include cultural evolution or memetics as well? We discovered that both Donald (1991, 2001) and Tomasello (1999) have developed models for the emergence of language in which culture plays a dominant role and that Christiansen (1994) and Deacon (1997) have developed models in which language itself evolves and is affected by cultural phenomena.

There is no doubt that culture has influenced the origin and development of language, but it is also true that language is an essential component of culture. I would, therefore, like to explore in this chapter the symbolic nature of culture and religion and the idea that language and culture have cross-impacted upon each other's development and, hence, co-evolved. We begin our discussion by defining the exact nature of culture.

## What Is Culture? An Ideational Definition

Culture is an important adaptive mental tool that is more or less unique to humans, whereby the learning of previous generations is passed on to the next generation through communication and social interactions. As suggested by Boyd and Richerson:

> Individual learning ... can be costly and prone to errors. Learning trials occupy time and energy that could be allocated to other components of fitness, and may entail a considerable risk to the individual as well. Because

of these costs, the investments of individuals in determining the locally favored behavior must be limited, and individual learning can lead to errors. Individuals may fail to discover an adaptive behavior, or a maladaptive one maybe retained because it was reinforced by chance. When these costs are important, selection ought to favor shortcuts to learning – ways that an organism can achieve phenotypic flexibility without paying the full cost of learning. Cultural inheritance is adaptive because it is such a shortcut. If the locally adaptive behavior is more common than other behaviors, imitation provides an inexpensive way to acquire it. (1985, 14)

Edward Tylor introduced the notion of culture as a subject of academic study with the publication of his book *Primitive Culture* in 1871 in London. He became the first professor of anthropology ever when he was appointed to teach the subject at Oxford University. His *definition* of culture, which is still used by many anthropologists, is 'that complex whole which includes knowledge, belief, art, law, morals, customs, and any other capabilities and habits acquired by man as a member of society' (1871, 1).

The problem with this definition according to Lee Cronk (1999, 4) is that it includes behaviour through the use of the word 'habit' and, as such, is too general. If one wants to explain behaviour in terms of culture then culture cannot include behaviour or else one's argument becomes circular. Cronk never explicitly defines culture but implicit in his text is the notion that culture is 'socially transmitted information' and that it takes its 'physical form ... as mental representations inside people's heads' (ibid., 13–14).

Others have been more explicit about the notion that culture is purely ideational. Clifford Geertz defines culture as 'an historically transmitted pattern of meanings embodied in symbols, a system of inherited conceptions expressed in symbolic forms by means of which men communicate, perpetuate and develop their knowledge about and attitudes towards life.' He goes on to add that 'culture is patterns for behavior not patterns of behavior' (1973, 8). Boyd and Richerson have a similar definition of culture: 'The essential feature of culture is social learning, the nongenetic transfer of patterns of skill, thought, and feeling from individual to individual in a population or society ... Learning and other modes of phenotypic flexibility do have features in common with culture, but it is the social transmission of culture that gives it an evolutionary dynamic different from ordinary learning and its analogs' (1985, 34).

Durham defines culture in the following way: 'The new consensus in anthropology regards culture as a system of symbolically encoded conceptual phenomena that are socially and historically transmitted within and between populations. As Keesing has pointed out, this view contrasts markedly with earlier conceptualizations of culture as adaptive behavioral systems, for which human populations maintain themselves in local environments' (1991, 8–9).

Although culture must be distinguished from 'adaptive behavioral systems' it should be recognized that culture is highly adaptive in that it encodes all of the lessons of survival from one's ancestors.

Johnson and Earle stress the importance of symbols for creating cohesion within a culture:

> To sustain economic integration beyond the capacity of the biological bonds that underpin the famialistic group, it is necessary to extend the individual's sense of 'self-interest' to broader social units. This extension of self is based on symbols. The evolution of the political economy represents the elaboration of this symbolizing capacity in order to overcome the individualistic, competitive, divisive, centrifugal stresses that continually threaten to defeat efforts to cooperate beyond the family level ... the economic integration beyond the family level is stabilized through the elaboration of public symbols. This process begins in the symbolic extension of famialistic relations via classificatory kinship, expands in the ceremonial construction of collective consciousness, as in totemism, and finds spectacular expression in 'big man' feasts. Far from being economically irrelevant, these symbolically rich events and institutions create channels of economic support, identify economically important groups, and advertise such crucial information as property ownership, group strength, and alliance formation. (1987, 322)

Culture provides an extrasomatic form of instruction that provides individual human organisms with an added margin of survival benefit. The information is extra-genetic and plays a role like genetically transmitted instincts. Just as instinctual behaviour is subject to change and evolution, so too is culturally constrained behaviour. Just as instinct supports survival, so does culture. Without a culture a human being or a small social group would be unable to survive. If the environment undergoes a dramatic change, the instincts that were inherited from a previous time could be detrimental to survival, and they will certainly undergo a change and evolution if the species is to survive. The same is true of culture.

As the environment changes, so will the culture so as to be a benefit to those who possess it. If not the society will not survive. There are, indeed, historical examples of cultures that were unable to adapt to changing conditions, which perished or were transformed into very different cultures. The culture of hunting had positive survival benefits and made for an easy life until game was depleted by overhunting. When this happened the hunters-gatherers supplemented their wild food with domesticated plants and/or animals. Hunting cultures evolved into pastoral societies in which animals were not slaughtered to extinction, but domesticated and culled in a controlled way. This required more effort than hunting because of the care that had to be given to the animals. The Garden of Eden story in Genesis is an explanation of this need to earn one's bread by the sweat of one's brow.

## Religion and Culture

One of the ways that symbols are used to create social cohesion in a culture is through ritual and religion. At the purely family-level of organization ceremonies were part of family rituals and were largely ad hoc and non-hierarchical. The ceremonies had a celebratory feeling to them, but they served an economic function as well. They brought members of a family that were generally dispersed together at certain seasons for cooperative foraging and consumption of a rich seasonal resource, and they allowed families to share information about the location of other resources. Such events had a social role, as the following account of the Kung San indicates: 'When several camps gather for all-night trance dancing and curing ceremonies, marriage brokering, socializing, and exchange make and strengthen ties within and between camps' (Johnson and Earle 1987, 50). At the local level ceremonies were used functionally to develop intragroup identity between families and intergroup identity to promote cooperation and integration; they integrate groups by dissipating factional tensions and brokering marriages.

At the regional level ceremony was used to legitimize authority and unequal access to resources. As societies became more complex, there was a general trend that for stratification and ceremonialism to emerge, become more elaborate, and grow in importance. Religion is a way in which ruling elites establish their authority over the commoners. This is true of both chiefdoms and states: 'Religious institutions helped to consolidate the chief's control' (Johnson and Earle 1987, 235). 'An institutionalized state religion' is a prerequisite for the formation of a state: 'The state religion serves to both organize production and to sanctify state rule' (ibid., 246). David Sloan Wilson comes to a similar conclusion in his treatment of the evolution of religion in *Darwin's Cathedral*: 'Around the world and across history, religions have functioned as mighty engines of collective action for the production of benefits that all people want' (2002, 187).

## The Relationship of Language and Culture

If culture consists of 'symbolically encoded' concepts, as claimed by Durham (1991, 8), then it is very much like language, which also consists of 'symbolically encoded' concepts, namely, words. It therefore follows that many of the characteristics that we have discerned and posited for language may apply to culture as well. Language is an explicit part of culture and it is also the medium for the transmission of culture. Culture, on the other hand, is the medium for the transmission of language. Let us for the moment focus on language as a medium for the transmission of culture both explicitly and implicitly.

As for the acquisition of explicit knowledge, Tomasello points out that 'beyond fundamental skills of primate cognition ... children's domain-specific knowledge and expertise depend almost totally on the accumulated knowledge of their cultures and its "transmission" to them via linguistic and other symbols, including both writing and pictures. The amount of knowledge that any individual organism can gain by simply observing the world on its own is extremely limited' (1999, 165). Tomasello also indicates that language is not only essential for explicit knowledge but it also provides a subliminal framework for organizing both the percepts of the observed world and the concepts of the inner mental world of the mind: '[Children's] continuing use of the language conventional in their culture leads children to construe the world in terms of the categories and perspectives and relational analogies embodied in that language, and perhaps to use these highly exercised skills of categorization, analogizing, and perspective-taking in other domains such as mathematics' (ibid., 189). Tomasello's observation indicates that language contains many subliminal cultural artifacts, a point originally made by both Sapir (1921) and Whorf (1964). A language is one of the media by which a culture is transmitted and preserved, and culture plays a role similar to the one that McLuhan (1964) described with his famous aphorism, 'the medium is the message.'

Like most good aphorisms, McLuhan's famous dictum has more than one meaning. For one, independent of its content or messages, a medium has its own intrinsic effects on our actions, perceptions, and concepts, which are its unique message. 'The message of any medium or technology is the change of scale or pace or pattern that it introduces into human affairs.' McLuhan cites the way the railway created 'totally new kinds of cities and new kinds of work' (1964, 8). What McLuhan wrote about the railroad applies with equal force to the media of spoken language, writing, print, television, the microcomputer, and the Internet. 'The medium is the message' because it is the 'medium that shapes and controls the scale and form of human association and action' (ibid., 9).

'The medium is the message' also carries the notion that a medium transforms its message or content. A movie shown on television or a play that is filmed affects its audience differently from the original live production. A lesson that is learned from a peer is different from a lesson learned from an adult or authority figure, as Tomasello points out. The essence of this second aspect of 'the medium is the message' is that the message is still the message but it is transformed by the medium. We may, therefore, formulate the relationship between language and culture as follows: Language is the medium and culture is the message. The message transmitted in the same language within two cultures that differ from each other even ever so slightly will have different meanings. This is the source of many misunderstandings. The problem when translating from one language to another is even more difficult: 'The ready-made categories of language ... provide the child with a starting point for conceptually grouping and interrelating entities of various types to one another. Cultural transmission of this type, of course, is only possible because children have the primate skills of perception, memory, categorization, and the like, but uniquely human cultural learning skills enable them to use these individually based skills to benefit from the knowledge and skills of others in their social group in uniquely powerful ways' (Tomasello 1999, 197).

Tomasello supports the notion, developed in the Extended Mind Model, that language represents a transition from percept-based to concept-based thinking and representation (1999, 118). In addition, he complements the idea expressed in the Extended Mind Model that words act as strange attractors for all of the percepts associated with a concept with his notion that words provide a multi-perspectival way of looking at events and objects, which 'is an integral part of the view of language known as Cognitive or Functional Linguistics,' and has been developed by Langacker (1987) among others:

> The symbolic representations that children learn in their social interactions with other persons are special because they are (a) intersubjective in the sense that a symbol is socially 'shared' with other persons; and (b) perspectival, in the sense that each symbol picks out a particular way of viewing some phenomenon (categorization being a special case of this process). The central theoretical point is that linguistic symbols embody the myriad ways of construing the world intersubjectively that have accumulated in a culture over historical time, and the process of acquiring the conventional use of these symbolic artifacts, and so internalizing these construals, fundamentally transforms the nature of children's cognitive representations. (Tomasello 1999, 95–6)

An interesting relationship between language and culture has been posited by Nettle to explain human cooperation and altruism. He argues 'that the creation of distinct languages and dialects is a way of maintaining solidarity in cooperating groups' (1999, 224). Speech acts as a social marker identifying and differentiating those who can be trusted to reciprocate altruistic acts from those who might be social free loaders. He cites evidence that 'the closer the stranger's speech is to that of the subject, the more likely he is to obtain cooperation' (ibid., 223).

## Nature versus Nurture

The nature versus nurture debate is based on a false dichotomy, as Hurford (2003) and Tomasello (1999) contend. Hurford (2003) argues that nature and nurture are intertwined: 'Cultural evolution, mediated by learning, has a different dynamic from biological evolution; and, to make matters even more complex, biological and cultural evolution can intertwine in a co-evolutionary spiral ... Children are taught to be "team-players." No concerted instruction in cooperation exists outside humans ... Dispositions to cooperation and maintenance of group cohesion are pragmatic cognitive pre-adaptations for language' (2003, 40 and 43).

Cooperation is essential to language and also to culture. But without language, culture and shared knowledge would have been at a much lower level, as is the case with other primates. Since the first human groupings were likely kin groups, those who cooperated enhanced group survival. Even if cooperation lowered the fitness of an individual it enhanced kin fitness. Those groups that did not cooperate achieved less fitness as a group, even where some individuals thrived at the expense of others:

> Learning is ... a product of evolution – one of its strategies, if we may anthromorphize the process a bit – as are culture and cultural learning as special cases of the 'extended ontogeny' evolutionary strategy. There is thus no question of opposing nature versus nurture; nurture is just one of the many forms that nature may take.(Tomasello 1999, 212)

> But the human cultural world is not thereby free of the biological world, and indeed human culture is a very recent evolutionary product, having existed in all likelihood for only a few hundred thousand years. The fact that the culture is a product of evolution does not mean that each one of its specific features has its own dedicated genetic underpinnings; there has not been enough time for that ... Modern adult cognition of the human kind is the product not only of genetic events taking place over many millions of years in evolutionary time but also of cultural events taking place over many tens of thousands of years in historical time and personal events taking place over many tens of thousands of hours in ontogenetic time. The desire to avoid the hard empirical work necessary to follow out these

intermediate processes that occur between the human genotype and phenotype is a strong one, and it leads to the kinds of facile genetic determinism that pervades large parts of social, behavioral, and cognitive sciences today. Genes are an important part of the story of human cognitive evolution, perhaps even from some points of view the most important part of the story since they are what got the ball rolling. (ibid., 216–17)

It is not nature versus nurture but rather nature and nurture working together, where nurture is actually a part of nature. The mechanism of evolution is not just genetic, but rather it also involves cultural or symbolic artifacts acting as memes. All symbolic artifacts, words, and syntactical structures, are memes.

**Symbolic Culture**

We have already discussed the intimate relationship between language and culture and it should therefore be no surprise that one of the bases of culture is symbolism. Philip Chase goes even further to suggest that symbolism infuses culture, asserting that 'symbolism really consists of two different phenomena. The first of these is symbolic reference, the use in language and elsewhere of arbitrary (i.e. conventional) signs to refer to things and concepts. The second, which I will call "symbolic culture," is the extension of symbolism beyond reference to the creation of an intellectual environment populated by phenomena that owe their very existence to symbolism and where every thing and every action has significance in an all-encompassing symbol system' (1999, 3).

Chase uses the notion of symbolic culture to explain how cooperation and altruism came into existence: 'We organize very large social systems, networks of interaction that require cooperation between individuals who may never have seen one another before and who may expect never to see one another again. It is not at all clear that humans could do this without symbolic culture' (1999, 37). Chase argues that altruism in a society where not every member is related by kinship cannot be explained as occurring if the environment in which an individual operated was a purely natural one like that of non-human animals, that is, a non-symbolic environment. Symbolic culture provides an unnatural environment in which humans would be willing to make sacrifices for strangers. The imperatives to act in such a selfless manner must be constructed culturally because such behaviour contradicts natural selection. The roots of such behaviour can, therefore, be traced to the emergence of language in which symbolism first emerged.

Given the importance of culture to human thinking, perhaps we need to revisit our notion that the mind is an extension of the brain due to language. Perhaps we need to add culture to the equation and consider the mind as an extension of the brain due to both language and culture. Our new formulation, then, is:

$$mind = brain + language + culture.$$

This notion that I formulated before reading Andy Clark (1997, 2003) is, nevertheless, reinforced by his ideas about culture contributing to scaffolded cognition, where both language and culture provide the scaffolding. Just as language provides a framework for conceptualization, culture does the same thing as it stores all of the lessons that a society has acquired over the years. Given that language is a cultural artifact, it makes sense that other cultural artifacts and processes would also contribute to the way humans would think and, hence, to the construction of their mind.

Donald has come to a similar conclusion: 'Culture distributes cognitive activity across many brains and dominates the minds of its members. Despite this, cognitive science studies the mind as if it were confined entirely within a single brain. Culture is not usually included in cognitive theory, except as part of the environment.' (2001, 149–50). According to Donald, language is the product of the interaction of brains and not the product of the operation of an isolated brain: 'Translated into a neural context, this implies that symbols evolved to mediate transactions between brains, rather than to serve as an internal thought code for individual brains' (ibid.). Once acquired through the emergent process of the interaction of two or more brains, language becomes the medium for internal thought.

Culture has an effect on the development of the human mind, both through the emergence of symbolic communication and through the content of that symbolic communication. As Donald points out, 'the specific form of the modern mind has been determined largely by culture. The creative collision between the conscious mind and distributed cultural systems has altered the very form of human cognition. It has also changed the tools with which we think. Language, art, and all our symbolic technologies have emerged from this collective enterprise' (2001, 153). Donald carries this argument even further claiming that 'without culture, we could never have become full-fledged symbolizing organisms ... We connect with and learn from others to a unique degree. Symbolic thought is a by-product of this fact, so is language. Both result from the collision of conscious minds in culture' (ibid., 202 and 253). In other words, culture gave rise to language and not language to culture. Donald argues that to understand human development one needs to consider, in addition to phylogeny and ontogeny, enculturation.

To illustrate the way in which culture affects the mind or thinking of those that possess it we will compare English Canadian and American cultures. American and Canadian English cultures share much in common. English Canadians and Americans enjoy, for the most part, the same movies and television shows starring both Canadian and American performers. The two countries share the world's longest undefended border. Despite these similarities the way English Canadians and Americans think about certain things is quite different in a number of ways. Their attitude to health care is one example. Canadians value their universal health care system, which some Americans envy but which most Americans consider to be a form of socialized medicine, and hence, undesirable. Canada has a relatively small army, which it deploys primarily for peacekeeping missions, whereas Americans invest a much greater percentage of their gross national product in their armed forces, which they use aggressively to pursue what they consider to be their national interest. Canada is officially bilingual and multicultural, a mosaic of its constituent cultures, whereas the United States prides itself on being a melting pot. These are a few of the ways in which Canadian and American cultures differ and affect the thinking of their citizens.

There are many other examples where people with the same language have different cultures. The difference in the cultures of different Latin American societies is one example. Another example would be the cultures of different religious communities in the same society. Still another would be the cultural differences of different work or professional communities embedded in the same society.

# 13 Altruism and the Origin of Language and Culture

In the last chapter we began to explore the relationship between culture, language, and cooperation or altruism. There is a strong connection between altruism and the origin of language. I am supported in this by Ingar Brinck and Peter Gärdenfors, who claim 'that the pressure for future-directed co-operation was a major force behind the evolution of language' (2003, 484). This position flies in the face, however, of those who make the contra-claim that altruism could not have arisen according to standard Darwinian thinking. The argument made goes something like this: An altruistic individual who helps another conspecific is helping someone with whom they are in competition for the propagation of their genes: 'Given this perspective, speech (and many other forms of cooperative behaviour) can be difficult to account for' (Noble 2000, 40). The emergence of culture is another form of cooperative behaviour that needs to be accounted for and which seems to arise from altruism and cooperation.

If the emergence of language and culture can be tied to the emergence of altruism, then instead of three mysteries, namely, the individual emergence of altruism, language, and culture we would be left with only one mystery requiring an explanation. The thrust of this chapter is to show that these three mysteries are somehow interrelated and that altruism, language, and culture somehow co-evolved and represent different facets of a unified phenomenon, which makes our species unique. If the life-history strategy of the genus Homo was one of coalitions and collaboration, then one would have a unified explanation of altruism, language, and culture. I am not alone in suggesting an intimate connection between language and altruism. Let me call upon Brinck and Gärdenfors once more: 'We submit that a major reason for the evolution of language is that it enhances co-operation. Language is the tool by which agents can make their imaginations, desires, and evaluations known to each other' (2003, 492).

Before plunging into the main thrust of this chapter, let us first address the issue of whether (and to what extent) altruism, language, and culture are unique to the human species. The issue arises because some scholars argue that each of the three aspects of altruism, language, and culture occur with non-human animals. I do not totally disagree with this claim but would counter by claiming that the level of altruism, language, and culture achieved by our species represents a major discontinuity over that of non-human animals and that their emergence with humans represents a saltation. Consider language, which many claim for apes, dolphins, and even parrots. I agree that many animals communicate and that certain acculturated chimps and bonobos (but not apes living in the wild) have even developed some form of symbolic communication, but they have never been able to master syntax, invent a new symbol, or use language to express their needs or plan for the future: 'All evidence for planning in non-human animals concerns planning for present needs. Humans seem to be the only animal that can plan for future needs' (Brink and Gärdenfors 1999, 100). Given the limited use that non-human animals make of their communication, it would be difficult to dispute that there exists a tremendous gap between human language and any form of non-human communication.

A similar kind of argument can be made for the uniqueness of human culture. As is the case for language, few would dispute that human culture represents a major discontinuity with non-human culture. Tomasello has pointed out that certain forms of non-human cultural transmission exists when, for example, 'fledgling birds imitate their parents species-typical songs, rat pups eat only the food eaten by their mothers, ants locate food by following the pheromone trail of other ants, and young chimps imitate tool use skills of their parents' (Tomasello 1999, 4). But, as Tomasello further points out, these are isolated cases and none of these species build on the accomplishments of their earlier cultural achievement to create, as is the case with humans, a constantly evolving and progressing culture which builds on earlier accomplishments, producing what Tomasello, Kruger, and Ratner (1993) have dubbed 'the ratchet effect.' I have independently identified a similar mechanism, 'the cognitive, social and technological interplay of language' in my studies of the evolution of notated language (Logan1995, 2004b) when I suggested:

> Cognitive tools and physical technology are two resources at the disposal of human innovators, and the needs or demands of society are often the motivating force. Necessity is the mother of invention, yet invention does not occur in a vacuum. All of the previous innovations in a culture provide the resources, both cognitive and physical, for the next level of innovation. The previous innovations also contribute to changes within the socio-economic system that give rise to new social demands. Each new invention, technological innovation, or discovery gives rise to new technical capabilities, new cognitive abilities, and new social conditions. These then interact with the existing economic, political, social, cultural, technical, and cognitive realities of the culture to set the stage for the next round of innovation. Thus, technological change in our model is part of an ongoing iterative process. It began with the inception of Homo sapiens and continues to this day at an ever-quickening pace. (1995, 125–32)

Finally, I turn to altruism in which I include sharing, cooperation, and collaboration. When discussing altruism in evolutionary terms there is a tendency to think of altruism strictly in terms of sacrifice, which is only one form of altruism. Operating with fellow humans in a cooperative and/or collaborative manner is also altruistic in the sense that one does not act immediately upon one's short-term needs but one learns to defer one's short-term needs in order to belong to a community where one's long-term goals will be satisfied. De Waal observes that reciprocal altruism is such that 'giving is contingent on receiving' and 'there is a time lag between giving and receiving' (1996, 24).

Altruistic behaviour is found in both non-human species and human beings, but that the level of human sharing, cooperation, and collaboration goes far beyond that of non-humans. The 'ratchet effect' or 'the cognitive, social and technological interplay of language' would not have been possible without the level of altruism, sharing, cooperation, and collaboration achieved by our species. Examples of non-human altruism, sharing, cooperation, and collaboration abound in nature, but it is with humans that new levels are achieved, which are different in nature from that of non-human animals, as has been argued by Charles Lumsden:

> In surveying the patterns of social organization among all species whose members are known to live in groups, Edward Wilson (1975, 1978) noted four pinnacles, or high points of evolutionary complexity, among the range of possibilities: the colonial invertebrates (the corals, sponges, colonial jellyfish); the social insects (ants, bees, wasps, termites); monkeys, apes, and social mammals excluding human beings; and us. Wilson also pointed out that, a seeming paradox: as one climbs a scale arranged on the basis of nervous system organization and behavioral complexity, one actually descends in the quality of many traits we intuitively associate with sociality, such as altruism, sharing, cooperation, division of labor, and social integration. With the appearance of the human mind in evolutionary history, however, this downswing in societal coherence is abruptly reversed – a phylogenetic event that has been of enormous consequence to our place in the global ecosystem and our impact on the environment. (2002, n.p.)

Having established that the level of language, culture, and altruism achieved by humans is unique to our species, I now turn to address the primary thesis of this chapter, namely, that (1) language, culture, and altruism co-evolved, and (2) the mystery of the origin of these three unique features of *Homo sapiens* is not three separate mysteries but can be simplified to a single mystery because language, culture, and altruism form an autocatalytic set of ideas. Another way of expressing this is to say that human language, culture, and altruism form a complex adaptive system or are a set of ideas that have a positive feedback loop. We cannot at this stage of our understanding of these three phenomena describe the process by which they emerged and interacted with each other. There are, however, a number of interesting analyses from linguistics, child psychology vis-à-vis language acquisition, hominid archaeology, and cultural anthropology that point to a strong interrelation between these three facets of human existence supporting the hypothesis that they may form an autocatalytic set of human behaviours.

Let me begin by cataloguing the results of the research of others that led me to postulate my theory and perhaps later try to synthesize or weave together these different strands into a coherent argument. By way of the history of these arguments I would like to mention that these ideas which had been kicking around in my head congealed at the Evolang 5 Conference in Leipzig in March 2004 where within the space of three days I was exposed to a number of fascinating results that led me to conclude that altruism was an essential factor in the emergence of language and culture.

Tomasello (1999), and later together with his co-workers in, showed that children from about one year of age begin to understand 'persons as intentional agents, which enables skills of cultural learning and shared intentionality. This initial step is "the real thing" in the sense that it enables young children to participate in cultural activities using shared, perspectival symbols with a conventional/normative/reflective dimension – for example, linguistic communication and pretend play – thus inaugurating children's understanding of things mental' (Tomasello and Rakoczy 2003, 121).

At the Leipzig conference, Tomasello reported evidence that children will engage in joint attentional activities and that they will show things to their parents or caregivers not only to obtain something they want, which they do, but also just for the pleasure of doing it because they want to share interest. Human children as opposed to non-human primates understand communicative intentions. They readily engage in joint actions and joint attention to such a greater extent than non-human primates that this quantitative difference becomes a qualitative one. Apes can follow someone reaching for something, but they cannot understand why a human is pointing at something, an ability that dogs possess even as puppies not exposed to humans. In other words, although apes can understand the intentions of conspecifics, such as the desire of a conspecific to obtain some food, they are unable to understand communicative intentions. Children understand what adults want, and they want to help adults achieve their objectives. They collaboratively engage in joint actions, which is something that apes are not capable of. In other words, children can understand the adult perspective (Tomasello 2004). All of these abilities of children are indicative of their innate altruistic or collaborative attitude.

The innate desire to share interest and to be collaborative is a prerequisite for language and cultural transmission, because without the motivation to share there is no motivation to communicate. What cannot be teased out of this argument, however, is whether the motivation to share motivates communication or vice versa: Does the desire to communicate motivate sharing? Perhaps sharing and communicating both motivate and support each other and as a result altruism and language emerged together.

Chris Knight points out that, according to the Darwinian view that if language is 'a system designed for communicating good information to trusting listeners,' then 'this implies that speech has been co-operative from its inception.' He goes on to observe that 'in accounting for the necessary honesty, it is tempting to draw on Darwinian reciprocal altruism theory (Trivers 1971): if you lie to me, I'll never again listen to you – so be honest. But even accepting this, we need to explain why the dynamic did not lead to volitional, conventional signaling among those apes, which appear cognitively capable of reciprocal altruism' (1998b, 75). Tomasello and Donald independently provide the same answer, namely, apes lack an understanding of the intentionality of others: 'This capacity (understanding of the intentionality of others) seems to be absent in apes' (Donald 1998, 56). 'Nonhuman primates are themselves intentional and causal beings, they just do not understand the world in intentional and causal terms' (Tomasello 1999, 19). This being the case, it is understandable why apes never developed reciprocal altruism – they could not conceive of a conspecific having the intention to treat them kindly.

Knight (1998b) makes his position for the relationship between altruism and 'communicating good information' by referring to Trivers's (1971) work. More recently Laland, Odling-Smee, and Feldman (1999) have critiqued Trivers, arguing persuasively that altruism is better accounted for by understanding the role of niche construction. Even if they are correct, Knight's point remains valid – language and altruism are interconnected whether altruism arises from reciprocity or niche construction. Ib Ulbaek also connects reciprocal altruism and social communication: 'The function of language in modern Homo sapiens and in the species' language using ancestors is to communicate thoughts ... language evolved in the Homo lineage not because of superior hominid intelligence, but because of special social conditions: the development of reciprocal altruism as a way of gaining fitness by sharing and helping' (1998, 41).

We have argued that humans, as opposed to apes, are capable of altruistic behaviour because they are capable of understanding the intentionality of others. But perhaps this argument is circular. One can equally argue that humans are capable of understanding the intentionality of others because they need to collaborate. We, therefore, need to identify some reasons that might have motivated genus Homo to be collaborative and, hence, capable of understanding the intentionality of others. Bickerton (2002, 209) suggests three, namely, group foraging, predator avoidance, and the instruction of the young. To these, following the work of Donald (1991), I would add (1) toolmaking and the sharing of that skill; (2) the maintenance of the hearth, once the control of fire was mastered; (3) the need to live harmoniously in large groups sharing the hearth; (4) large-scale coordinated hunting; and (5) mimetic communication.

A further area that links altruism and language is the connection between altruism and encephalization. Although the exact link between language and encephalization is not known, much evidence from neuroscience and hominid physical archaeology suggests that there is some sort of correlation between language and encephalization. When this correlation is coupled with archaeological evidence of hominid settlement sites that shows a connection between encephalization and food sharing, a form of cooperation or altruism, one has another link between language and altruism. James Steele (2004) has persuasively argued, from energy considerations, that in order for the brain to have grown in size it was necessary for the gut to have become smaller because the human brain which represents only a small percentage of body weight uses up 20 per cent of the body's energy resources. The diet of early hominids was made up of low-quality foods such as leaves, ripened and unripened fruits, insects, and small game – this diet required large guts and a lot of energy devoted to digestion. With dietary improvements due to the inclusion of large game animals, hominids were able to devote more energy to servicing a larger brain and less to digestion. Thus, a positive feedback loop was initiated.

Archeological records show that more advanced hominids emerged where there was a large quantity of game. The more intelligent the hominids were the more they would succeed in finding large game, which would in turn promote greater encephalization, and in turn greater intelligence and a better diet, and so on and so forth. Food sharing, a form of altruism and cooperation or collaboration, was essential for reducing variance in the high-quality foods essential for brain growth. Through group selection, food sharing and altruism, as well as encephalization would be selected for. Steele (2004) presented evidence for food sharing from analyses of animal bones found at hominid archaeological settlement sites. These analyses indicate that a site accommodated a small kin group of about a hundred people. It is surmised that as groups exceeded this number, they would have split off to keep the size of the group not much larger than a hundred.

Here is another connection between language, encephalization, and high-quality food: Because the range of large game is quite vast, successfully hunting them requires good communication between hunters and the need for a large-scale coordinated hunt. Still another connection between language, encephalization, and high-quality food has been developed by Buckley and Steele (2002). They tested three evolutionary ecological models for the emergence of language against existing archaeological and paleontogical data and concluded that the following model provides the best explanation of the data:

> The first set of models emphasizes the stabilization of kinship networks and the extension of provisioning effort for the rearing of offspring to include both males and female kin (e.g. 'grandmothers'). In this model, the effectiveness of alliance networks enables a mother to rely on other individuals, envisaged as close kin relations, to assist in the provisioning and nurturing of the female's offspring. The supposed benefit of such a situation is to ensure the gene survival over multiple generations. Language serves both to optimize the task of co-operative food search and to enforce social contracts linking provisioning effort to reproductive success.
>
> The most plausible social explanation for the evolution of language is intensely negotiated co-operation within small stable groups, based on family or kinship ties. Language enhances efficiency in co-operative foraging

tasks ... Language also enables the negotiation of food sharing ... Social sta-
bility is reinforced by the symbolic development of classificatory kinship
terms that discriminate between degrees of relatedness and therefore
degrees of co-operation. Language is consequently vital to distinguish
between members of the kinship group and the importance of their relatedness to an individual – and the social contracts that are entailed in the
relations between individuals of defined kinship categories.

Another direct link between language and altruism is suggested by
Jean-Louis Dessalles, who claims that 'relevance is a requirement of
language' from which it follows that language conveys 'valuable information, and thus ... any relevant utterance is potentially altruistic'
(1998, 130–1). 'Sharing information, like sharing food, is altruistic'
(ibid., 135). But this presents a paradox which requires an explanation
because Dessalles claims that 'if it is altruistic, the communicative
behaviour of human beings should not exist, unless we are able to show
that some cheating detection device is systematically employed by talking people' (ibid.). In fact, all human societies do have a system for
detecting and punishing cheaters. It is one of the cultural universals of
human society. The ability to detect cheaters allows reciprocal altruism
(Trivers 1971) or niche-constructed altruism (Laland et al. 1999) to
emerge, which according to Ulbaek allows 'information sharing [to]
take place without loss of fitness to the speaker. In the human lineage,
social co-operation based on obligatory reciprocal altruism has evolved,
a system, which rewards people for co-operating and punishes them
(morally and physically) for cheating. In such an environment language is finally possible' (1998, 41). We have just learned that the emergence of speech required a system for detecting cheaters but that such a
system would have, in turn, required a system of speech to detect cheaters. This leads us to the conclusion that speech, reciprocal altruism and
the detection of cheaters must have co-evolved and emerged together
as an autocatalytic system.

Dessalles does not invoke the universality of justice systems to explain
the paradox he has formulated. Rather his approach is to explain that
the motivation to share information comes from the desire of the
speaker to forge a collaborative relationship with the persons with
whom he or she shares information and that linguistic behaviour 'is a

form of trade: relevant information is given in exchange for status' (1998, 146). The status obtained is instrumental in forming collaborative alliances that obviously have a survival advantage. The instinct to form collaborative alliances is something we might have inherited from our non-human primate ancestors who regularly create such alliances: 'In the social domain, primates, but not other mammals, understand something of the third-party social relationships that hold among other individuals; for example, they understand such things as the kinship and dominance relations that third parties have with one another. Thus, primates are selective in choosing their coalition partners, selecting as an ally, for instance, an individual who is dominant to their potential adversary – indicating their understanding of the relative dominance ranks of these two individuals' (Tomasello 1999, 17).

### The Origin of Social Norms

So far our discussion has centred on the role of altruism in the origin of language and culture. In this section we will examine the origin of social cooperation and norms, which some have claimed are contrary to natural selection. There is, in fact, a rather large literature from social thinkers who consider the emergence of altruism to be a consequence of natural selection in the form of emergence theory rather than a phenomenon that contradicts natural selection.

If we consider the earliest stages of human development, then the formulation of laws or rules of conduct or social norms had to await the origin of speech. Once language emerged, then laws or rules could be formulated. But even before speech came into existence, however, social norms had to exist in order for the level of hominid cooperation described earlier to have emerged. These social norms were a form of proto-laws, which were followed automatically without much, if any, forethought. This connection between social norms and cooperation or the emergence of altruism has been suggested by a number of researchers.

Frank Ryan (2002) argues that cooperative arrangements have been a driving force in evolution at all levels of biology from the migration of mitochondria and chloroplasts to human culture. An example of this for humans is provided by Robert Axelrod, who asserts that 'a norm exists in a given social setting to the extent that individuals usually act in a certain way and are often punished when seen not to be acting in this way' (1997). Norms emerge in competitive situations when players can observe each other and imitate successful strategies, which hominids were capable of. We know that monkeys are able to imitate successful strategies, as was the case with potato washing monkeys on a Japanese island. Axelrod (1985) makes extensive use of game theory and the prisoner's dilemma to argue for human cooperation.

Steven Strogatz (2004) argues that 'coupled oscillations' are often the underlying process of patterned behaviour in situations where there is no obvious conscious control or even intention. This could explain the emergence of social norms before the existence of language and conceptual thought. Social norms or proto-laws emerged as patterned behaviour without the intentions of a lawmaker. We think of law as being legislated because we live in a verbal and literate society in which laws are conceived, formulated, and then recorded. Hominid proto-law was an emergent phenomenon not something thought out. An example of the emergence of rules without intention in contemporary society is the way in which the open source movement for the creation of shared code emerged from the interaction of players through the Internet. Another example of rules without legislators is the way the laws of science, as encompassed in the scientific method, emerged by consensus of its players.

The medium for Strogatz's 'coupled oscillations' can be any medium of communication. For prehuman hominid society it was mimetic communication. But for human society it could be any of the six languages of speech, writing, mathematics, science computing, and the Internet, which according to Logan (1995, 2004b), form an evolutionary chain of languages.

Ernst Fehr and Joseph Henrich (2003) note that rewarding those that follow social norms and punishing those that do not plays an important role in creating common goods and altruistic behaviour. They show that this is not maladaptive, as some others have argued. They suggest that their explanation does not require any of the standard arguments for altruism, including kin selection, reciprocal altruism, indirect reciprocity, or costly signalling. Henrich and al. (2004) point out that people will reward fairness and punish cheaters even at a cost to themselves. Prosecution of lawbreakers is at a significant cost to society and individuals through the justice system of police, courts, and prisons, as is the punishment of invaders or international lawbreakers. Law evolves or emerges from punishing cheaters and non-reciprocators of social norms. This is essential for a society pervaded by cooperation and altruistic behaviour.

Other authors have maintained that altruism is consistent with natural selection. Peter Corning (2003) argues that synergy, as in combined or cooperative effects of individuals, is a key driver of human biological and cultural evolution. He shows that this is true throughout the entire biological range from bacteria to humans: 'Synergy has played a key role in the progressive evolution of complex systems in nature. However, complexity is not an end in itself; it's a consequence of the innovations that produce more potent forms of synergy. Synergy is the driver' Matt Ridley (2003, 1998) claims that human emotions, customs, and institutions enable humans to survive and compete effectively through cooperative social norms such as laws. Donna Hart and Robert Sussman (2005) point out that hominids were prey, not predators, and that cooperation was a necessity for survival.

# 14 Culture as an Organism and the Emergence of Universal Culture

## Is Culture an Organism?

In this chapter we will examine the possibility that culture, like language, evolved as an organism that was easy for the human mind to grasp and, as a result, gave rise to Universal Culture just as language evolved in such a way as to give rise to Universal Grammar. Because culture is essentially symbolic – a set of ideas, beliefs, and knowledge, its acquisition by the human mind (like with language) must be simple and straightforward if it is to be transmitted and, hence, survive. It is therefore logical to posit that culture like language evolved in such a way as to be easily acquired by humans. Thus, I am tempted to extend Christiansen's (1994) idea that language is an organism to culture itself and suggest that culture is also an organism, a 'nonobligate symbiant.' If we accept this hypothesis then it follows by analogy that many of the conclusions that Christiansen reached regarding language would apply to culture as well.

I have taken the liberty of transforming a paragraph by Christiansen, Dale, Ellefson, and Conway (2002) that I quoted in chapter 8 by replacing the word 'language' with the word 'culture' to arrive at some thoughts about the nature of culture and its evolution. By making this substitution I have generalized and expanded Christiansen's (1994) notion of 'language as an organism' to the idea that culture can also be considered as an organism in the same metaphorical sense:

Cultures exists only because humans can learn, produce, and process them. Without humans there would be no culture. It therefore makes sense to construe *cultures* as organisms that have had to adapt themselves through natural selection to fit a particular ecological niche: the human brain. In order for *cultures* to 'survive,' they must adapt to the properties of the human learning and processing mechanisms. This is not to say that having a *culture* does not confer selective advantages onto humans. It seems clear that humans with superior *cultural* abilities are likely to have a selective advantage over other humans ... What is often not appreciated is that the selection forces working on *culture* to fit humans are significantly stronger than the selection pressures on humans to be able to use *culture*. In the case of the former, a *culture* can only survive if it is learnable and processable by humans. On the other hand, adaptation toward *culture* use is merely one out of many selective pressures working on humans (such as, for example, being able to avoid predators and find food). Whereas humans can survive without *culture*, the opposite is not the case. Thus, *culture* is more likely to have adapted itself to its human hosts than the other way around. *Cultures* that are hard for humans to learn simply die out, or more likely, do not come into existence at all. (adapted from Christiansen, Dale, Ellefson and Conway, 166–7)

The above excerpt from Christiansen, Dale, Ellefson, and Conway has been altered by substituting the word *culture(s)* for *language(s)*. It suggests that culture like language can also be regarded as an organism that evolved to be easily acquired and preserved.

### The Culture of Each Individual in the Society Is an Organism

When we speak of culture as an organism, we must decide if we are speaking of the culture of the whole society or of individuals within the society: 'People learn as individuals. Therefore, if culture is learned, its ultimate locus must be in individuals rather than in groups ... If we accept this, then cultural theory must explain in what sense we can speak of culture as being shared or as the property of groups ... and what the processes are by which such sharing arises' (1981, 54). Based on this insight of Ward Goodenough we will assume that the culture of each individual of that group is an organism, the culture of the group is a species, and the cultures of individuals are conspecifics.

The culture of each individual in a society can be quite different from every other individual because there are components which depend on the family they are members of, the locale and country in which they live, their profession, the company or organization for which they work, their religious beliefs, their hobbies, and a large number of other factors. We can further bolster this assumption by applying to culture the arguments, made in chapter 8 regarding language as an organism. Stuart Kauffman defines a living organism as 'a system of chemicals that has the capacity to catalyze its own reproduction' (1995, 49). Let us generalize Kauffman's definition to apply to the idea of culture operating as an organism. A culture operating as a living organism is a system of symbols, ideas, beliefs, and knowledge that has the capacity to catalyze its own reproduction. If we consider the culture produced and comprehended by each individual as an organism, then we may regard culture to be reproducing itself each time a child acquires the culture similar to his or her parents, together with other cultural conspecifics.

By defining the culture of each individual in the society as an organism, not only do we meet Kauffman's criteria that an organism catalyzes its own reproduction but we are able to consider the evolution of this organism using Darwin's simple one-line definition of evolution, namely, 'descent with modification.' By descent Darwin meant reproduction. The only way we can speak of a culture reproducing itself is by considering the culture of each individual in the society as an organism. Then, as was the case with the language of individuals, the inheritance or descent is not by diploidy but the polyploidy of parents, siblings, peers, teachers, relatives, and society in general. One can now apply the concept of natural selection to the culture organism of each individual in a society.

But what are we to make of the culture of the society as a whole? It is not an organism because it cannot reproduce itself. The solution to this dilemma is simple and parallels the way we treated the language of a society. The culture of the society is not an organism but a species whose member conspecifics are the culture of the individuals comprising the society. Just as conspecifics of a biological species are able to reproduce among themselves, the conspecifics of a cultural species are able to communicate with each other, cooperate, collaborate, and share certain basic values and assumptions. So English and French cultures are cultural species. American, English-speaking Canadian, and British cultures are subspecies of English-speaking culture, as are the many different social groups within these three countries. They may be regarded as subspecies in that they are distinct in some ways but their members share certain values and assumptions, just as members of biological subspecies are distinct but can interbreed.

The cultural ideas, beliefs, and knowledge of each individual represents an organism with its own unique culture that can share values and assumptions with members of the same cultural species. The culture possessed by each individual can be characterized the way Christiansen and Ellefson characterize language, namely, as 'a kind of beneficial parasite – a nonobligate symbiant – that confers some selective advantage onto its human hosts without whom it cannot survive' (2002, 339) The way in which the culture that belongs to the community or society rather than the individual evolves is through the mutations that arise in the idiosyncratic use and modification of culture by individuals. Those idiosyncratic mutations can then be reproduced by being incorporated into the individual cultures of other individual members of the cultural community through cultural transmission.

A person may possess more than one cultural profile depending on her religion, her profession, or her hobbies, to name a few examples. An individual who is a member of more than one cultural community can act as a cross-pollinator between cultures, as he borrow an idea or belief from one cultural group and use it in the context of another. An example is the way many aspects of African-American culture have now become part of mainstream American culture, as well as of youth culture worldwide. From this perspective there are two meanings to culture: the culture of the individual and the common culture of a society. The cultural community can be a nation state, a local region such as a city, a tiny village or a neighbourhood, a profession, a community of practice, or even an extended family.

Pursuing this line of thought of treating culture as an organism we may expand on our notion of the autocatalysis of language, social skills, and cognition, which we developed in Question 2 in chapter 9 to, include culture. We may also entertain the notion of the co-evolution of culture, language, and genetics. The mechanism by which culture and language for that matter could affect genetic evolution is through the Baldwin effect by which certain biological changes are selected for as a result of behavioural changes. Language and culture create a new behavioural environment and, therefore, affect the biological characteristics that are selected for, namely, they increase innate cognitive skills, as suggested by Tomasello (1999).

In *The Origin of the Modern Mind*, Merlin Donald traces the evolution of culture through three distinct stages representing ape, hominid, and human culture respectively: The most primitive stage, is episodic culture, which functions as 'a series of concrete episodes' in which the apes live their lives 'entirely in the present' (1991, 148). Mimetic culture of Homo habilis and Homo erectus is one of toolmaking, control of fire, social structures, and generative intentional non-verbal communication through gesture, hand signals, body language, and vocalizations. Mimetic culture was still very much focused on the present, as it was based on perceptual thinking, but it did allow for 'intentional expression' and the 'comprehension of social relationships.' The third culture of *Homo sapiens* is semiotic, abstract, and based on integrative thought which allowed the construction of 'conceptual models of the human universe' and 'symbolic invention' (ibid., 215–16). The three stages of cultural evolution which Donald sketches illustrate the autocatalysis of culture, language, cognition, and social-communicative skills. Actually, as pointed out by Linnda Caporael: 'Donald argues that a fourth phase, based on the external symbolic storage and symbol manipulation as in print and computers is beginning' (2001, 612). I would add writing and mathematical notation to Caporael is list, before print and the Internet after computers, as I have done in chapter 2 which described the evolution of notational language. We might wish to call this fourth phase of culture notational culture, which could be broken down further into literate, electric mass media, and digital culture.

Although we have assumed that the culture of each individual in a society may be regarded as an organism, and the culture of the society as a whole as the species of these cultural organisms, another interpretation is also possible. Just as societies of social insects such as ants, bees, and termites may be regarded as biological superorganisms (Wilson 1971), Donald (2001, 151–3) hints at the notion that human cultures may be regarded as biological superorganisms. There is something to be said about the way a cultural collectivity acts as though it has a life of its own, but as Donald (ibid.) points out, it is not conscious of itself – but then neither is a superorganism like an ant colony. Although our cultural inheritance resides in our mind, we are most often unaware of it as it guides our choices and actions much the way a fish is unaware of the water in which it lives and acts. Each action or choice we make is a figure embedded in the ground of our culture. We are aware of the figure but not the ground, which melts into our consciousness and is taken for granted.

## Universal Culture

There is still another, I might add highly speculative, consequence that I would like to explore as a result of extending to culture Christiansen's (1994) metaphor of language as an organism. Christiansen claims that language in order to survive had to evolve in such a way as to adapt itself 'to fit the human learning and processing mechanism' (1995, 9). He then argues that this was the mechanism that led to the universality of the characteristics of human language or to the Universal Grammar (UG), as first identified by Chomsky. If natural selection acting on language as an organism led to the UG, then we should expect that natural selection acting on culture as an organism should lead to a universal set of rules that govern the social interactions within a culture, which we might wish to call Universal Culture (UC), that is, the set of universal elements that characterize all human cultures. The universals include such elements as language, marriage, kinship relations, gossip, and taboos.

The notion of Universal Culture has certain parallels with Universal Grammar, as pointed out by Robin Fox: 'The parallel search by linguists had some important lessons: the search for substantive universals seems barren; if there were universals they were at the level of *processs* ... They [cultures] may be unique at the level of specific content – like languages – but at the level of the *processes* there are remarkable uniformities – like language again ... Each outcome of a universal process can look very different. But it is nowhere written that universal processes should have identical outcomes' (1989, 113). The outcomes or outputs of cultures are different because the inputs are different – the environment, history, interactions with neighbours, natural disasters, and so forth, are all sources of different inputs which can affect the evolution of a culture. Jared Diamond, in his book *Guns, Germs, and Steel* (1999), illustrates how the environment, and in particular the distribution of native plants and animals that could be domesticated, played a major role in the way that cultures and civilizations developed. We should expect to see variations in the way culture expresses itself in different societies, but as is the case with language because of the universality of human cognitive skills, we should be able to detect some similarities in the overall pattern of human cultures. And if we do, we certainly will not suggest that Universal Culture is hard-wired or there exists a Culture Acquisition Device or CAD. Rather we will adopt a stance similar to cognitive grammar and suggest that the universal elements of culture are due to the universality of human cognition. Langacker suggests that linguistic structure should be 'analyzed in terms of more basic systems and abilities (e.g., perception, attention, categorization) from which it cannot be dissociated' (1998, 1), and the same should apply to the analysis of culture.

As pointed out in the *Stanford Encyclopedia of Philosophy* (2001):

> part of the difficulty in understanding cognitive behavior as the product of evolution is that there are at least three very different evolutionary processes involved. First, there is the biological evolution of cognitive and perceptual mechanisms via genetic inheritance. Second, there is the cultural evolution of language and concepts. Third, there is the trial-and-error learning process that occurs during an individual's lifetime. Moreover, there is some reason to agree with Donald T. Campbell that understanding human knowledge fully will require understanding the interactions between these processes. This requires that we be able to model both processes of biological and cultural evolution. There are by now a number of well-established models of biological evolution. Cultural evolution presents more novelty.

It should be pointed out, however, that the notion of a universality of human culture runs counter to the main stream of the field of anthropology, where the traditional focus has been on the description of primitive and exotic cultures. Anthropology, once known as Tylor's science, was launched with the publication of Edward Tylor's book, *Primitive Culture* (1871). The bias of anthropology has been towards uncovering the variety and diversity of human cultures. A number of anthropologists, however, contend that there are more things that cultures have in common than they have that are different and that the basic structures of human culture are actually very similar and it is only the details that are different.

Lee Cronk suggests that the great diversity of cultures is perhaps an illusion because anthropologists are biased to look for differences rather than similarities. Languages are very different from each other, but they presumably share a Universal Grammar according to Chomsky and Chomskyites. Cronk considers that maybe the same is true of culture. He cites Donald E. Brown's book *Human Universals* (1991), and in particular the chapter titled 'Universal People,' which details

> universals appearing in everything from the details of language and grammar to social arrangement to the ubiquity of music, dance, and play. The list includes some surprises. Every society has gossip, all societies understand the idea of a lie, they all have special types of speech for special occasions, they all use narrative, and they all have poetry with lines that take about three seconds to say. Men are everywhere on average more aggressive and likely to kill than women, though individual men and women do differ significantly from the average. Everyone has taboos on certain statements and certain foods. All societies are at least aware of dancing (though it is prohibited in some of them) and have some sort of music. Remarkably, everyone has children's music. If as cultural determinist dogma would have it, culture is all-diverse and all-powerful, why are there any such universals? Why aren't human cultures more diverse than they apparently are? (Cronk 1999, 25)

Cronk suggests that to explain cultural universality 'we have to look closely at the forces that shape cultural and social patterns and ask which of them are sources of uniformity rather than diversity' (1999, 26). One possibility is 'that only certain pathways through ethnographic hyperspace are actually possible. Once a society is started on a path, it may not be able to leave it easily, and changing directions or jumping to nonadjacent points may be difficult.' It is constrained by its history and, like biological evolution, designs cannot be created from scratch but emerge by a process of bricolating or tinkering. As Cronk (ibid., 27) points out, baboons cannot grow wings no matter how useful they would be. Cronk suggests that one factor that might account for the universality of human culture is procreation: 'Because the one imperative of natural selection is to reproduce, we ought to expect that the most fundamental commonalities among different people will be found in those institutions and practices that relate most closely to procreation. Those parts of the human endeavor that do not have much direct influence on reproduction – perhaps including art, music, and many aspects of religion – ought to display the greatest diversity' (1999, 30). The institution of the family, in particular, is notable for its importance in reproduction and for its universality, which Cronk defines as 'a social unit with a mother and child at its core and in which a male, often though not always the biological father of the child, usually has an important role' (ibid.). Cronk cites the failure of the social experiments of the kibbutzim and the Oneida utopian religious colony to destroy the family unit plus the Nayar mercenary Indian soldiers polygynandrous culture that returned to monogamy after British rule (ibid., 30–2).

Allen Johnson and Timothy Earle also regard the family as a universal and integral institution of all human cultures:

> So resilient and adaptive is the family group that it has survived the most momentous changes in the economy and society, changes that in some cases reach to the heart of the family economy. Family groups remain the basis of the subsistence economy, as primary units of production and consumption, at all the evolutionary levels we have discussed … The social organization of the family group is based on the nurturance and trust generated in the daily give and take of family life. (1987, 315)
>
> Riding a wave of optimism for a future classless society, the Maoists attempted to convert China's family-based economic and social relations to a system characterized by collectivization and direct state control. They failed; and their failure bears out one message of this book, namely, that self-serving individuals and families, far from being the recent products of a depraved capitalism, are the fundamental economic unit in all societies. (ibid., 291)

As a way of explaining the diversity of human culture but yet its essential universality, Tiger and Fox 'argued that the important universals are not at the 'substantive' level where anthropologists usually seek them, but at the level of 'process' … Processes may be universal even though their results are highly variable' (1971, cited by Brown 1991, 81).

There is an analogy that can be drawn between Universal Grammar and Universal Culture, as we have defined it. The languages of the world are quite diverse especially with respect to their lexicons, yet the deep structure of their grammars seems to be universal. The same can be said of cultures. In detail cultures are quite diverse but they seem to share a common deep structure. Another analogy is that the syntax of languages falls into categories depending on the order in which the subject (S), verb (V), and object (O) appear. Some languages have an SVO structure or ordering and some have an SOV ordering, but once a language demonstrates a particular pattern it more or less sticks to that pattern and has certain common grammatical features with all other languages that share the same ordering of S, O, and V. The same might be said of cultures: some are patrilineal and some are matrilineal, but once a society adopts one of these patterns a number of other regularities can be predicted which become fixed parts of that culture.

Tiger and Fox (1971, 7) have created the notion of 'biogrammar' that links the lexical elements of social action to create a language of human behaviour. Just as the lexicons of verbal languages differ but their grammars reveal a universal deep structure, so it is that the lexicons of social action of different societies differ but the deep structure of their biogrammars seems to be universal.

## A Catalogue of Cultural Universals

Brown has attempted to catalogue all those aspects of human culture that are universal or in his words are 'near-universal.' He asks, 'What do all people, all societies, all cultures, and all languages have in common?' (1991, 130) He attempts to provide an answer in terms of what he calls 'the Universal People (UP)':

> The UP are aware of this uniqueness (i.e. their possession of culture) and posit a difference between their way – culture – and the way of nature. A very significant portion of UP culture is embodied in their language, a system of communication without which their culture would necessarily be very much simpler. With language the UP think about and discuss both their internal states and the world external to each individual ... With language, the UP organize, respond to, and manipulate the behavior of their fellows ... UP language is of strategic importance to those who wish to study the UP. This is so because their language is, if

not precisely a mirror of, then at least a window into, their culture and into their minds and actions. (1991, 130)

Brown lists over a hundred items that human cultures right across the planet share in common on a universal or near-universal basis. His list includes a number of universal features of culture associated with language including:

prestige for good use of language,
gossip,
lies,
humour,
insults, and
language change. (1991, 130–41, 157–201)

'There are features of language at all basic levels – phonemic, grammatical, and semantic – that are found in all languages' (ibid., 131). In addition to these features Brown lists the following set of universal or near-universal aspects of language:

nouns and verbs,
the possessive form,
marking (good is never solely expressed as not bad),
special speech for special occasions,
narrative,
poetry, with a pause approximately every three seconds,
figurative speech,
metaphor,
metonymy,
onomatopoeia,
gender,
temporal duration,
units of time, such as days, months, seasons, and years,
cyclicity or rhythmicity,
tense (past, present, and future),
similar classification categories (e.g., parts of the body, inner states, behavioural properties, flora, fauna, weather conditions, tools, space),
proper nouns,
pronouns (first, second, and third person),
topographic and place names,
antonyms and synonyms,
numerals,
kin terms, distinguishing gender and generation,
semantic categories such as motion, speed, location, dimension,

more often used words are shorter, binary discrimination (e.g., black and white, nature and culture, male and female, good and bad, and ordered continua with a concept of a middle),
measures and distances, but not always with uniform units,
taxonomies,
logic terms such as *not, and, same, equivalent,* and *opposite,*
symbols,
conjectural reasoning,
causality,
subject-object distinction,
mimetic elements such as hand signals, and
gestures that can be mimicked, masked, or modified and which are universally recognized. (ibid., 130–41, 157–201)

In addition to these universal associated with language, Brown finds the following psychological and behavioural features of human culture universal:

trial-and-error learning,
a theory of mind,
concept of self and others, self-awareness,
understanding intentions,
fear, especially of loud noises, strangers, and snakes,
sexual attraction,
homosexuality,
flirting,
jealousy,
envy,
recognition of others,
prolific toolmaking and use (levers, containers, materials for tying, spears, weapons, the use of fire),
cooking,
drugs,
shelter,
preparation for birth,
post-partum natal care,
group living such as the family,
groundedness in a locality,
marriage and courtship,
adultery,
family,
child rearing,
juvenile delinquency,
traditional restraints on the rebelliousness of young men,
nepotism,
sex taboos,
Oedipus complex,
ascribed and achieved social status,
social states,
domination,
prestige,
labour division,
male dominance, male rulers,
male activities that exclude females,
cooperative labour,

trade, gifts, food sharing,
predicting and planning for the future,
triangular relationships,
government or public affairs,
authority,
power,
collective decision-making,
leaders, never completely demo- cratic nor totally autocratic,
admiration of generosity,
altruism,
loyalty,
rules,
dispute settlement,
proscription against rape, violence, and murder with sanctions,
suicide,
conflict,
control of disruptive behaviour,
ingroup-outgroup classification,
ethnocentrism,
recognizing and employing prom- ises,
morality,
values, ideals, and standards,
empathy,
pride,
shame,
sorrow,
need,
daily routines,
etiquette,
hospitality,
sex and excretion modesty,
religion or belief in supernatural things,
anthropomorphization,
medicine,
magic,
divination,
theories of fortune and misfortune,
ritual,
rites of passage,
mourning,
world-view,
dreams and interpretation,
possessive case,
property,
rules of inheritance,
aesthetic standards,
art,
imagination,
story telling, narratives, and myths,
a need to explain the world,
adornment,
grooming,
hairstyles,
dance,
music (instrumental, vocal, and children's),
play, and
games of skill and chance. (Brown 1991, 130–41, 157–201)

Some aspects of culture such as the domestication of dogs; notation systems; the association of poetry and ritual; the belief in spiritual entities such as the soul; the symbolism of red, white, and black; capital punishment; and abortion are near-universals.

The list of universals that I have listed here comes from the literature and for the most part from the work of Brown (1991) who originally compiled these lists. There is one universal that I believe should be added and that is a justice system to detect and punish cheaters. Although capital punishment is a near-universal, almost every society has other forms of punishment for those that transgress against their society by cheating in one form or another.

## Memes as the Replicators of the Organism of Culture

If culture is an organism, as we have posited, then its replication requires something analogous to genes, the replicators of biological systems. Richard Dawkins in his book *The Selfish Gene* (1989, but first published in 1976) has identified an analogue to genes with his introduction of the meme as a cultural replicator. Dawkins considers the cultural meme as a way of extending Darwin's theory of evolution from biological systems to cultural or social systems: 'I developed the idea of the 'cultural meme' as a way of dramatizing the fact that genes aren't everything in the world of Darwinism ... The meme, the unit of cultural inheritance, ties into the idea of the replicator as the fundamental unit of Darwinism. The replicator can be anything that replicates itself and exerts some power over the world to increase or decrease its probability of being replicated' (1996, 80–1).

If language and culture are regarded as living entities rather than the behaviours of humans, one can then consider their evolution using analogies with Darwinian evolution or with Dawkins's notion of meme or cultural replicators (or artifacts). Dawkins's notion of the meme as a cultural replicator and the analogue of biological genes helps us solidify our notion of culture as an organism. The meme not only accounts for the reproduction of culture, it is also the entity that undergoes natural selection as it competes with other memes for existence in the human mind. Just as a biological organism can be defined in terms of its genetic composition, so a cultural organism can be defined in terms of its memetic composition. The words of a language and its grammatical structures may also be regarded as memes, as language is an integral part of culture.

Other analogies can be identified. Like biological species and language species (such as Latin, Anglo-Saxon, Aramaic, English, French, and Arabic), cultural species come into existence and they die out or become extinct. Cultural organisms reproduce themselves when children inherit the culture of their parents, teachers, and other members of their society who influence their thinking and their values. New species come into existence when two cultures encounter each other, and a new cultural species is born which carries characteristics of both of its parent cultures. Mexican culture was born form the combination of aboriginal Meso-American and Spanish culture.

Independent of the consideration of language, any study of memetics or the evolution of cultural replicators must deal with the transition from the purely biological evolution of hominids before the emergence of human culture and language to the joint biological and memetic evolution of *Homo sapiens* and their languages and cultures. It would be difficult to envision a sharp boundary between the time that human evolution was purely biological-genetic to the time when it was principally cultural-memetic. In fact, there is no reason to believe that human biological evolution has suddenly come to a stop. It is clear, however, that the rate of cultural evolution which includes the evolution of language, technology, socioeconomic institutions, and culture far outstrips the rate of human biological evolution.

In developing our ideas regarding the evolution of culture and its treatment as an organism, we have argued by analogy with our treatment and evolution of language as an organism à la Christiansen (1994). One justification for making this analogy is that language is actually an element or subset of culture, and hence, the conclusions we can draw about the origin and evolution of language apply to culture and vice versa: the conclusions we can draw about the origin and evolution of human culture apply to language.

## The Universal Pattern of the Evolution of Political Economies

In addition to the catalogue of cultural universals we identified above to support the notion of Universal Culture, Johnson and Earle, in their book, *The Evolution of Human Societies*, have identified a universal pattern in the evolution of political economies, based on society's need for sustenance:

Subsistence intensification, political integration and social stratification are three interlocked processes observed again and again in historically unrelated cases. Foragers diversify and gradually adopt agriculture; villages form and integrate into regional polities; leaders come to dominate and transform social relationships ... We see the evolutionary process as an upward spiral. At the lowest level the pressure of an increased population on resources evokes a set of economic and social responses that interact to create a higher level of economic effort capable of sustaining an increased population. The process repeats itself until eventually a growing population becomes possible only with the increasing involvement of leadership, with its concomitants of increasing dependence and political development. (1987, 4 and 15)

Human behaviour can only be explained by understanding both the biological and cultural factors, and they are interdependent. Although biological factors dominated human-hominid existence at first, with the emergence of technology, language, and culture, these factors can no longer be disentangled from biology: 'Population and technology have a feedback relationship; population growth provides the push, technology change the pull. But ... it is fundamentally population growth that propels the evolution of the economy' (Johnson and Earle 1987, 5).

As we learned earlier the family was the first economic unit among humans, the ground zero of cooperation. As population increased the following problems arose, which gave rise to universal extra-family strategies to counter the problems that single families working in isolation could not solve. Such problems include:

1 Production risk – countered by risk management strategies such as centralized storage and distribution
2 Increased resource competition – countered by alliances to help defend resources and for protection against war
3 Demand for capital for technology to support increased resource production – countered by group contributions through tributes, taxes, and rent
4 The depletion of local resources – countered by trade.

These extra-family strategies that required leadership and management opened the possibility for control by a 'big man,' a chief or a king, who limited access to these strategies to an elite loyal to him.

Johnson and Earle (1987) identified the following stages of socialization that emerged with each incremental increase in population density: (1) *family-level groups*, which divided into either the family camp or the family hamlet; (2) *local groups* of five to ten times the number of families of the family-level group, which came together for the purpose of defence or food storage; and (3) *regional polities* that arose out of local groups and at moderate populations formed into a *chiefdom* and at large population levels into a *state*.

## Family-Level Groups: Foragers and Domesticators

The post-Pleistocene period was characterized by the spread of humans throughout the world, increasing human populations, and the need for the intensification of food procurement, which led to exploitation of suboptimal habitats, diversification of diet, and then the domestication of plants and animals. Intensification also led to increased integration and the universal emergence of the camp (consisting of four to five families). Family-level groups came together for some joint activities but once the group foraging, which required cooperation, had been completed the individual families dispersed so as to reduce unnecessary resource competition.

Intensification also led to territoriality to defend valuable resources and hence to alliances, greater integration, and stratification, arrangements not characteristic of family-level foragers. One of the solutions to intensification was domestication, which eventually led to more complex social and economic strictures but there are many examples of domesticators, which retained the same social structures as the family-level foragers. The key to family-level society was the family's access to land, labour, and technology, which was easy when resources were rich and population densities low. Family-level society is characterized by simple tools, a pattern of aggregation and dispersion, social organization based exclusively on kinship, weak territoriality, a lack of warfare, family-based ceremony, and ad hoc leadership.

*Local groups*

Local groups are composed of multi-family groups, subdivided along kinship lineages. They either form villages or larger groups led by a network of 'big men' who act on behalf of their local group, coordinating defence and food storage. Subsistence is based on agriculture, pastoralism, or extremely productive sources of wild food. The three forms of local groups (village, clan, and 'big man' collectivity) have moderate population densities and the settlement pattern is sedentary. Local groups form for defence as population growth leads to conflicts and competition for resources. They also entail the social management of risk, technology, and to some extent trade: 'The local group forms a ritually integrated political group and may have a headman; but it typically fragments into its constituent kin groupings either seasonally or periodically as a result of internal disputes. Ceremonialism is important for publicly defining groups and their interrelationships. Resources are held exclusively by kin groups, and territorial defense is common' (Johnson and Earle 1987, 20). A 'big man' exists for larger local groups. He is important for internal dispute resolution, risk management, trade, and intergroup alliance. He is a charismatic leader who rules at the pleasure of his followers and can be replaced by a rival.

THE FAMILY AND THE VILLAGE
The economy is still family-level, but because of crowding and overpopulation there is a need for defence of precious resources. This gives rise to villages for mutual protection and defence. Ceremony is used to identify the local group. Families have to sacrifice a certain amount of individual self-interest to group self-interest in exchange for greater security, but they are free to leave the collectivity if dissatisfied to find another.

THE VILLAGE AND THE CLAN
The same problem of defending valuable resources through the organization of villages still exists but now the family structure, while still the basic social unit, gives way to greater integration through clans and lineages. Local villages are now interconnected through 'extensive interpersonal networks of exchange and personal support' and ceremonies

'to define groups and their interrelationships' (Johnson and Earle 1987, 158). This sometimes involves cooperative ventures such as whale hunts or sharing risk in the case of pastoralists.

THE CORPORATE GROUP AND THE 'BIG MAN' COLLECTIVITY

Leadership emerges at this level 'to integrate the village-sized community into a regional economy' (Johnson and Earle 1987, 158). Intensification now requires the cooperation of many villages and, hence, a manager. The 'big man' coordinates economic activities, such as the construction and use of group-wide technologies. He is also responsible for the greater integration of the new polity by negotiating alliances and trading relationships, organizing ceremonies, and accumulating wealth as a form of risk management. This role of the 'big man' who controls certain resources leads, for the first time, to a stratification of the society but he only rules at the pleasure of the group and can be easily replaced if he does not deliver.

*The Regional Polity*

The regional polity, consisting of chiefdoms and archaic states, is characterized by: very high population densities; environmental diversity; technology requiring major capital investments; hierarchical settlement patterns 'with a center providing economic, political, and religious services for outlying settlements'; hierarchical social organization with a ruling elite, and central and regional organizations dominating local ones; territoriality, with ownership by elites; warfare with groups outside the polity; ceremonialism to legitimize social stratification; and institutionalized leadership in offices open only to the elite (Johnson and Earle 1987, 302–3).

*Simple Chiefdom and Complex Chiefdoms*

The chiefdom is similar to the local group in terms of the economy, but there is enough richness so that a surplus is generated often through capital investments such as irrigation, fishing boats, or trade. The surplus is used to support the chief's activities, which include conquest of other local groups which are incorporated into the polity rather than excluded as in the case of local groups. Leadership is controlled by a hereditary elite at both the local and regional levels and is legitimized by ceremonies. With the death of a chief a competition begins to succeed him which results in a new regime of officeholders.

The intensification required to support ever-increasing population densities gives rise to technologies that allow a chief to create a monopoly and control the centralized economy of the polity. The chief owns the wealth, which is redistributed and also serves as a form of risk management. The redistribution of wealth also provides a way for the chief to finance the various activities that he carries out, which include the coordination of trade, the management of the production economy, the mediation of disputes, the conduct of defence, and warfare. The society stratifies into a ruling elite and commoners. The chief is assisted by other members of his elite cohort. Ceremonies are used to legitimize his power: 'We can identify the main "causes" of evolution of centralized societies as being risk management, warfare, technological complexity, and trade. Whether alone or in combination, it is argued, these prime movers, themselves, an outcome of population growth and intensification, require central management and thus underlie the evolution of complex societies. This functionalist logic sees cultural evolution as adaptation, the solution of particular problems brought about by population growth under particular environmental conditions' (Johnson and Earle 1987, 244). One of the forms of risk management was centralized storage supervised by the 'big man' or chief and the exchange of gifts between different groups so as to establish ties that could be called upon in time of need.

## STATES

The state or empire involves the conquest of more groups so that a multi-ethnic polity of considerable size and population is created through conquest. Hereditary elites manage and control the resources and technology of the polity, which are treated as their personal property legitimized by a formal legal system. Commoners work the land and provide the lord with tributes and/or rents: 'Integration on a massive regional or interregional scale is a defining characteristic of states. Minimally this integration involves a bureaucracy, a military establishment, and an institutionalized state religion ... a judiciary, and a police force' (Johnson and Earle 1987, 270 and 319).

*The Role of Markets in the State*

Another characteristic of the state is the emergence of markets and their management by the state. Markets determine the many ways in which material and human resources are deployed. The market makes for the more efficient use of resources as prices are determined by supply and demand, and hence, resources are not wasted because they are cheap and underpriced. The market acts as 'an efficient means of storage,' as surpluses can be sold on the market and stored in the form of money (Johnson and Earle 1987, 299) Markets plus a good transportation system can even out shortages in locales under stress by shipping resources from areas where there is abundance. The market system also encourages specialization and, hence, the most efficient use of human resources. The family subsistence, however, is now at the mercy of a faceless market system. There is no longer a 'big man' or chief who can take a personal interest in their plight, only an impersonal bureaucracy and market system:

> Basic to both state finance and stratification is this element of control. As we have seen, there are two main kinds of control: control over production made possible by such technological developments as irrigation or more weakly by short-fallow, carefully managed farm lands; and control over distribution (trade), made possible by market development and the generation of mercantile wealth. In the first instance stratification is defined by two classes: a ruling and landowner elite class, and a producer class of commoners. In the second instance a third class is also present: a merchant class, often attached in one way or another to the ruling class. (Johnson and Earle 1987, 270)
>
> The economy [of the state] is now so huge that any effort to move labor and goods through the system by use of personal hierarchical chains of command is necessarily less efficient than reliance on the 'impersonal free market.' In essence the evolution from the complex chiefdom and the archaic state into a market-integrated nation-state is characterized by the increasing dominance of the economy by a competitive, price-fixing market, a dominance made possible by an institutional framework largely devoted to nurturing and protecting the market system. (ibid., 272)

As we have seen, at each evolutionary stage existing organizational units are embedded within new, higher-order unifying structures. Hamlets are made up of families, local groups of hamlets, regional chiefdoms of local groups, and states of regional chiefdoms. The earlier levels continue to operate but with modified functions. Thus the local group of a stateless society, which had formerly been a unit of defense, is transformed into a unit of taxation and administration as it becomes incorporated into the state. (ibid., 322)

## The Emergence and Evolution of Polities: Complexity and the 'Ratchet Effect'

As human societies succeeded in their ability to procure natural sources of food, their population density increased which led in the long run to a depletion of their food supply. The population overload led to new challenges and chaos. From this chaos far from equilibrium a new level of order emerged à la Ilya Prigogene (1997) in the form of the domestication of plants and animals. This pattern of domestication occurred throughout the world in isolated communities. While it is true that at the local level one society might learn domestication from its neighbours, it is also true that agriculture and pastoralism emerged independently on every continent and in almost every ecosystem in the world. The explanation of the emergence of domestication out of chaos of population overload parallels the model I have previously used to explain the emergence of speech (chapter 3), and its subsequent evolution into writing, mathematics, science, computing, and the Internet (chapter 2).

If we consider Tomasello's (1999, 5) 'ratchet effect' in combination with the emergence of domestication, we can develop a deeper understanding of the pattern of the evolution of economic polities that Johnson and Earle (1987) have sketched for us. The domestication of plants and animals led to new challenges and new levels of complexity, which in turn gave rise to new levels of increasing order in the form of family-level groups (camps and villages), local groups ('big man' systems), and regional polities (chiefdoms and states). Each new political system emerged from the population overload of the previous political system, just as new forms of language emerged from the information overload of the previous forms of language. It was through cultural transmission and the 'ratchet effect' that the features of the previous political system were incorporated into the new political order.

I have suggested earlier that if we treat the language of each individual as an organism à la Christiansen (1994) this can explain the regularities of the world's languages as formulated by the Universal Grammar. I then extended this idea to treat the culture of each individual as an organism, which led to the idea of cultural regularities, which I labelled Universal Culture. If we now generalize once again and regard economic polities as organisms that evolved so as to be easily acquired by a society, we have an explanation of the universal forms of the family-group camp and village, the 'big man' collectivity, the chiefdom, and the state. Not all villages, 'big man' collectivities, chiefdoms, and states are identical, just as not all languages or cultures are totally identical either but certain regularities can be discerned in the patterns of polities, as Johnson and Earle (1987) have demonstrated.

# Epilogue:
# The Propagating Organization
# of Language and Culture

After completing the manuscript of this book but before it went to press I had the good fortune to work on the problem of the nature of information in biotic systems with a team headed by Stuart Kauffman that included Robert Este, Randy Goebel, Ilya Shmulevich, and David Hobill (in press). I would like to report on the findings of our study, Propagating Organization: An Enquiry (hereafter referred to as POE), as it sheds additional light on the nature of language and culture. I will also add a few new thoughts on the way language and culture propagate their organization.

One of the central themes of this book has been the notion that language and culture can be treated like living organisms that (1) evolve through a process of descent, modification, and selection, and (2) are emergent phenomena that arise from autocatalytic processes.

The third way that language and culture behave like living organisms is that they too propagate their organization. Stuart Kauffman (2000) in his book *Investigations* introduced the notion that living organisms propagate their organization. In POE Kauffman et al. (in press) extended this notion to language and culture.

What motivated our study of propagating organization in POE was an attempt to understand the nature of information in a biotic system. Kauffman (2000) in *Investigations* observed that living organisms are autonomous agents that must perform thermodynamic work cycles in order to maintain and replicate themselves. Work is the constrained release of free energy but as Kauffman observed it takes constraints to do that work and work to build those constraints. The constraints are built into the propagating organization of the autonomous agent by autocatalysis. In POE we have identified those constraints as instructional or biotic information and showed that they differ from Shannon information.

Based on Kauffman and Clayton (2006) we argued in POE that biology cannot be reduced to physics and that this implies that 'the future evolution of the biosphere cannot be finitely prestated' (Kauffman et al. in press). It is for this reason that Shannon information does not apply to biotic systems. Shannon information is defined as the reduction of uncertainty from a source with a set of messages over which a well-defined probability distribution might be attributed. The 'reduction of uncertainty, hence the lowering of the entropy of the source, constitutes the amount of information transmitted' (ibid.). Shannon information does not apply to the biosphere therefore, because one cannot prestate all possible Darwinian preadaptations. In other words, the configuration space cannot be defined, as is the case with a physical gas, for example, where the $N$ is the number of molecules in the gas and the number of variables is $6N$ in order to define the position and velocity of each particle in the three-dimensional gas.

To define information that is appropriate for living organisms we need to consider the work cycles of living cells:

Cells carry out propagating work linking spontaneous processes, constraints, work, and non-spontaneous processes, and more broadly ... the propagating organization of process. In doing so, the cell carries out a set of interlocked tasks that achieve a closure of tasks whereby the cell literally builds a rough copy of itself ... This closure of work, constraints, tasks, and information ... is a new form of matter, energy, information, and organization that constitutes the living state.

The new insight that we explore in this article is that the constraints that allow autonomous agents to channel free energy into work are connected to information: in fact, simply put, the constraints *are* the information, are partially causal in the diversity of what occurs in cells, and are part of the organization that is propagated. (ibid.)

The symbolosphere consisting of language and culture. It differs from the biosphere in two distinct ways. For one, the symbolosphere is a totally abstract non-material symbolic domain. The second difference is that the organisms of language and culture are symbiant parasites that derive their energy from their human hosts. That being said, language and culture are emergent phenomena that propagate their organization and evolve by a process of descent, modification, and selection. In the same way that biology cannot be reduced to physics it is also the case that the symbolic conceptual aspects of human behaviour, namely, language and culture, cannot be reduced to, derived from, or predicted from human biology. Nor can the future evolution of language and culture be finitely prestated. For example, one could never have predicted the emergence of Proto-Indo-European nor its divergence into its many descendants such as English, Sanskrit, Greek, Latin, and Italian. Nor could one prestate the preadaptations of the cultures of the world, their technologies, economies, and forms of governance, all of which depend on the physical environment and the biology of the human organism.

The same inability to prestate all the possible states into which the symbolosphere could evolve means that language and culture cannot be described in terms of Shannon information; they are, however, subject to a set of constraints, which represents their information and propagating organization. As for language, the constraints seem to be those of Universal Grammar, which arose not through hard wiring but through the evolution of the language organism so that it could be easily acquired by its human host as we discussed in Chapter 8. As for the culture organism, the constraints are those that give rise to what we defined in chapter 14 as Universal Culture, a concept that is not yet fully understood and will require further study.

In *Investigations*, where the notion of propagating organization of the biosphere was first developed, Kauffman (2000) also introduced three other related themes:

1  the biosphere's persistent probing of the adjacent possible,
2  the biosphere's maximization of variety and hence Kauffman's putative fourth law of thermodynamics, and
3  the population of the biosphere with self-constructing systems.

The adjacent possible is defined in the following manner: 'autonomous agents forever push their way into novelty – molecular, morphological, behavioral, organizational. I will formalize this push into novelty as the mathematical concept of an "adjacent possible," persistently explored in a universe that can never, in the vastly many lifetimes of the universe, have made all the possible protein sequences even once, bacterial species even once, or legal systems even once. Our universe is vastly nonrepeating; or ... nonergodic' (ibid., 22).

We have maintained that words representing concepts are strange attractors because their meaning is constantly changing depending on the context of their use. Strange attractors never return to the same place in phase space, and hence the use of language is nonergodic.

Kauffman (2000, 143) claims that 'the biosphere has been expanding, on average, into the adjacent possible for 3.8 billion years' and as a result 'there are now a standing diversity of 100 million species' with an estimated 10 trillion different genes representing a diversity that 'is likely to be hundreds of trillions or more' organic chemical species (ibid., 11).

The symbolosphere, on the other hand, has existed by most accounts only 50 thousand to 150 thousand years (some will claim a million or two years) but has generated an enormous amount of diversity. There are extant some 6,000 languages, not counting various local dialects. There were also many languages that became extinct.

How many words in each language? English has approximately one million. Assuming the others have on average only 100,000 then the sum total of extant words in all the languages of the world is over half a billion words. But this is not the extent of the variety in the symbolosphere. We must also take into account all of the propositions or sentences that have been constructed from these words since the beginning of language. Let us assume a population of 6 billion people (we are only counting those alive today) with an average lifetime of 50 years uttering 100 sentences per day. This yields some 10,000 trillion sentences since the symbolosphere came into existence. Each year the number of sentences will increase by 200 trillion at today's population level. And this reckoning only takes into account language. There is also the variety in technology, economics, law, and cultural artefacts such as clothing, jewelry, art objects, and soon.

As we saw in the last section, by probing the adjacent possible 'autonomous agents forever push their way into novelty' with the result that there is a 'persistent evolution of novelty in the biosphere' (ibid., 5, 22). The same dynamic holds in the symbolosphere, which for example increases linguistic novelty or variety in a number of ways including the creation of new words (neologisms) and new grammatical elements through grammaticalization and by bifurcating into myriad accents, dialects, and new languages such as the way Latin diverged into French, Italian, Spanish, Portuguese, Catalan, and Romanian. The symbolosphere is also increasing its novelty through the diversification of culture, a fact Kauffman acknowledges for the economy: 'the economy, like the biosphere, is about persistent creativity in ways of making a living' (ibid., 229). It is worth noting that the persistent economic creativity is in part due to conceptualization and the use of language.

Kauffman formulates a putative Fourth Law of Thermodynamics based on the persistent emergence of novelty in the adjacent possible for both the biosphere and the econosphere. 'Biospheres maximize the average secular construction of the diversity of autonomous agents ... On average, biospheres persistently increase the diversity of what can happen next' (ibid., 3–4). Our claim is that this putative fourth law applies with equal validity to all elements of the symbolosphere as is evidenced by the persistent novelty of technology, science, law, literature, music, and the visual arts.

A central theme in *Investigations* (Kauffman 2000) is the notion that the universe and the biosphere are self-constructing systems. 'A coevolving biosphere accomplishes th[e] coconstruction of propagating organization' (ibid., 5). We wish to posit that the symbolosphere is also a self-constructing system. As we pointed out in chapter 3 (see pp. 59–60), it takes concepts or thoughts to create words and words to create thoughts or concepts. Just as autonomous agents emerge in the biosphere through autocatalysis, a similar mechanism works in the symbolosphere.

The driving force of the self-construction of the biosphere is autocatalysis, which Kauffman (ibid., 37) attributes to a phase transition. He argues that, 'as molecular diversity of a reaction system increases, a critical threshold is reached at which collectively autocatalytic, self-reproducing chemical reaction networks emerge spontaneously' (ibid., 16).

We can extend this argument to the symbolosphere. Perhaps with the increased lexical/conceptual diversity of Bickerton's (1990) protolanguage system a critical threshold is reached at which collectively autocatalytic, self-reproducing symbolic networks emerge spontaneously with a full-blown syntax and grammar.

For language the basic units are the words that comprise the semantics of a language, whereas the constraints are the grammar or syntax. The autocatalysis of language arises from the fact that it takes concepts and grammar to make words and words to make concepts and grammar. Semantics and grammar are autocatalytic within the context of the lexical hypothesis, which posits that the lexicon is at the core of language (Donald 1991, Levelt 1989, and Hudson 1984). Also as pointed out by Deacon (1997, 136) words can only be defined in terms of other words and hence they form a semantic web of symbol-symbol relationships.

We conclude by pointing out that like living organisms, language and culture are autocatalytic, emergent self-constructing systems that propagate their organization and constantly probe their adjacent possibles, persistently increasing their novelty and variety.

# References

Abler, W. 1989. On the particulate principle of self-diversifying systems. *Journal of Social and Biological Structures* 12: 1–13.

– 1997. Gene, language, number: The particulate principle in nature. *Evolutionary Theory* 11: 237–48.

Aitchison, Jean. 1998. On discontinuing the continuity-discontinuity debate. In James Hurford, Michael Studdert-Kennedy, and Chris Knight (ed.), *Approaches to the Evolution of Language*. Cambridge: Cambridge University Press, 17–29.

Albright, W.F. 1957. *From the Stone Age to Christianity*, 2$^{nd}$ ed. Garden City, NY: Doubleday Anchor.

Alexander, R. 1987. The origin and dispersal of modern humans. *Science* 236: 668–9.

Anderson, John R. 1980. *Cognitive Psychology and Its Implications*. San Francisco: W.H. Freeman.

Arbib, Michael. 2003. The evolving mirror system: A neural basis for language readiness. In Morten Christiansen and Simon Kirby (ed.), *Language Evolution*. Oxford: Oxford University Press, 182–200.

Ashby, Ross. 1957. *An Introduction to Cybernetics*, 2$^{nd}$ ed. New York: Wiley.

Axelrod, Robert. 1985. *The Evolution of Cooperation*. New York: Basic Books.

– 1997. *The Complexity of Cooperation*. Princeton, NJ: Princeton University Press.

Bach, Emmon. 1989. *Informal Lectures on Formal Semantics*. Albany, NY: SUNY Press.

Bak, Per. 1996. *How Nature Works: The Science of Self-Ordered Criticality*. New York: Copernicus.

Baldwin, J.M. 1896. A new factor in evolution. *American Naturalist* 30: 441–51.

Bandle, O., H. Klingenberg, and H. Mauer. 1958. *Kategorien Lehre vom Satz*. Hamburg, n.p.

Barton, R. 1996. Neocortex size and behavioural ecology in primates. *Proceedings of the Royal Society of London* B263: 173–7.

Barton, R., and R. Dunbar. 1997. Evolution of the social brain. In R. Byrne and A. Whiten (ed.), *Machiavellian Intelligence,* vol. 2, 240–63.

Batali, John. 1994. Innate biases and critical periods: Combining evolution and learning in the acquisition of syntax. In R. Brooks and P. Maes (ed.), *Artificial Life,* vol. 4. Cambridge, MA: MIT Press, 160–71.

– 1998. Computational simulations of the emergence of grammar. In Hurford et al., *Approaches to the Evolution of Language,* 405–26.

– 2000. The negotiation and acquisition of recursive grammars as a result of competition among exemplars. In E.J. Briscoe (ed.), *Linguistic Evolution through Language Acquisition: Formal and Computational Models.* Cambridge: Cambridge University Press, chapter 5.

Bates, Elizabeth, and Brian MacWhinney. 1982. Functionalist approach to grammar. In E. Wanner and L. Gleitman (ed.), *Language Acquisition: The State of the Art.* Cambridge: Cambridge University Press, 173–218.

Bates, E., D. Thal, and V. Marchman. 1989. A Darwinian approach to language development. In N. Krasnegor, D. Rumbaugh, M. Studdert-Kennedy, and R. Schiefelbusch (ed.), *The Biological Foundations of Language Development.* Oxford: Oxford University Press.

Benno, R. H., 1990. Development of the nervous system: Genetics, epigenetics and phylogenetics. In S.H. Broman and J. Grafman (ed.), *Atypical Cognitive Deficits in Developmental Disorders.* London: Erlbaum, chapter 7.

Berk, L., and R. Garvin. 1984. Development of private speech among low-income Appalachian children. *Developmental Psychology* 20(2): 271–86.

Berwick, Robert. 1998. Language evolution and the Minimalist Program: The origins of syntax. In Hurford et al., *Approaches to the Evolution of Language,* 320–40.

Bickerton, Derek. 1990. *Language and Species.* Chicago: University of Chicago Press.

– 1995. *Language and Human Behaviour.* Seattle: University of Washington Press; 1996 ed. published in London by University College London Press.

– 1998. Catastrophic evolution: The case for a single step from protolanguage to full human language. In Hurford et al., *Approaches to the Evolution of Language,* 341–58.

– 2000. How protolanguage became language. In C. Knight, M. Studdert-Kennedy, and J. Hurford (ed.), *The Evolutionary Emergence of Language.* Cambridge: Cambridge University Press, 264–84.

– 2002. Foraging versus social intelligence in the evolution of protolanguage. In A. Wray (ed.), *The Transition to Language.* Oxford: Oxford University Press, 207–25.

– 2003. Symbol and structure: A comprehensive framework for evolution. In Christiansen and Kirby, *Language Evolution*, 77–93.

Bloomfield, L. 1933. *Language*. New York: Holt.

Boyd, R., and P.H. Richerson. 1985. *Culture and the Evolutionary Process*. Chicago: University of Chicago Press.

Bradshaw, J.L. 1988. The evolution of human lateral asymmetries. *Journal of Human Evolution* 17: 615–37.

Bresnan, Joan W. 2001. *Lexical-Functional Syntax*. Oxford: Blackwell.

Bresnan, Joan W. (ed.). 1982. *The Mental Representation of Grammatical Relations*. Cambridge, MA: MIT Press.

Brinck, Ingar, and Peter Gärdenfors. 1999. Representations and self-awareness in intentional agents. *Synthese* 118: 89–104.

– 2003. Co-operation and communication in apes and humans. *Mind and Language* 18 (5): 484–501.

Briscoe, E.J. 2000. Evolutionary perspectives on diachronic syntax. *Proceedings of DIGS5*. Oxford: Oxford University Press.

– 2002. *Linguistic Evolution through Language Acquisition: Formal and Computational Models*. Cambridge: Cambridge University Press.

Brockman, John. 1996. *The Third Culture*. New York: Touchstone.

Brown, Donald E. 1991. *Human Universals*. New York: McGraw-Hill.

Bruner, Jerome S. 1974/5. From communication to language: A psychological perspective. *Cognition* 3: 255–78.

Buckley, Carina, and James Steele. 2002. Evolutionary ecology of spoken language: Co-evolutionary hypotheses are testable. *World Archaeology* 34(1): 26–46.

Burling, Robbins. 1986. The selective advantage of complex language. *Ethology and Sociobiology* 7: 1–16.

– 2000. Comprehension, production and conventionalisation in the origins of language. In Knight et al., *The Evolutionary Emergence of Language*, 27–39.

– 2002. The slow growth of language in children. In Wray, *The Transition to Language*, 297–310.

Bybee, Joan. 2003. Cognitive processes in grammaticalization. In Michael Tomasello (ed.), *The New Psychology of Language: Cognitive-Functional Perspective on Language Structure*, vol. 2. Mahwah, NJ: Erlbaum, 177–202 .

Byrne, R. 1995. *The Thinking Ape: Evolutionary Origins of Intelligence*. Oxford: Oxford University Press.

Byrne, R., and A. Whiten (ed.). 1988. *Machiavellian Intelligence: Social Expertise and the Evolution of Intelligence in Monkeys, Apes and Humans*. Oxford: Clarendon Press.

–1997. Machiavellian Intelligence, vol. 2. Cambridge: Cambridge University Press.

Calvin, William. 1983. A stone's throw and it's launch window: Timing precision and its implications for language and hominid brains. *Journal of Theoretical Biology* 104: 121–35.

– 1990. *The Cerebral Symphony.* New York: Bantam.

Campbell, Donald. 1965. Variation and selective retention in socio-cultural evolution. In Herbert Barringer, George Blanksten, and Raymond Mack (ed.), *Social Change in Developing Areas: A Reinterpretation of Evolutionary Theory.* Cambridge, MA: Schenkman, 19–49.

– 1997. From evolutionary epistemology via selection theory to a sociology of scientific validity. *Evolution and Cognition* 3:5–38.

Cann, R.L. 1993. *Formal Semantics: An Introduction.* Cambridge: Cambridge University Press.

Cann, R.L., M. Stoneking, and A.C. Wilson. 1987. Mitochondrial DNA and human evolution. *Nature* 325: 31–6.

Caporael, Linnda. 2001. Evolutionary psychology: Towards a unifying theory and a hybrid science. *Annual Review of Psychology* 52: 607–28.

Carruthers, Peter. 1996. *Language, Thought and Consciousness.* Cambridge: Cambridge University Press.

Carstairs-McCarthy, Andrew. 1998. Synonymy avoidance, phonology and origin of syntax. In Hurford et al., *Approaches to the Evolution of Language*, 279–96.

– 2000. The distinction between sentences and noun phrases: An impediment to language evolution? In Knight et al., *The Evolutionary Emergence of Language*, 248–63.

Cavalli-Sforza, L.L., and M.W. Feldman. 1981. *Cultural Transmission and Evolution.* Princeton, NJ: Princeton University Press.

Chafe, Wallace. 1998. Language and the flow of thought. In Tomasello, *The New Psychology of Language*, vol. 1, 93–111.

Chase, Philip. 1999. Symbolism as reference and symbolism as culture. In Robin Dunbar, Chris Knight, and Camilla Power (ed.), *The Evolution of Culture: An Interdisciplinary View.* New Brunswick, NJ: Rutgers University Press, 113–46.

Cheney D., and R. Seyfarth. 1990. *How Monkeys See the World: Inside the Mind of Another Species.* Chicago: University of Chicago Press.

Chomsky, N.A. 1957. *Syntactic Structures.* The Hague: Mouton.

– 1965. *Aspects of the Theory of Syntax.* Cambridge, MA: MIT Press.

– 1966. *Cartesian Linguistics.* New York: Harcourt, Brace and World.

– 1972a. *Studies on Semantics in Generative Grammar.* The Hague: Mouton.

– 1972b. *Language and Mind,* enlarged ed. New York: Harcourt Brace Jovanovich.

– 1975. *Reflections on Language.* New York: Pantheon.

– 1980. *Rules and Representation.* New York: Columbia University Press.

– 1981. *Lectures on Government and Binding.* Dordrecht: Foris.

- 1982. *The Generative Enterprise: A Discussion with Riny Huybregts and Henk van Riemsdijk.* Dordrecht: Foris.
- 1986. *Knowledge of Language.* New York: Praeger.
- 1995. *The Minimalist Program.* Cambridge, MA: MIT Press.
- 2000. *New Horizons in the Study of Language and Mind.* Cambridge: Cambridge University Press.

Chomsky, N.A., and Howard Lasnik. 1993. The theory of principles and parameters. Reprinted in Chomsky, *The Minimalist Program*, 13–127.

Christiansen, Morten. 1994. Infinite languages finite minds: Connectionism, learning and linguistic structure. Unpublished doctoral dissertation, Centre for Cognitive Studies, University of Edinburgh.

- 1995. Language as an organism: Implications for the evolution and acquisition of language. Unpublished manuscript, Washington University.

Christiansen, M., and J. Devlin. 1997. Recursive inconsistencies are hard to learn: A connectionist perspective on universal word order correlations. In *Proceedings of the 19th Annual Cognitive Society Conference.* Mahwah, NJ: Erlbaum, 160–71.

Christiansen, M., R. Dale, M. Ellefson, and C. Conway. 2002. The role of sequential learning in language evolution: Computational and experimental studies. In A. Cangelosi and D. Parisi (ed.), *Simulating the Evolution of Language.* London: Springer-Verlag, 165–88.

Christiansen, M., and M. Ellefson. 2002. Linguistic adaptation without linguistic constraints: The role of sequential learning in language evolution. In Wray, *The Transition to Language*, 335–58.

Christiansen, Morten, and Simon Kirby (ed.). 2003a. *Language Evolution.* Oxford: Oxford University Press.

- 2003b. Language evolution: The hardest problem in science? In Christiansen and Kirby, *Language Evolution*, 1–15.

Clahsen, H. 1999. Lexical entries and rules of language: A multidisciplinary study of German inflection. *Behavior and Brain Sciences* 22: 980–99.

Clark, Andy. 1997. *Being There: Putting Brain, Body, and World Together Again.* Cambridge, MA: MIT Press.

- 1998. Magic words: How language augments human computation. In P. Carruthers and J. Boucher (ed.), *Language and Thought: Interdisciplinary Themes.* Cambridge: Cambridge University Press, 162–83.

- 2003. *Natural-Born Cyborgs.* Oxford: Oxford University Press.

Clark, Andy, and David Chalmers. 1998. The extended mind. *Analysis* 58: 10–23.

Clark, Herbert. 1996. *Using Language.* Cambridge: Cambridge University Press.

Clayton, Philip. 2004. *Mind and Emergence: From Quantum to Consciousness.* Oxford: Oxford University Press.

Comrie, Bernard (ed.). 1990. *The World's Major Languages.* Oxford: Oxford University Press.

– 2003. On explaining language universals. In Tomasello, *The New Psychology of Language,* vol. 2, 195–209.

Corballis, Michael. 1991. *The Lopsided Ape.* Oxford: Oxford University Press.

– 1992. On the evolution of language and generativity. *Cognition* 44: 197–226.

– 2003. From hand to mouth: Gestural origins of language. In Christiansen and Kirby, *Language Evolution,* 201–18.

Corning, Peter. 2003. *Nature's Magic: Synergy in Evolution and the Fate of Humankind.* Cambridge: Cambridge University Press.

Croft, W. 1998. Syntax in perspective: Typology and cognition. Presentation at DG6S Summer School 31 Aug to 11 Sept in Mainz, Germany.

Cronk, Lee. 1999. *The Complex Whole: Culture and the Evolution of Human Behavior.* Boulder, CO: Westview.

Crow, T.J. 2002. Candidate gene for cerebral asymmetry. In Wray, *The Transition to Language,* 93–112.

Culicover, Peter. 1999. *Syntactic Nuts: Hard Cases in Syntax.* Oxford: Oxford University Press.

Cziko, G. 1995. *Without Miracles: Universal Selection Theory and the Second Darwinian Revolution.* Cambridge, MA: MIT Press.

Darwin, Charles. 1859/1968. *The Origin of Species by Means of Natural Selection.* Harmondsworth: Penguin.

– 1871. *The Descent of Man, and Selection in Relation to Sex.* London: J. Murray (reissued in facsimile 1981 by Princeton University Press)

Davidson, I., and W. Noble. 1989. The archaeology of perception: Traces of depiction and language. *Current Anthropology* 30: 125–55.

Dawkins, R. 1989. *The Selfish Gene.* Oxford: Oxford University Press. (Originally work published in 1976).

– 1996. The survival machine. In John Brockman (ed.), *The Third Culture.* New York: Touchstone, 74–95.

De Boer, Bart. 2000. Emergence of sound systems through self-organization. In Knight et al., *The Evolutionary Emergence of Language,* 177–98.

De Saussure, F. 1966. *Course in General Linguistics.* New York: McGraw-Hill.

– 1967. *Grundfragen der allgemeinen Sprachwissenschaft.* [Basic Questions of Linguistics] 2nd ed. Berlin: de Gruyter.

Deacon, Terrence W. 1992. Brain-language coevolution. In J.A. Hawkins and M. Gell-Mann (ed.), *The Evolution of Human Language.* Santa Fe Studies in the Science of Complexity II. Reading, MA: Addison-Wesley, 49–83.

– 1997. *The Symbolic Species: The Co-evolution of the Brain and Language.* New York: W.W. Norton.

Deacon, Terrence. 2003. Universal Grammar and semiotic constraints. In Christiansen and Kirby. *Language Evolution.*

Demsky, Aaron. 1972. *Scroll.* Jerusalem: Encyclopedia Judaica.

Dennet, Daniel C. 1991. *Consciousness Explained.* New York: Little, Brown.

– 1995. *Darwin's Dangerous Idea: Evolution and the Meaning of Life.* New York: Simon and Schuster.

Dessalles, Jean-Louis. 1998. Altruism, status and the origin of relevance. In Hurford et al., *Approaches to the Evolution of Language,* 130–47.

– 2000. Language and hominid politics. In Knight et al., *The Evolutionary Emergence of Language,* 62–80.

De Waal, F. 1996. *Good-natured: The Origin of Right and Wrong in Humans and Other Animals.* Cambridge, MA: Harvard University Press.

Diamond, Jared. 1999. *Guns, Germs, and Steel: The Fates of Human Societies.* New York: W.W. Norton.

Donald, Merlin. 1991. *The Origin of the Modern Mind.* Cambridge, MA: Harvard University Press.

– 1998. Mimesis and the executive suite. In Hurford et al., *Approaches to the Evolution of Language,* 44–67.

– 2001. *A Mind So Rare: The Evolution of Human Consciousness.* New York: W.W. Norton.

Dryer, M. 1997. Are grammatical relations universal? In J. Bybee, J. Haiman, and S. Thompson (ed.), *Essays on Language Function and Language Type.* Amsterdam: John Benjamins, 343–66.

Dunbar, Robin. 1992. Neocortex size as a constraint on group size in primates. *Journal of Human Evolution* 20: 469–93.

– 1996. *Grooming, Gossip an the Evolution of Language.* London: Faber and Faber.

– 1998. Theory of mind and the evolution of language. In Hurford et al., *Approaches to the Evolution of Language,* 92–110.

Durham, William H. 1991. *Coevolution: Genes, Culture and Human Diversity.* Stanford, CA: Stanford University Press.

Eldredge, N., and S.J. Gould. 1972. Punctuated equilibria: An alternative to phyletic gradualism. In T.J.M. Schopf (ed.), *Models in Paleobiology.* San Francisco: Freeman, 82–115.

Elman, Jefferey. 1991. Incremental learning, or the importance of starting small. *13th Annual Conference of Cognitive Science Society.* Hillsdale, NJ: Erlbaum.

– 1993. Learning and development in neural networks: The importance of starting small. *Cognition* 48: 71–99.

Elman, Jeffrey, Elizabeth Bates, Mark Johnson, Annette Karmiloff-Smith, Domenico Parisis, and Kim Puckett. 1996. *Rethinking Innateness: A Connectionist Perspective on Development.* Cambridge, MA: MIT Press.

Falk, D. 1987. Hominid paleoneurology. *Annual Review of Anthropology* 16: 13–30.

Fehr, Ernst, and Joseph Henrich. 2003. Is strong reciprocity a maladaptation? – on the evolutionary foundations of human altruism. In P. Hammerstein (ed.), *Genetic and Cultural Evolution of Cooperation*. Cambridge: MA, MIT Press, 55–82.

Fernald, Anne. 1984. The perceptual and affective salience of mother's speech to infants. In L. Feagan, C. Garvey, and R. Golinkoff (ed.), *The Origin and Growth of Communication*. New Brunswick, NJ: Ablex.

Fillmore, Charles. 1968. The case for case. In E. Bach and R. Harms (ed.), *Universals in Linguistic Theory*. New York: Holt, Rinehart and Winston, 1–90.

Fillmore, Charles, Paul Kay, and Mary Catherine O'Connor. 2003. Regularity and idiomaticity in grammar constructions: The case of let alone. In Tomasello, *The New Psychology of Language*, vol. 2, chapter 10.

Fisher, R.A. 1930. *The Genetical Theory of Natural Selection*. Oxford: Clarendon Press.

Fitch, W. Tecumseh. 2005. The evolution of language: A comparative review. *Biology and Philosophy* 20: 193–230.

Flinn M.V., and R.D. Alexander. 1982. Culture theory: The developing synthesis from biology. *Human Ecology* 10: 383–400.

Fodor, J. 1975. *The Language of Thought*. New York: Thomas Crowell.

Fox, Robin. 1989. *The Search for Society*. New Brunswick, NY: Rutgers University Press.

Frank, Robert, and Anthony Kroch. 1995. Generalized transformations and the theory of grammar. *Studia Linguistica* 49: 103–51.

Gärdenfors, Peter. 2004. Cooperation and the evolution of symbolic communication. In K. Oller and U. Griebel (ed.), *The Evolution of Communication Systems*. Cambridge, MA: MIT Press, 237–56.

Garstang, Walter. 1922. The theory of recapitulation: a critical restatement of the biogenetic law. *Journal of the Linnaean Society* (Zoology) 35: 81–101.

Geertz, Clifford. 1973. *The Interpretation of Culture*. New York: Basic.

Gell Mann, Murray. 1996. Plectics. In Brockman, *The Third Culture*. New York: Touchstone.

Giddens, Anthony. 1984. *The Constitution of Society*. Berkeley: University of California Press.

Givo´n, T. 1979. *On Understanding Grammar*. New York: Academic Press.

– 1995. *Functionalism and Grammar*. Amsterdam: John Benjamins.

Goodenough, Ward. 1981. *Culture, Language and Society*. McCaleb Module in Anthropology. Menlo Park, CA: Benjamin/Cummings.

Goldberg, Adele. 1995. *Constructions: A Construction Grammar Approach to Argument Structure*. Chicago: University of Chicago Press.

Goodwin, William. 1912. *A Greek Grammar*. New York: Macmillan.

Gopnik, M., and M.B. Crago. 1991. Familial aggregation of a developmental language disorder. *Cognition* 39: 1–50.

Gould, S.J. 1979. Panselectionist pitfalls in Parker and Gibson's model of the evolution of intelligence. *Behavioral and Brain Sciences* 2: 385–6.

– 1996. The pattern of life's history. In Brockman, *The Third Culture*, 49–73.

Gould, S.J., and N. Eldredge. 1977. Punctuated equilibria: The tempo and mode of evolution reconsidered. *Paleobiology* 3: 115–51.

Gould, S.J., and R.C. Lewontin. 1979. The spandrels of San Marco and the Panglossian paradigm: A critique of the adaptationist programme. *Proceedings of the Royal Society of London* 205: 281–8.

Greenfield, P.M. 1991. Language, tools and brain: The ontogeny and phylogeny of hierarchically organized sequential behavior. *Behavioral and Brain Sciences* 14: 531–95.

Gregory, W.K. 1951. *Evolution Emerging: A Survey of Changing Patterns from Primeval Life to Man*, 2 vols. New York: Macmillan.

Groenendijk, Jeroen, Martin Stokhof, and Frank Veltman. 1996. Conference and modality. In S. Lappin (ed.), *The Handbook of Contemporary Semantic Theory*. Oxford: Blackwell, 179–213.

Gumperz, J.J. 1982. *Discourse Strategies*. Cambridge: Cambridge University Press.

Halliday, M.A.K. 1989. Spoken and Written Language, 2nd ed. Oxford: Oxford University Press.

Hamilton, W.D. 1964. The evolution of social behavior. *Journal of Theoretical Biology* 7: 1–52.

Harris, Marvin. 1977. *Cannibals and Kings*. New York: Random House.

Harris, Zellig. 1968. *Mathematical Structures of Language*. New York: Wiley.

Hart, Donna, and Robert Sussman. 2005. *Man the Hunted: Primates, Predators, and Human Evolution*. New York: Basic.

Hauser, Marc, Noam Chomsky, and Tecumseh Fitch. 2002. The faculty of language: What is it, who has it, and how did it evolve? *Science* 298: 1569–79.

Havelock, Eric. 1963. *Preface to Plato*. Oxford: Oxford University Press.

– 1978. The alphabetization of Homer. In Havelock and Hershbell, *Communications Arts in the Ancient World*, 3–21.

Hawkes, Kristen. 1993. Why hunter-gatherers work: An ancient version of the problem of the public goods. *Current Anthropology* 34(4): 341–61.

Heim, Irena. 1989. *The Semantics of Definite and Indefinite Noun Phrases in English*. New York: Garland.

Henrich, Joseph, Robert Boyd, Samuel Bowles, Colin Camerer, Ernst Fehr, and Herbert Gintis. 2004. *Foundations of Human Sociality: Economic Experiments and Ethnographic Evidence from Fifteen Small-Scale Societies*. New York: Oxford University Press.

Hershbell, J. 1978. The ancient telegraph: War and literacy. In Havelock and Hershbell, *Communications Arts in the Ancient World.*

Hertzler, Joyce. 1965. *A Sociology of Language.* New York: Cooper Square Publishers.

Heylighen, F., and C. Joslyn. 2001. The law of requisite variety. http://pespmcl.vub.ac.be/REQVAR.html. Accessed 12 December 2005.

Hickerson, Nancy. 1980. *Linguistic Anthropology.* New York: Holt, Rinehart and Winston.

Hill, J.H. 1974. Possible continuity theories of language. *Language* 50: 134–50.

Hockett, Charles. 1960. The origin of speech. *Scientific American* 203: 88–111.

Horgan, John. 1995. The new social Darwinists. *Scientific American* 273(4): 174–81.

Hudson, R. 1984. *Word Grammar.* London: Basil Blackwell.

Hurford, J.R. 1989. Biological evolution of the Sassaurean sign as a component of the language acquisition device. *Lingua* 77: 187–222.

– 1998. Introduction: The emergence of syntax. In Hurford et al., *Approaches to the Evolution of Language,* 299–304.

– 2000. Introduction: The Emergence of Syntax. In Knight et al., *The Evolutionary Emergence of Language,* 219–30.

– 2002. The roles of expression and representation in language evolution. In Wray, *The Transition to Language,* 311–34.

– 2003. The language mosaic and its evolution. In Christiansen and Kirby, *Language Evolution,* 38–57.

Hurford, J., M. Studdert-Kennedy, and C. Knight (ed.). 1998. *Approaches to the Evolution of Language.* Cambridge: Cambridge University Press.

Innis, Harold. 1972. *Empire and Communication.* Toronto: University of Toronto Press.

Isaacs, F.J. 1983. Aspects of human evolution. In D.S. Bendall (ed.), *Evolution from Molecules to Men.* Cambridge: Cambridge University Press.

Itard, Jean-Marc-Gaspard. 1962. *The Wild Boy of Aveyron.* Trans. George Humphrey. New York: Meredith Publishing.

Jacob, F. 1977. Evolution and tinkering. *Science* 196: 1161–6.

Jackendoff, Ray. 2002. *Foundations of Language: Brain, Meaning, Grammar, Evolution.* New York and Oxford: Oxford University Press.

Johnson, Allen W., and Timothy Earle. 1987. *The Evolution of Human Societies: From Foraging Group to Agrarian State.* Stanford: Stanford University Press.

Joshi, Aravind. 1987. An introduction to tree-adjoining grammars. In A. Manaster-Ramer (ed.), *Mathematics of Language.* Amsterdam: John Benjamins, 87–114.

Kalma´r, I. 1985. Are there really no primitive languages? In D.R. Olson, N. Torrance, and A. Hilyard (ed.), *Literacy, Language and Learning:*

*The Nature and Consequences of Reading and Writing*. Cambridge: Cambridge University Press, 148–66.

Kamp, Hans, and U. Reyle. 1993. *From Discourse to Logic*. Dordrecht: Kluwer.

Kauffman, Stuart. 1995. *At Home in the Universe*. Oxford: Oxford University Press.

Kauffman, Stuart A. 2000. *Investigations*. Oxford: Oxford University Press.

Kauffman, Stuart, Robert K. Logan, Robert Este, Randy Goebel, Phil Hobill, and Ilya Shmulevich. (Forthcoming.) The propagation of organization: An enquiry. *Biology and Philosophy*. Available at: http://dx.doi.org/10.1007/s10539-007-9066-x

Kimura, D. 1976. The neurological basis of language qua gestures. In Whitaker, H. & H. A. Whitaker (ed.), *Current Trends in Neurolinguistics*. San Diego, CA: Academic Press, 145–56.

– 1979. Neuromotor mechanisms in the evolution of human communication. In Stelkis, H.D. and M.J. Raleigh (ed.), *Neurobiology of Social Communication in Primates*. San Diego, CA: Academic Press.

Kirby, Simon. 1998. Fitness and the selective adaptation of language. In Hurford et al., *Approaches to the Evolution of Language*, 359–83.

– 2000a. Syntax without natural selection: how compositionality emerges from vocabulary in a population of learners. In Knight et al., *The Evolutionary Emergence of Language*, 303–21.

– 2000b. Learning, bottlenecks and the evolution of recursive syntax. In Briscoe, *Linguistic Evolution through Language Acquisition*, 173–204.

Kirby, Simon, and James Hurford. 1997. Learning, culture and evolution in the origin of linguistic constraints. In *Proceedings of the Fourth European Conference on Artificial Life*. Cambridge, MA: MIT Press, 493–502.

Knight, Chris. 1998a. Introduction: Grounding language function in social cognition. In Hurford et al., *Approaches to the Evolution of Language*, 9–16.

– 1998b. Ritual/speech coevolution. In Hurford et al., *Approaches to the Evolution of Language*, 68–91.

– 2000a. Introduction: Evolution of co-operative communication. In Knight et al., *The Evolutionary Emergence of Language*, 19–26.

– 2000b. Play as the precursor of phonology and syntax. In Knight et al., *The Evolutionary Emergence of Language*. 99–119.

Knight, C., M. Studdert-Kennedy, and J. Hurford. 2000a. Language: A Darwinian adaptation? In Knight et al., *The Evolutionary Emergence of Language*, 1–15.

– 2000b. *The Evolutionary Emergence of Language*. Cambridge: Cambridge University Press.

Konner, M. 1982. *The Tangled Wing: Biological Constraints on the Human Spirit*. New York: Harper.

Kramer, S.N. 1959. *Life Begins at Sumer*. New York: Doubleday Anchor.

Krebs, J.R., and R. Dawkins. 1984. Animal signals: Mind-reading and manipulation. In J.R. Krebs, and N.B. Davies (ed.), *Behavioural Ecology: An Evolutionary Approach*, (2nd ed.) Oxford: Blackwell, 380–402.

Kuhn, Thomas. 1972. *The Structure of Scientific Revolutions*. Chicago: University of Chicago Press.

Lakoff, George. 1987. *Women, Fire and Dangerous Things*. Chicago: University of Chicago Press.

Laland, Kevin, John Odling-Smee, and Marcus Feldman. 1999. *Niche Construction, Biological Evolution and Cultural Change*. Princeton: Princeton University Press.

Lamb, Sydney. 1966. *Outline of Stratification Grammar*. Washington: Georgetown University Press.

Langacker, Ronald. 1987. *Foundations of Cognitive Grammar*, vol. 1. Stanford, CA: Stanford University Press.

– 1991. *Foundations of Cognitive Grammar*, vol. 2. Stanford, CA: Stanford University Press.

– 1992. The symbolic nature of cognitive grammar. In M. Pütz (ed.), *Thirty Years of Linguistic Evolution*. Amsterdam: John Benjamins, 483–502.

– 1998. Conceptualization, symbolization, and grammar. In Tomasello, *The New Psychology of Language*, vol. 1, 1–39.

Lee, N., and Schumann, J.H. 2003. The evolution of language and the symbolosphere as complex adaptive systems. Paper presented at the conference of the American Association for Applied Linguistics, Arlington, VA, 22–5 March.

Lenneberg, E.H. 1967. *Biological Foundations of Language*. New York: Wiley.

Levelt, W.J.M. 1989. *Speaking: From Intention to Articulation*. Cambridge, MA: MIT Press.

Lewis, David. 1972. General semantics. In D. Davidson and G. Harman (ed.), *Semantics for Natural Language*. Dordrecht: Reidel, 169–218.

Lieberman, P. 1973. On the evolution of human language: A unified view. *Cognition* 2: 59–94.

– 1975. *On the Origins of Language: An Introduction to the Evolution of Human Speech*. London: Macmillan.

– 1984. *The Biology and Evolution of Language*. Cambridge, MA: Harvard University Press.

– 1989. Some biological constraints on universal grammar and learnability. In M. Rice & R.L. Schiefelbusch (ed.), *The Teachability of Language*. Baltimore, MD: Paul H. Brookes, 199–225.

– 1991. *Uniquely Human: The Evolution of Speech, Thought and Self-less Behavior*. Cambridge, MA: Harvard University Press.

– 1992. Could an autonomous syntax module have evolved? *Brain and Language* 41: 768–74.

Lightfoot, David. 2000. The spandrels of the linguistic genotype. In Knight et al., *The Evolutionary Emergence of Language*, 231–47.

Livingston, David, and Colin Fyfe. 2000. Modeling language-physiology coevolution. In Knight et al., *The Evolutionary Emergence of Language*, 199–215.

Locke, John. 1998. Social sound-making as a precursor to spoken language. In Hurford et al., *Approaches to the Evolution of Language*, 190–201.

Logan, Robert K. 1979. The mystery of the discovery of zero. *Etcetera* 36: 16–28.

– 1995. *The Fifth Language: Learning a Living in the Computer Age*. Toronto: Stoddart.

– 1997. The extended mind: Understanding language and thought in terms of complexity and chaos theory. Presented at the 7th Annual Conference of the Society for Chaos Theory in Psychology and the Life Sciences at Marquette University, Milwaukee, WI, 1 Aug.

– 2000. The extended mind: understanding language and thought in terms of complexity and chaos theory. In Lance Strate (ed.), *Communication and Speech Annual* 14. New York: New York State Communication Association, 63–80.

– 2004a. *The Alphabet Effect*. Cresskill, NJ: Hampton. (Original work published in 1986 by William Morrow).

– 2004b. *The Sixth Language: Learning a Living in the Internet Age*. Caldwell, NJ: Blackburn. (Original work published in 2000 by Stoddart)

– 2006a. The extended mind model of the origin of language and culture. In Nathalie Gontier, Jean Paul Van Bendegem, and Diederik Aerts (ed.). *Evolutionary Epistemology, Language and Culture*. Dordrecht: Springer, 149–68.

– 2006b. Neo-dualism and the bifurcation of the symbolosphere into the mediasphere and the human mind. *Semiotica* 160: 229–42.

Logan, Robert K., and John Schumann. 2005. The symbolosphere, conceptualiztion, language and neo-dualism. *Semiotica* 155: 201–14.

Logan, Robert K., and Louis W. Stokes. 2004. *Collaborate to Compete: Driving Profitability in the Knowledge Economy*. Toronto and New York: Wiley.

Ludwig, O. 1983. Writing systems and written language. In F. Coulmas and K. Erlich (ed.), Writing in *Focus*. New York: Mouton, 31–43.

Lumsden, Charles. 2002. Fit To Be Eyed: Genes, Culture and Creative Minds. http://www.apa.org/divisions/div10/articles/lumsden.html. Accessed 18 Nov. 2005.

MacNeilage, Peter. 1998. Evolution of the mechanism of language output: Comparative neurobiology of vocal and manual communication. In Hurford et al., *Approaches to the Evolution of Language*, 222–41.

MacNeilage, Peter, and Barbara L. Davis. 2000. Evolution of speech: The relation between ontogeny and phylogeny. In Knight et al., *The Evolutionary Emergence of Language*, 146–60.

Malinowski, B. 1923. The problem of meaning in primitive languages. In C.K. Ogden and I.A. Richards (ed.), *The Meaning of Meaning*. London: Routledge and Kegan Paul, 296–336.

Marshack, Alexander. 1964. Lunar Notation on Upper Paleolithic Remains. *Science* 146: 743–5.

Maynard Smith, J., and E. Szathmary. 1995. *The Major Transitions in Evolution*. Oxford: Freeman.

Mayr, E. 1982. *The Growth of Biological Thought*. Cambridge, MA: Harvard University Press.

McLuhan, Marshall. 1962. *The Gutenberg Galaxy*. Toronto: University of Toronto Press.

– 1964. *Understanding Media*. New York: McGraw-Hill.

– 1967. Anonymous voice heard on the audio album available on CD: *The Medium Is the Massage*.

McLuhan, Marshall, and R.K. Logan. 1977. Alphabet, Mother of Invention. *Etcetera* 34: 373–83.

Meyers, E. 1960. *Education in the Perspective of History*. New York: Harper.

Miller, J., and R. Weinert. 1998. *Spontaneous Spoken Language*. Oxford: Oxford University Press.

Mithen, Steven. 1999. Symbolism and the supernatural. In Dunbar et al., *The Evolution of Culture*, 147–69.

Mithun, M. 1984. How to avoid subordination. *Berkeley Linguistic Society* 10: 493–523.

Moravcsik, Julius. 1967. Aristotle's theory of categories. In J. Moravcsik (ed.), *Aristotle: A Collection of Critical Essays*. Garden City: Anchor, 125–45. Books.

Murdock, George Peter. 1967. *Ethnographic Atlas*. Pittsburgh: University of Pittsburgh Press.

Needham, Joseph. 1979. *Grand Titration*. Toronto: University of Toronto Press.

Nettle, Daniel. 1999. Language variation and the evolution of societies. In Dunbar et al., *The Evolution of Culture*, 214–27.

Newmeyer, Frederick. 1991. Functional explanations in linguistics and the origins of language. *Language and Communication* 11: 3–28.

– 1998. On the supposed counterfunctionality of Universal Grammar: Some evolutionary implications. In Hurford et al., *Approaches to the Evolution of Language*, 305–19.

– 2000. On the reconstruction of 'proto-world' word order. In Knight et al., *The Evolutionary Emergence of Language*, 372–88.

– 2002. Uniformitarian assumptions and language evolution research. In Wray, *The Transition to Language*, 359–75.

– 2003. What linguistics can tell us about the origins of language. In Christiansen and Kirby, *Language Evolution*, 58–76.

Newport, Elissa L. 1990. Maturational constraints on language learning. *Cognition Science* 14: 11–28.

– 1991. Contrasting conceptions of the critical period for language. In S. Carey and R. Gelman (ed.), *Epigenesis of Mind: Essays on Biology and Cognition*. Hillsdale, NJ: Erlbaum, 111–30.

Newport, Elissa L., Henry Gleitman, and Lila R. Gleitman. 1977. Mother I would rather do it myself: Some effects and non-effects of maternal speech style. In C. Snow and C. Ferguson (ed.), *Talking to Children: Language Input and Acquisition*. New York: Cambridge University Press, 109–49.

Noble, Jason. 2000. Cooperation, competition and the evolution of prelinguistic communication. In Knight et al., *The Evolutionary Emergence of Language*, 40–61.

Nowak, M.A., J.B. Plotkin, and V.A. Jansen. 2000. The evolution of syntactic communication. *Nature* 404: 495–8.

Okanoya, Kazuo. 2002. Sexual display as a syntactical vehicle. In Wray, *The Transition to Language*, 46–63.

Ong, Walter. 1982. *Orality and Literacy: The Technologizing of the Word*. London and New York: Methuen.

Pagel, Mark. 2000. The history, rate, and pattern of world linguistic evolution. In Knight et al., *The Evolutionary Emergence of Language*, 391–416.

Paivio, A., and I. Begg. 1981. *Psychology of Language*. Englewood Cliffs, NJ: Prentice-Hall.

Palermo, D. 1978. *The Psychology of Language*. New York: Scott Foresman.

Perlmutter, David M. 1983. *Studies in Relational Grammar*, vol. 1. Chicago: University of Chicago Press.

Perlmutter, David M., and Carol G. Rosen (ed.). 1984. *Studies in Relational Grammar*, vol. 2. Chicago: University of Chicago Press.

Piaget, Jean. 1970. Piaget's theory. In P. Mussen (ed.), *Manual of Child Development*. New York: Wiley.

Pinker, Steven. 1989a. Language acquisition. In M.I. Posner (ed.), *Foundations of Cognitive Science*, 359–99.

– 1989b. *Learnability and Cognition: The Acquisition of Argument Structure*. Cambridge, MA: MIT Press.

– 1999. *Words and Rules*. New York: Wm. Morrow.

– 2003. Language as an adaptation to the cognitive niche. In Christiansen and Kirby, *Language Evolution*, 16–37.

Pinker, Steven, and Paul Bloom. 1990. Natural language and natural selection. *Behavioral and Brain Sciences* 13(4): 707–84.

Pinker, Steven, and Ray Jackendoff. 2004. What's special about the human language faculty? *Cognition* 95: 201–36.

Plunkett, Kim, and Virginia Marchman. 1991. U-shaped learning and frequency effects in a multi-layered Perceptron: Implications for child language acquisition. *Cognition* 49: 21–69.

Pollard, Carl, and Ivan Sag. 1994. *Head-driven Phrase Structure Grammar.* Chicago: University of Chicago Press.

Power, Camilla. 1998. Old wives' tales: The gossip hypothesis and the reliability of cheap signals. In Hurford et al., *Approaches to the Evolution of Language,* 111–29.

– 2000. Secret language use at female initiation: Bounding gossiping communities. In Knight et al., *The Evolutionary Emergence of Language,* 81–98.

Premack, D. 1986. *Gavagai!* Cambridge, MA: MIT Press.

Prigogine, Ilya. 1997. *The End of Certainty.* New York: Free Press.

Prigogine, Ilya, and I. Stengers. 1984. *Order Out of Chaos.* New York: Bantam.

Ragir, Sonia. 2002. Constraints on communities with indigenous sign language: Clues to the dynamics of language genesis. In Wray, *The Transition to Language,* 272–94.

Ridley, Matt. 1998. *The Origin of Virtue: Human Instincts and the Evolution of Cooperation.* New York: Penguin.

Rose, M. 1980. The mental arms race amplifier. *Human Ecology* 8: 285–93.

Ryan, Frank. 2002. *Darwin's Blind Spot: Evolution Beyond Natural Selection.* Boston: Houghton Mifflin.

Sadock, Jerrold. 1991. *Autolexical Syntax.* Chicago: University of Chicago Press.

Saffran, Jenny R., Richard N. Asslin, and Elissa L. Newport. 1996. Statistical learning by 8–month old infants. *Science* 274: 1926–8.

Samuels, M.L. 1972. *Linguistic Evolution.* Cambridge: Cambridge University Press.

Sanderson, Stephen K. 1990. *Social Evolutionism.* Cambridge, MA: Basil Blackwell.

Sapir, Edward. 1921. *Language.* New York: Harcourt Brace.

Savage-Rumbaugh, Susan. 1986. *Ape Language: From Conditioned Response to Symbol.* New York: Columbia University Press.

Sawaguchi, T., and Kudo H. 1990. Neocortical development and social structure in primates. *Primates* 31: 283–90.

Sawyer, J., and R.A. LeVine. 1966. Cultural dimensions: A factor analysis of the world ethnographic sample. *American Anthropologist* 68: 701–31.

– 1978. The Earliest Precursor of Writing. *Scientific American* 238: 50–9.

Schmandt-Besserat, D. 1974. The use of clay before pottery in the zagros. *Expedition* 16(2): 11–17.

– 1979. An Archaic Recording System in the Uruk-Jemdet Nasr Period. *American Journal of Archeology* 83: 19–48.

– 1981. The envelopes that bear the first writing. *Technology and Culture* 21(3): 351–85.

– 1981. From tokens to tablets: A re-evaluation of the so-called numerical tablets. *Visible Language* 15: 321–44.

– 1984. Before numerals. *Visible Language* 18: 48–60.

– 1985. Clay symbols for data storage in the VIII millennium b.c. In *Studi di Palentologia in onore di Salvatore M. Puglisi.* La Spaienza: Universita di Roma.

– 1986a. An ancient token system: The precursors to numerals and writing. *Archeology* 39(6): 32–9.

– 1986b. The origins of writing. *Written Communication* 3: 31–45.

– 1986c. Tokens at Susa. *Oriens Antiquus* 25(1–2): 93–125.

– 1987. *Oneness, Twoness, Threeness: The Sciences.* New York: Academy of Sciences.

– 1988a. Quantification and Social Structure. In D.R. Maines and C.J. Couch (ed.), *Communication and Social Structure.* Springfield, IL: C.C. Thomas.

– 1988b. Tokens at Uruk. *Bagdader Mitteilungen* 19: 1–175.

– 1992. *Before Writing,* vol. 1, *From Counting to Cuneiform.* Houston: University of Texas Press.

Schumann, John H. 2003a. The evolution of language: What evolved? Paper presented at the Colloquium on Derek Bickerton's Contributions to Creolistics and Related Fields, the Society for Pidgin and Creole Linguistics Summer Conference, University of Hawaii, Honolulu, 14–17 Aug.

– 2003b. The evolution of the symbolosphere. Great Ideas in the Social Sciences Lecture, UCLA Center for Governance, 21 Nov.

Shankland, M., and E.R. Macagno (ed.) 1992. *Determinants of Neuronal Identity.* San Diego, CA: Academic Press.

Slobin, D. 1985. The language making capacity. In D. Slobin (ed.), *The Cross-Linguistic Study of Language Acquisition* vol. 2. Hillsdale, Erlbaum, 1157–1256.

Smith, Frank. 1982. *Writing and the Writer.* New York: Holt, Rinehart and Winston.

Sontag, Susan. 2003. From a talk given at the Living Literacy Conference, York University, Toronto, 14–16 Nov.

*Stanford Encyclopedia of Philosophy.* 2004. Evolutionary Epistemology (6 Jan.). http://plato.stanford.edu/entries/epistemology-evolutionary. Accessed 22 Nov. 2005.

Steele, James. 2004. Plenary talk at Evolang5 Conference in Leipzig, 30 March to 3 April.

Steels, Luc. 1998. Synthesizing the origins of language and meaning using coevolution, self-organization and level formation. In Hurford et al., *Approaches to the Evolution of Language,* 384–404.

Stringer, C.B., and Andrews, P. 1988. Genetic and fossil evidence for the origin of modern humans. *Science* 239: 1263–8.

Stringer, C., and R. McKie. 1996. *African Exodus: The Origins of Modern Humanity.* London: Johnathan Cape.

Strogatz, Steven. 2004. Sync: How Order Emerges from Chaos in the Universe, Nature, and Daily Life. *Theia,* 14 April.

Stubbs, Michael. 1980. *Language and Literacy.* London: Routledge and Kegan Paul.

Studdert-Kennedy, Michael. 1998. The particulate origins of language generativity: From syllable to gesture. In Hurford et al., *Approaches to the Evolution of Language,* 202–21.

– 2000a. Introduction: The emergence of phonetic structure. In Knight et al., *The Evolutionary Emergence of Language,* 123–9.

– 2000b. Evolutionary implications of the particulate principle: Imitation and the dissociation of phonetic form from semantic function. In Knight et al., *The Evolutionary Emergence of Language,* 161–76.

Symon, D. 1979. *The Evolution of Human Sexuality.* Oxford: Oxford University Press.

Talmy, Leonard. 2003. Concept structuring systems in language. In Tomasello (ed.), *The New Psychology of Language,* Cognitive-Functional Perspective on Language vol. 2,: 15–46.

Teal, T.K., D. Abro, E. Stabler, and C.E. Taylor. 1999. Compression and Adaptation. In D. Floreano, J. Nicoud and F. Mondada, (ed.), *ECAL99.* Berlin: Springer-Verlag, 709–19.

Tiger, Lionel, and Robin Fox. 1971. *The Imperial Animal.* New York: Holt, Rinehart and Winston.

Tinbergen, N. 1963. On the aims and methods of ethology. *Zeitschrift für Tierpsychologie* 20: 410 – 33.

Tobias, P.V. 1981. The emergence of man in Africa and beyond. *Philosophical Transactions of the Royal Society of London* B 292: 43–56.

Tomasello, Michael. 1998. Introduction: A cognitive-functional perspective on language structure. In Tomasello, *The New Psychology of Language,* vol. 1, 1–39.

– 1999. *The Cultural Origins of Human Cognition.* Cambridge, MA: Harvard University Press.

– 2000. Do young children have adult syntactic competence? *Cognition* 74: 209–53.

– 2003a. Introduction: Some surprises for psychologists. In Tomasello, *The New Psychology of Language,* vol. 2, 1–14.

– 2003b. On the different origins of symbols and grammar. In Christiansen and Kirby, *Language Evolution,* 94–110.

– 2004. Plenary talk at Evolang5 Conference in Leipzig, 30 March to 3 April.

Tomasello, Michael, A.C. Kruger, and H.H. Ratner. 1993. Cultural learning. *Behavioral and Brain Sciences* 16: 495–552.

Tomasello, Michael, and H. Rakoczy. 2003. What makes human cognition unique? From individual to shared to collective intentionality. *Mind and Language* 18(2): 121–47.

Tooby, J., and L. Cosmides. 1990. On the universality of human nature and the uniqueness of the individual: The role of genetics and adaptation. *Journal of Personality* 58: 17–67.

Tooby, J., and J. DeVore. 1987. The reconstruction of hominid evolution through strategic modeling. In W.G. Kinzey (ed.), *The Evolution of Human Behavior: Primate Models*. New York: SUNY Press.

Toulmin, Stephen. 1972. *Human Understanding*, vol. 1. Oxford: Clarendon Press.

Trivers, R.L. 1971. The evolution of reciprocal altruism. *Quarterly Review of Biology* 46: 35–7.

Tylor, Edward. 1871. *Primitive Culture*. London: J. Murray.

Ulbaek, Ib. 1998. The origin of language and cognition. In Hurford et al., *Approaches to the Evolution of Language*, 30–43.

Van Valin, Robert, and Randy LaPolla. 1997. *Syntax: Structure, Meaning and Function*. Cambridge: Cambridge University Press.

Vihman, Marilyn M., and Rory A. Depaolis. 2000. The role of mimesis in infant language development: Evidence for phylogeny? In Knight et al., *The Evolutionary Emergence of Language*, 130–45.

Von Humboldt, W. 1836/1972. *Linguistic Variability and Intellectual Development*. Trans. G.C. Buck and F.A. Raven. Philadelphia: University of Pennsylvania Press.

Vygotsky, Lev. 1962. *Thought and Language*. Cambridge, MA: MIT Press.

– 1978. *The Mind in Society: The Development of Higher Psychological Processes*. Edited by M. Cole, V. John-Steiner, S. Scribner, and E. Souberman. Cambridge, MA: Harvard University Press.

Watson, John B. 1913. Psychology as the behaviorists view it. *Psychological Review* 20: 158–77.

Whiten, A., and R. Byrne. 1988. Tactical deception is primates. *Behaviour and Brain Sciences* 11: 233–73.

– 1997. *Machiavellian Intelligence*. Vol. 2. *Evaluations and Extensions*. Cambridge: Cambridge University Press.

Whorf, Benjamin Lee. 1964. *Language, Thought and Reality: Selected Writings*. Cambridge, MA: MIT Press.

Wilkins, W.K., and J. Wakefield. 1995. Brain evolution and neurolinguistic preconditions. *Behavioral and Brain Sciences* 18: 161–226.

Wilson, David Sloan. 2002. *Darwin's Cathedral: Evolution, Religion, and the Nature of Society*. Chicago: University of Chicago Press.

Wilson, Edward. 1975. *Sociobiology: The New Synthesis*. Cambridge, MA: Belknap Press.

– 1978. *On Human Nature*. Cambridge, MA: Harvard University Press.

Worden, R.P. 1995. A speed limit for evolution. *Journal of Theoretical Biology* 176: 137–52.

– 1998. The evolution of language from social intelligence. In Hurford et al., *Approaches to the Evolution of Language*, 148–68.

– 2000. Words, memes, and language evolution. In Knight et al., *The Evolutionary Emergence of Language*, 353–71.

Wray, Alison. 1998. Protolanguage as a holistic system for social interaction. *Language and Communication* 18: 47–67.

– 2000. Holistic utterances in protolanguage: the link from primates to humans. In Knight et al., *The Evolutionary Emergence of Language*, 285–302.

– (ed.). 2002. *The Transition to Language*. Oxford: Oxford University Press.

Zipf, G.K. 1935. *The Psycho-biology of Language: An Introduction to Dynamic Philology*. Boston: Houghton Mifflin.

# Index